SYRIA ON THE BRINK

Cover Photo from Istock.com
Cover Design by Fiona Jayde Media, www.FionaJaydeMedia.com
Interior Design by The Deliberate Page, www.DeliberatePage.com

ISBN 978-1-7338668-2-8

Printed and bound in the United States of America

SYRIA ON THE BRINK

US NATIONAL SECURITY AND A COUNTRY IN TURMOIL

CHRISTOPHER J HILL

To the Founders' Vision for America

CONTENTS

*Peace comes from
understanding, not agreement.*

Arab Proverb[1]

INTRODUCTION

In 2014, the Islamic State controlled 34,000 square miles of territory within Syria and Iraq, slightly bigger than the state of South Carolina. With its taxes, oil, and black market for art and historical artifacts, the Islamic State was also generating nearly $2 billion in annual revenue.[2] It was able to do so initially, in part, due to the nature of the sectarian fighting that had erupted in Iraq, rather than any vacuum left by withdrawing US forces specifically; the nasty civil war raging in Syria allowed for its rise and spread.

This civil war has resulted, as of December 2018, in the deaths of 560,000 people, including 111,330 civilians and 104,000 that had been tortured to death while in Syrian jails.[3] In addition to those killed, millions have been forced to flee the fighting: 5.6 million have fled Syria, while another 6.6 million remain internally displaced.[4] Growing from relatively small street demonstrations in 2011, the Syrian Civil War has morphed into a fierce battleground, littered, not only with government and opposition fighters, but also an International Coalition, headed by the United States, and fighters, in one form or another from: Israel, Turkey, Russia, Iran, Kurdish groups, and numerous terror organizations. With all this attention and effort, over eight years of conflict has yet to result in a peaceful solution.

This is difficult to do with so many state and non-state actors, each with varying degrees of motivation and influence. Bashar al-Assad wants to regain control and reunite the country, in his image, while the opposition is attempting to make their case for Assad's removal and a political transition, in their own. Russia is assisting Assad, perhaps to maintain influence in the region, perhaps to counter American hegemony, while Iran is assisting Assad to keep its pipeline to Hezbollah in Lebanon open through Syria and, in turn, expand its own hege-monic ambitions. Terror groups want what terror groups want: power, control, and influence, while the United States undoubtedly wants to maintain its experiment in Iraq, failed or otherwise. Couple this with the US's desire to undermine Iran and Russia, is the political neces-sity of maintaining the appearance of combatting the Islamic State.

While the United States has done so many great things for the world, it has not been so successful in the Middle East. Despite nearly two decades in Iraq, the United States still does not have an adequate understanding of the Middle East: the languages, demo-graphics, cultures, or religions. While the Syrian government invited Russia and Iran to assist in its fighting, the United States received no such invitation. It utilized the fighting against the Islamic State that emanated from Iraq, as justification, despite the fact that this group poses no substantial threat to the United States. Furthermore, the US move is unconstitutional, as no war has been declared and no Congressional debates on the validity of the matter have taken place. This is important in order to gain an understanding of the cost, both in lives and taxpayer funds, not for future blame games.

As of January 2019, the United States was $22 trillion dollars in debt; divided up amongst all federal income taxpayers in the US, each person would owe $180,000 each. Given that US military spending makes up one of the largest expenses in the federal budget (about $670 billion), the military (through the President and the Congress, of course) essentially have carte blanche to operate around the world. And of course, the military further justifies its budget by all of the oper-ations it conducts around the world. It is a revolving cycle. Limiting this role will in no way impact US national defense (with a presence in nearly 180 countries, how could it?), but it will endear the US to the world (an increase in soft power) and rightfully return tax dollars to the American taxpayer (an increase in freedom at home). To put it in perspective, the United States spends more on "defense" than the next seven countries combined.

Reducing military operations will have the added benefit of increasing the efficiency of the Veteran's Administration (VA). With fewer service members being committed to austere and hostile cli-mates, their need for VA services will be dramatically reduced. Over time, the number of veterans seeking VA assistance will decrease, allowing for increased efficiency, as the VA will be able to concentrate on the present veterans without an influx of new enrollees, thereby reducing costs as well.

In addition to the great costs, the presence of the United States can add fuel to a volatile situation, much of what has been done in Syria. From September 2014 through November 2018, coalition forces had killed nearly 13,000 people, of which 3,416 were civilians, including 1,400 women and children.[5] Despite the US's vast technological "advantages" in its military hardware, 25% of those killed were still non-combatants. This only adds to the complexity and devastation throughout Syria, while boosting the recruitment efforts of terror groups. The only way to truly defeat the Islamic State in Syria, and any other terror groups, is by having peace and stability in Syria, and this can only be done with a healthy, functioning government. With Russia and Iran clearly assisting the Assad government, the US's fight against the Islamic State is also indirectly assisting the Syrian government and its allies by eliminating IS from the battlefield. This, however, increases tensions between the international players involved, further endangering the geo-political climate.

This, however, is only a portion of the story, one that goes back to the splintering of the Middle East, in a post-World War I breakup of the Ottoman Empire. Springing from this were Syrian feelings of betrayal at being promised land that they had fought to liberate, only to be subjected to a French mandate in addition to Great Britain's approval of Zionist immigration into, and takeover of, Palestine. Despite the withdrawal of the European powers, and subsequent independence of Syria, grievances remained, in the form of European, followed by American support, of Israel, and the interference in Syria's domestic affairs. In order for one to know how Syria arrived at its present position, it is important to look to the past to help chart a path into the future. This is the dilemma that the United States faces in its fight against terrorism, its role in Syria (past and present), and its attempts to mediate an Arab-Israeli peace: it has forgotten how it arrived at its present situation, and therefore, its current way forward is bound to fail.

It is this past that we must look to first.

CHAPTER 1
THE ORIGINS OF MODERN SYRIA

By the early 20th century, the Ottoman Empire maintained control of the lands of the eastern Mediterranean, comprising modern Lebanon, Syria, Israel, Palestine, and Jordan, while Great Britain had a number of troops garrisoned for the defense of Egypt, specifically to safeguard its own logistics route through the Suez Canal. The British had gained control of the Suez Canal zone in the 1880s, just over ten years after the canal had been opened. At the outbreak of war in 1914, the Suez Canal became even more strategically important to Great Britain, as it linked England with its overseas territories, particularly in India, but also in Iraq, Iran, and along the Persian Gulf. With World War I breaking out in July 1914, these lines-of-communication were of increased importance for Great Britain to maintain.

With global hostilities exploding, the Arabs began petitioning the nearby British for assistance in gaining their independence from the Ottomans. In a letter from Sharif Hussein of Mecca to the High Commissioner of Cairo, Sir Henry McMahon, the Sharif outlined the Arab desire to be free of this Ottoman oversight and pledged to undertake an amicable relationship with Great Britain, as the Sharif believed it was in their mutual interests. The Sharif was seeking an Arab country in its entirety, essentially everything south of present-day Turkey, east of the Mediterranean Sea, west of present-day Iran, and the entire Arabian Peninsula, excluding Aden, which would remain a British possession (another point along its route to India); the Arabs could control this territory without undermining British interests. The Sharif of Mecca proposed an alliance and cooperation between the two powers for a term of 15 years. Furthermore, he requested a timely response from McMahon, and stated that "if this period should lapse before they [the Arab nation] receive an answer, they [the Arab nation] reserve to themselves complete freedom of action."[6] This threat seemed a real possibility for the British to be faced with, as the Ottoman sultan was the spiritual head of all Sunni Muslims at the time, a position that, the British feared, he might use to rouse, not only his Muslim subjects, but global Muslims. At this time, half of the world's Muslim population lived under British, French, or Russian rule, so the British were faced with a possible domestic crisis: assist the Arabs and give hope to British subjects that independence could soon be obtained, or stand by and allow the Ottoman sultan to provide that opportunity to those subjects.

The Ottomans could understand the British position and quickly offered full independence to the Arabs in exchange for their support in fighting the British.[7] While their statement about a "complete freedom of action" was not an empty threat, the Arabs evidently did not fully trust the Ottomans to deliver such a promise, and were willing to work with the British towards an amicable solution. However, there was a disagreement between the Arabs and the British concerning control of the vilayets of Beirut and Aleppo as they possessed relatively large Christian populations (for administrative purposes, the Ottomans established vilayets throughout the lands they controlled; in 1865, they adopted the name Syria to denote the vilayet of Damascus).[8] The Sharif held no distinctions about these Christian population centers, later stating that there was "no difference between a Moslem and a Christian Arab: they are both descendants of one forefather."

In addition, McMahon listed the vilayets of Baghdad and Basra, roughly the southern two-thirds of modern-day Iraq, as a special interest of Britain, as they "necessitate special administrative arrangements in order to secure…from foreign aggression" while overseeing the overall welfare of the people. Aside from the vilayets of Beirut and Aleppo, and Iraq, McMahon assured the Sharif that "Great Britain is prepared to recognize and support the independence of the Arabs in all the regions within the limits demanded by the Sharif of Mecca." However, he could not make assurances concerning the areas of Beirut and Aleppo, "as the interests of our ally, France, are involved in them both."

Furthermore, McMahon inserted, somewhat ambiguously, the statement that "Great Britain is free to act without detriment to the interest of her ally, France." The Sharif did not address this last statement, but was willing to allow British oversight in the vilayets of Baghdad and Basra, assuming that it was a temporary situation, and the Arab nation was justly compensated for such an inconvenience, a compensation they trusted the British to decide. The Sharif acknowledged the difficult position of Great Britain in this regard, stating the desire "to avoid what may possibly injure the alliance of Great Britain and France," yet also that "it is impossible to allow any derogation that gives France, or any other Power, a span of land in those regions."[9]

The ball was in the British court; war was raging. British forces were slugging it out on the Western Front of France while conducting a tough Mesopotamian Campaign in Iraq, and the possibility of losing control of its empire was becoming more of a possibility as tensions progressed. With the Arabs ready to usurp the Ottomans throughout the Middle East, the British finally threw their full support behind the Arabs, sending T.E. Lawrence (the eventual Lawrence of Arabia) to assist in their endeavors and show the seriousness of the British position in aiding the Arabs. Part of Lawrence's help to the Arabs was searching out a leader amongst the Arabs, one with the charisma and leadership to unite the disparate tribes and clans, qualities he eventually found in Feisal bin Hussein. Describing his first encounter with Feisal bin Hussein, Lawrence stated that "I felt at first glance that this was the man I had come to Arabia to seek— the leader who would bring the Arab Revolt to full glory."[10] While impressed with Feisal's leadership capabilities, Lawrence wrote of the Arabs as a whole:

They were weak in material resources, and even after success would be, since their world was agricultural and pastoral, without minerals, and could never be strong in modern armaments. Were it otherwise, we should have had to pause before evoking in the strategic centre of the Middle East new national movements of such abounding vigour.[11]

This sentiment was expressed before such massive pockets of oil were discovered in the region.

Allied with the Germans against the British, the Ottomans could not afford an autonomous Arab people causing problems within their territories, therefore the Ottoman authorities appointed Jemal Pasha as Ottoman governor over the Arab lands. He was not interested in granting concessions, let alone independence, to the Arabs, and began cracking down and repressing the population. To this end, Jemal Pasha had 21 Arabs hanged in Beirut and Damascus on May 6, 1916, an event that became known as Martyr's Day, a national holiday in Lebanon and Syria. This event no doubt pushed the Arabs fully onto the British side, giving the British the confidence of Arab motivation in defeating the Ottomans, and sealing the eventual fate of the Ottomans.

With Feisal at the head of an Arab force, and Lawrence acting in an advisory capacity, the Arab forces began harassing the Ottomans to the great fortune of the British. With a stalemate steadily growing in the trenches of France, and the Russian Revolution pulling troops away from Germany's eastern line and towards British and French positions on the Western Front, the British grew concerned with a quick end to the fighting with the Ottomans and began contributing more and more resources to the Arabs throughout 1918. By the end of the year, the British troops, under the Egyptian Expeditionary Force, began moving north from Egypt, capturing large areas of the Arabian Peninsula, as well as the Levant, with the Arab armies finally capturing Damascus and Aleppo. T.E. Lawrence described it thusly: "Next in force had been a pugnacious wish to win the war: yoked to the conviction that without Arab help England could not pay the price of winning its Turkish sector. When Damascus fell, the Eastern war—probably the whole war—drew to an end."[12]

During the fighting throughout the First World War, the French and British came together, even before peace was a distinct possibility, to decide how best to divide and administer the lands of the Ottoman Empire. As Allied armies began rolling back Ottoman forces throughout the Middle East, it became apparent that a plan was needed to administer these areas. In 1916, the British and French governments, with Russian understanding, believing an Ottoman defeat imminent and the need to oversee the subsequent freedom of the Arab lands, came together in the signing of the Sykes-Picot Agreement. The agreement set out to establish the protectorate powers of their respective governments throughout the Arab lands, including the power to appoint advisors and functionaries for local administrations. Furthermore, the two governments agreed not to allow outside control of these lands without the other's consent, except for the creation of an Arab state or confederation. Per the agreement, France would have control over an area roughly comprising modern-day southern Turkey, Syria, and Lebanon; Great Britain would oversee modern day Iraq, Kuwait, Bahrain, northern Saudi Arabia, and Jordan; and an international force would control the current Palestinian Territories and Israel (a point insisted on by the Russians).[13]

They Sykes-Picot Agreement was initially kept secret, especially from the Arabs, but, according to Lawrence, McMahon and the Sharif as well. Lawrence was not a fan of Mark Sykes (describing him as "a bundle of prejudices, intuitions, half-sciences."),[14] and was less enthusiastic of the document. He described it as an

old-style division of Turkey between England, France, and Russia, made public by the Soviets. Jemal read the more spiteful paragraphs at a banquet in [Beirut]. For a while the disclosure hurt us; justly, for we and the French had thought to plaster over a split in policy by a formula vague enough for each to interpret in his divergent way.[15]

After Feisal learned of the betrayal, Lawrence assured him and the Arabs that England was a country which "kept her word in letter and spirit,"[16] and convinced Feisal "that his escape was to help the British so much that after peace they would not be able, for shame, to shoot him down in its fulfillment..."[17] With this, Lawrence was able to maintain the partnership between the British and Arabs, which led to Lawrence's feeling of being "continually and bitterly ashamed."[18] He knew that the Sykes-Picot Agreement was a betrayal of the Arabs, but also knew that without the Arab Revolt, the British might possibly have failed against the Ottomans.[19] Arab support was vital for success and he further believed that the fruition of the Arab Revolt "would prevent the creation—by us or others—in Western Asia of unduly 'colonial' schemes of exploitation.[20] This was not to be in Syria's future.

WAR'S END

World War I was concluded on November 11, 1918, the eleventh hour of the eleventh day of the eleventh month, but the victors had much work to conclude. On November 7, 1918 the French and British concluded the Anglo-French Declaration. This essentially ensured that Great Britain and France would commit to establishing governments in former Ottoman-lands. As the fighting had not quite ended, it seemed that the Allied governments did not want to alienate the people of these lands. They made it clear that their "only concern is to offer such support and efficacious help as will ensure the smooth working of the governments and administrations which those populations will have elected of their own free will to have."[21]

The two powers further reinforced the Sykes-Picot Agreement from 1916 by committing to the establishment of national governments in the former-Ottoman lands of the Arabs, determined by the exercise of a free people. To this end, on November 23, 1918, when the smoke from the still recent fighting had barely cleared, the British divided the region into three Occupied Enemy Territories by way of a military edict. Syria was divided between two: Occupied Enemy Territory West, composed of coastal Syria and controlled by France (this included Lebanon as well), while Occupied Enemy Territory East consisted of the interior of Syria, controlled by an Arab administration under Emir Feisal bin Hussein, whose leadership skills Lawrence of Arabia had recognized.[22]

While the British and French were cooperating to divide the Ottoman Empire, American President Woodrow Wilson desired to exert his influence as well. In a speech in January 1918, President Wilson outlined his Fourteen Points in an effort to not only see an end to World War I, but all future wars. His Twelfth Point concerned the Ottoman lands:

> The Turkish portion of the present Ottoman Empire should be assured a secure sovereignty, but *the other nationalities which are now under Turkish rule should be assured an undoubted security of life and an absolutely unmolested opportunity of autonomous development* [author's emphasis], and the Dardanelles {the area dividing the Aegean Sea from the Sea of Marmara} should be permanently opened as a free passage to the ships and commerce of all nations under international guarantees.[23]

World leaders next met in France for the Paris Peace Conference in January 1919 in order to hammer out details for the Central Powers' capitulation and to assign mandatory powers in the former Ottoman territory. France, Great Britain, the United States, and Italy[i] (the Big Four) were represented, respectively, by George Clemenceau, Lloyd George, Woodrow Wilson, and Vittorio Emanuele Orlando. While Germany's outcome weighed heavily on the Allies (including Germany's overseas possessions), the Arabs were also seeking their place in the world, free of foreign oversight, although if that were unavoidable, they would have preferred a US mandate, as the British and French had not maintained much credibility in the region.

Joining the war late put the US at a disadvantage in the process. The French and British were vying to extend their influences throughout the region while the Americans desired a means of gathering information on the conditions of the former Ottoman lands, officially publishing what came to be known as the King-Crane Commission. Taking shape after the Paris Peace Conference, the commission sought to gain "as accurate and definite information as possible concerning the conditions, the relations, and the desires of all the peoples and classes concerned in order" to assist the US government in formulating a policy towards the region. Their findings were presented on August 28, 1919, although not made public until 1922.

One of the most glaring findings of the commission was the multiculturalism of the region, a great concern for a land that was used to being dominated by a central, non-sectarian, authority. The commission concluded that,

It is not to be forgotten either, that, however they are handled politically the people of Syria are there, forced to get on together in some fashion. They are obliged to live with one another-the Arabs of the East and the people of the coast, the Moslems and the Christians. Will they be helped or hindered, in establishing tolerable and finally cordial relations, by a single mandatory? No doubt the quick mechanical solution of the problem of difficult relations is to split the people up into little independent fragments. And sometimes, undoubtedly, as in the case of the Turks and the Armenians, the relations are so intolerable as to make some division imperative and inevitable. But in general, to attempt complete separation only accentuates the

---

i   Italy was originally allied with the Central Powers, but switched allegiance in 1915, ending with the winning side.

differences and increase the antagonism. The whole lesson of the modern social consciousness points to the necessity of understanding "the other half," as it can be understood only by close and living relations. Granting reasonable local autonomy to reduce friction among groups, a single mandatary ought to form a constant and increasingly effective help to unity of feeling throughout the state, and ought to steadily improve group relations.[24]

Wise words, but of little value to the Arabs of Syria. According to this conclusion, splitting these various groups up along ethno-cultural lines could further hostility, but there could be times when this was necessary, but only in extreme circumstances. In the meantime, it would be the mandatory power's responsibility to entice these groups into cooperation, boosting "social cooperation," a "unity of feeling," and to "steadily improve group relations." It seems that all this was in fitting with President Wilson's progressive agenda, for the commission further concluded that "America is peculiarly fitted to be the single Mandatory Power for all Asia Minor [not just Syria], not only because of her national convictions, her international faith, and her record, but also because the course of duty for her would seem to lie in this direction."

The commission believed that this mixture of ethnicities and religions within Syria were played off of one another by their Ottoman overlords, and that the newly established government would institute respect and justice for all groups. They concluded that a constitutional monarchy would benefit the Syrian people best, and, as seemed evident from the majority of Syrians, Emir Feisal bin Hussein should head such a government.

MANDATE OVER SYRIA

The conclusions of the King Crane Commission were unnecessary and irrelevant to the British and the French, they largely ignored the findings and continued in their efforts to conclude the details of a mandate over the area. In April 1920, representatives of the Allied governments of Britain, France, Italy, and Japan met in San Remo, Italy to determine how best to carve up the former-Ottoman Arab lands. The precise boundaries were left open, to "be determined by the Principal Allied Powers," officially settled years later. As this San

Remo Conference did not necessarily concern itself with Syria, since the Anglo-French Declaration all but guaranteed an autonomous Syria (not to mention the word of T.E. Lawrence to the Arabs), it did lead to the French assuming the mandate over Syria, in exchange for their relinquishing any aspirations over Palestine.[25] The British were largely concerned with ensuring a Jewish homeland was seen through to the end. By the time of the San Remo Conference, British relations with the Zionists had soured. The British believed that the French had contributed to this, if only partially, and did not desire for a French threat calling for an international presence to be carried out in Palestine. The British raised no objections to French aspirations over Syria, despite knowing that granting France a mandate over Syria would amount to a betrayal of the Syrians, especially Emir Feisal bin Hussein.[26]

The conclusions reached at San Remo were carried forward and built upon in the Treaty of Sevres, which was concluded on August 10, 1920 between the Allied Powers (represented again, principally, by Great Britain, France, Italy, and Japan) and the Ottoman Empire; in it, the map was redrawn in order to accommodate the dissolution of the Ottoman Empire.[ii] According to Section VII, Article 94 of the Treaty of Sevres, the Ottoman Empire's administration over Syrian lands would come to an end, replaced "by a Mandatory until such time as they are able to stand alone."[27] An element of the treaty that was never implemented, but has had dreadful consequences into the present, was the providing for a free and independent Kurdish country. The present-day countries of Turkey, Syria, Iraq, and Iran have Kurdish populations, with Baghdad and Ankara having taken heavy-handed measures against their respective Kurdish populations throughout the years. The British were also concerned with oil interests, as was evinced in its keeping of Mosul, Iraq under its own mandate instead of granting it to the French, as originally planned. Also, the British

---

ii   The Treaty of Sevres was quickly undermined due to the Turkish War of
      Independence, and was superseded by the Treaty of Lausanne, concluded
      on July 24, 1923. With it, peace was finally concluded between the former
      Ottoman Empire, now Turkey, and the allied powers of World War I, with
      Turkey giving up any claims over its former Arab lands, and the allies rec-
      ognizing Turkish independence.

were interested in containing Russian ambitions, an expensive and risky endeavor that had consumed British foreign policy since at least around the time of the First Anglo-Afghan War in the 1830s.

The Arabs under Feisal did not initially accept a French mandate, having established a government of their own in Damascus after having been guaranteed independence by the British during the war, not to mention the Sykes-Picot Agreement. After the Arab armies marched into Damascus, Feisal became the military governor of the area, except for the coastal areas that had fallen under French control. Feisal began implementing infrastructure development and improvements to education, while forming a constitutional committee. The French, however, demanded Feisal accept the French mandate or they would force his consent, but proceeded anyhow with military forces, even after they received Feisal's acquiescence, albeit slightly after the deadline. The French sent the military to usurp Feisal, and the two sides met at the Battle of Maysulun on July 24, 1920, near Damascus; the French defeated the Arab army and entered the capital soon thereafter, thus officially establishing the French mandate over Syria. Originally, the French figured on dividing Syria along ethnic lines, with the Alawite in the north, the Druze in the south, and the Sunni in the middle in an effort to stamp out any nationalist sentiment or uprisings. This division was roughly maintained, except that the French divided their mandate into six provinces. The majority of the populace was not receptive to the French presence, with the exception of the Christians. Despite some improvement projects initiated through the French Mandate, the Syrians did not much warm to their presence, particularly as the French undermined free speech and political activism, leading to already disillusioned Syrians becoming more disenchanted.

Meanwhile, the British were presiding over their mandate in Iraq, leading to an elected assembly in March 1924. The Syrians took notice, realizing their progress was not coming near as fast as their Iraqi neighbor, and in 1925, led by Sultan Pasha al-Atrash, the Druze rebelled against the French rule. Other parts of Syria took heart, leading demonstrations of their own, and al-Atrash was convinced to march towards Damascus, getting as far as the region surrounding the capital. The French were intent on holding onto the mandate, and bombarded areas under rebellion, killing some 5,000 Syrians, and crushing the revolt by the end of the year.

Into and throughout the 1930s, conditions began to improve for the Syrian people. The French began relaxing their oversight, granting more autonomy to the Syrians and improving conditions throughout the country with increased education and improvements to infrastructure. While socio-economic conditions began improving, by the late 1930s, instability began creeping back into society, due to a continued French presence, economic woes, and mass immigration. The Syrians had always resented having their Feisal-led country undermined by the French mandate and the continued presence of French forces continued to kindle ill-feelings. The French franc (the adopted currency for its mandated areas) had depreciated, leading to some minor economic concerns throughout the region. Beginning in the 1920s through the 1930s, ethnic groups began immigrating into Syria in an effort to flee repressive policies of the newly created Turkish state. From about 1924-1938, the Kurds arrived in large numbers, and the twenty years from 1925-1945 brought the largest number of Armenians, while the Assyrians arrived in the largest numbers in 1933.[28] With such large numbers of immigrants arriving in the country in such a short period of time, foreign cultures were introduced in larger numbers, undermining the positive elements of assimilation, such as shared values, shared belief in government's role, and a shared language to understand it all.

Just as the King Crane Commission had reported, Syria was a hodgepodge of ethnicities, religions, and cultures, remaining so into the present. As of July 2016, Syria was a country of an estimated 17 million people, with just over 90% made up of Arabs and the remainder Kurds (who are primarily located in the northeast of the country), Armenians, and other minority ethnic groups. 74% of the population identifies as Sunni Muslim, while the Shi'a (which includes the Alawi and Ismaili) makeup 13%. Christians account for 10% of the population, the Druze compose 3%, and a very small population of Jews remain in areas in or around Damascus and Aleppo.[29] While the Alawi technically fall under the Shi'a umbrella, most Shi'a do not relate to the Alawi, viewing them as having deviated from the principles of Islam.[30]

The Kurds, for their part, are predominately Sunni Muslim, although a minority of them practice the Alevi faith. The Alevi are Shi'a (but also incorporate pre-Islamic and Sufism traditions), similar to the Alawi, but contain their own distinct practices and rituals (for one, they do not worship in mosques, but instead utilize the cemevi). This, however, has created problems throughout the fighting in Syria, as Turkish President Recep Tayyip Erdogan typically references the two groups as one in the same, claiming the Alevi take advantage of this "alliance" with the Alawi to undermine Turkish society.

Just like Christianity, Islam is composed of various denominations, each built around their own ideals of faith: the two largest groups are known as the Sunni and the Shi'a, and each of these are composed of various sub-groups. The Sunni are by far the largest Muslim population, with around 90% of all Muslims identifying as Sunni, while the remaining 10% identify as Shi'a. While Sunnis compose the majority throughout the entire Muslim world (not just in the Middle East), the Shi'a make up the majority of the populations within Iran, Iraq, Bahrain, and Azerbaijan. This Sunni-Shi'a split occurred in the early days of Islam, and while there are many, albeit subtle, differences, the fundamental split concerned the rightful successor of the Prophet Mohammed upon his death. According to the Quran, in the year 610 a merchant by the name of Mohammed ibn Abdallah began receiving the word of God in a mountain cave outside the city of Mecca in present-day Saudi Arabia (as a merchant, he made many forays into present-day Syria). During this time, the peoples of the Arabian Peninsula were largely polytheistic, although Judaism and Christianity had some minor influences. In 612, Mohammed began preaching to the masses and slowly developed a following; however, not all were convinced of Mohammed's words. Just as the Jewish leaders felt threatened by the teachings of Jesus, so too did the powerful families of Mecca feel threatened by Mohammed. These leaders enforced a policy with which no marriages or trading could take place with the newly converted Muslims, forcing them to leave Mecca in 622, and establish themselves in nearby Medina (this migration is known as the hijra and marks the beginning of the Muslim calendar).

From this period until his death in 632, Mohammed acted as a sort of military and political figurehead, as well as a religious leader. In order to ensure this continuation after his death, and thereby continue the spread and unification of this nascent faith, it was important to have strong and recognized leadership, and a successor was quickly chosen from a meeting of prominent Muslims in Medina. It was agreed that Abu Bakr, one of Mohammed's fathers-in-law, should succeed; however, Mohammed's cousin, Ali ibn Abi Talib, dissented. Ali believed, as a blood relative to the Prophet, that he was more rightly placed to succeed Mohammed; however, as he was attending to funeral arrangements for Mohammed, he was absent from the meeting, and therefore unable to have his voice heard. Ali and his supporters eventually relented and agreed to support Abu Bakr.

Along with Abu Bakr, the first four caliphs to succeed Mohammed were known as the Rashidun, or the rightly guided (at least to the Sunni), and reigned as follows: Abu Bakr (r. 632-634) was followed by Umar ibn al-Khatab (r. 634-644), who was responsible for spreading Islam into present-day Syria, reaching the area by 641. The third caliph was Uthman ibn Affan (r. 644-656), followed by Ali (r. 656-661). With Ali chosen, some semblance of vindication may have been felt, but was hardly enough to satiate the Shi'a, as they would come to be known (the word Shi'a, in Arabic, means follower or community). Following Ali's death, these Shi'a threw their support first to Hasan, then to Hussein, both sons of Ali. To the Shi'a, the successors of the Prophet were spiritual and religious leaders, whereas the Sunni believed that this role was more political.

However, problems had arisen for Hasan and Hussein upon their father's accession following the death of Uthman. As an Uthman-appointed governor of Damascus, Muawiyah refused to acknowledge Ali until Uthman's killer could be brought to justice. Muawiyah had accumulated men and wealth and confronted Ali at the Battle of Siffin in 657, in present-day Raqqa, Syria. The results were indecisive, but Ali was nonetheless caliph, while Muawiyah continued to gain in influence. Upon the death of Ali, Muawiyah was able to convince Hasan to side-step rule, in exchange for family rule returning upon Muawiyah's death, with Hussein becoming caliph. This, however, did not come to fruition; in 680, Muawiyah's son Yazid was declared caliph and Hussein fled Mecca for Iraq where many supporters were awaiting his arrival. This same year, the Sunni-Shi'a schism came to a head at the Battle of Karbala, where Hussein and a small party of followers were killed, ending the hope of Ali's descendants becoming the rightful heirs of Muhammed.

Despite these ethno-cultural issues facing Syrian society, and the problems under the French Mandate, the Syrian people were attempting to govern themselves throughout the time of the French Mandate. The National Bloc, a coalition of various nationalist groups within Syria, succeeded in drafting a Syrian constitution, effectively ignoring the French Mandate. The French Mandatory authorities dissolved this Constituent assembly in 1930, although the French forced one of their own upon the Syrians. Elections were held shortly thereafter with the National Bloc winning 25% of the seats in the Chamber of Deputies, the Syrian Parliament. As the British had granted Iraq independence in 1932, thereby ending, for all intents and purposes, the British Mandate in Iraq, the Syrian people began to believe independence for themselves was a legitimately viable possibility.

In 1933, a Franco-Syrian Treaty was signed, but was opposed by the Syrian Chamber of Deputies, leading to its suspension by the French authorities. For the next few years, the French Mandate attempted to break-up the National Bloc, closing down its offices and arresting its members. However, in 1936, the National Bloc called for demonstrations, resulting in many demonstrators being killed and martial law being imposed in some cities. By March 1936, the French agreed to negotiate and the National Bloc called for an end to the unrest, leading to the French-Syrian Treaty of Friendship and Alliance in September 1936. The Chamber of Deputies was reconstituted and ratified the treaty. Although this granted Syria its independence, the French failed to ratify the treaty on their own end. The rising power of Hitler and the Nazi Party in Germany was enough for France to postpone its plans for Syria for the moment; by the end of the decade the Chamber of Deputies was no more and Vichy France had taken control of Syria by 1940.

World War II was hard fought for the French, and by July 1945, the French had had enough with Syria and transferred control to an independent Syrian government, completing their withdrawal the following spring. According to noted Middle Eastern historian Bernard Lewis:

> In countries of still uncertain territorial definition and of shifting national identity, ethnic nationalism was much more understandable than patriotism. Similarly, radical and authoritarian ideologies had greater appeal than liberal and libertarian ideas. Communal and collective identities and rights

made better sense than the individualistic formulations of the West, which at that particular point seemed both irrelevant and inappropriate. There influences were to remain more active in Syria...than in Egypt, which had a stronger national identity, an older liberal tradition and a much more extensive and effective parliamentary experience.[31]

This did not prevent the West from supporting the newly independent Syria, which received international recognition and member state status into the United Nations (UN) on October 24, 1945. But even prior to this, in March 1945, Syria, together with Egypt, Iraq, Lebanon, Saudi Arabia, and Jordan, formed the League of Arab States. This league, later renamed simply the Arab League, is today composed of nearly two dozen member states, with the purpose of drawing "closer the relations between member States and coordinate their political activities with the aim of realizing a close collaboration between them, to safeguard their independence and sovereignty, and to consider in a general way the affairs and interests of the Arab countries." In particular, the Arab League's intent is to closely cooperate on matters of: economics, communication, culture, social welfare, health, and "matters connected with nationality, passports, visas, execution of judgements and extradition."[32] Through the building of viable Arab states, and the creation of the League of Arab States, the French mandate was no longer physically or politically necessary, and thus officially ended the French Mandate over Syria.

With the French gone, the Syrians celebrated, but they were on their own and needed to create a viable country; they did not have much time to affect such an undertaking. In 1948, along with the Arab League, Syria declared war against its newly established neighbor Israel, one day after it declared an independent country for itself, and in the process, carving out the lands of the Palestinians. As a member of the Arab League, Syria signed a pact, part of which guaranteed, under Article VI, in the event "of aggression or threat of aggression... against a member State," the Arab League "shall determine the necessary measures to repel this aggression." While Palestine was not technically a member of the Arab League, the pact signed between the members had a special provision concerning Palestine, which is worth quoting at length:

At the end of…[World War I], Palestine, together with the other Arab States, was separated from the Ottoman Empire. She became independent, not belonging to any other State.

The Treaty of Lausanne proclaimed that her fate should be decided by the parties concerned in Palestine.

Even though Palestine was not able to control her own destiny, it was on the basis of the recognition of her independence that the Covenant of the League of Nations determined a system of government for her.

Her existence and her independence among the nations can, therefore, no more be questioned de jure [by right] than the independence of any of the other Arab States.

Even though the outward signs of this independence have remained veiled as a result of force majeure ["superior force," or essentially, through no cause of their own], it is not fitting that this should be an obstacle to the participation of Palestine in the work of the [Arab] League.

Therefore, the States signatory to the Pact of the Arab League consider that in view of Palestine's special circumstances, the Council of the League should designate an Arab delegate from Palestine to participate in its work until this country enjoys actual independence.[33]

So, while Palestine was not technically a member, the Arab League viewed the Palestinians as the rightful heirs to the land, and through no fault of their own, were deprived of their just sovereignty when the State of Israel was declared. This act, therefore, was seen as a sign of aggression against an allied state amongst the Arab League, and hence, the declaration of war in self-defense.

The creation of Israel and the subsequent hostilities would create many years of tension for Syria, leading on a direct path towards the outbreak of its civil war in 2011. The intent of this book is not to delve into an in-depth account of the Arab-Israeli conflict specifically, but to fully understand Syria through its modern history leading to the civil war it is important to have a fundamental understanding of its relationship with Israel. This understanding can help shape a way forward for Syria and the entire region.

CHAPTER 2
ORIGINS OF ARAB-ISRAELI TENSION

While the Arabs were living under the thumb of the Ottoman Empire, the Jews of Europe were plotting their own escape. By the late-19th Century, Zionists began immigrating into Palestine from Europe, attempting to make theirs' the lands of the Bible. Spurred by the publication of Theodor Herzl's The Jewish State in 1896, Jews throughout Europe began immigrating to Palestine in ever larger numbers. Although Palestine seemed to be the popular choice, Herzl had actually questioned the ultimate location of a settled Jewish homeland: debating between Palestine and Argentina. He wrote:

> In both countries important experiments in colonization have been made, though on the mistaken principle of a gradual infiltration of Jews. An infiltration is bound to end badly. It continues till the inevitable moment when the native population feels itself threatened and forces the Government to stop a further influx of Jews. Immigration is consequently futile unless we have the sovereign right to continue such immigration.[34]

How prophetic these words would become for the Zionists and Arabs of Palestine. While Herzl described Argentina's mild climate and scattered population as a benefit to Jewish immigration, and how a Jewish presence would benefit Argentina (much like it had benefitted Palestine, according to the Zionists and the British of the time), he mentioned the historic homeland of the Jews as being in Palestine. This, to the Zionists, was their "sovereign right."

Herzl, no doubt utilizing the momentum of *The Jewish State*, became a vocal proponent of an actual Jewish state. In Basel, Switzerland in 1897, the first World Zionist Congress was held, establishing the World Zionist Organization, an entity with the express purpose of settling Palestine as the Jewish homeland. Prior to the outbreak of war in 1914, the Jewish population throughout Palestine numbered 85,000, or roughly 14% of the population, with half residing in Jerusalem. Although Ottoman records were not exact, these numbers are in stark contrast to estimates of the Jewish population prior to the Zionist movement: over 400,000 Muslims, 43,000 Christians, and about 15,000 Jews, or roughly 3% of the population.[35] So, in the approximate four decades of the Zionist movement, the Jewish population of Palestine had increased from 3% of the population to 14% approximately, and would continue to rise.

The Zionists had their first piece of real news in November 1917 with the Balfour Declaration. Early in 1917, things had appeared as promising for the British and the French as three years of fighting could bring. Russia was in the throes of a revolution, eventually signing an armistice with Germany in December 1917 (the Treaty of Brest-Litovsk), ending their participation in the war and allowing Germany to shift resources to the Western Front. The Italian Front was also not holding up well against the Central Powers, forcing the British and French to send troops to bolster the defenses there. The Germans also began increasing their U-boat campaign, ultimately bringing the United States into the fight, boosting hopes that the war would soon end. But, even with the United States joining the fight, it took time to mobilize, and victory for the Allies was not a forgone conclusion.

While many leading British statesmen supported the Zionist movement, the immediate concern was the war. It was against this backdrop that the British became desirous to court Jewish support for the war, and in a letter from Arthur Balfour (the British Foreign Secretary) to Lord Rothschild[iii], the British essentially pledged their support for a repatriation of the Jews into Palestine. While the Balfour Declaration was not a mandate or official policy of the British

---

iii   Rothschild was himself a Zionist and was associated with Chaim Weizmann, a noted Zionist and the first president of the State of Israel.

government at the time, Balfour himself, as a member of the British government, had a great deal of weight behind his words, much the same as the words of Sir Henry McMahon to the Arabs. Perhaps remembering their promise to the Arabs, Balfour declared "…that nothing shall be done which may prejudice the civil and religious rights of existing non-Jewish communities in Palestine…"[36] This would soon prove to be an ineffectual statement as the situation would come to expose the British as middlemen to the problem that would soon form between the Zionists and the Arabs of Palestine.

While the French were undermining the Arabs in Syria, the British Mandate was doing the same for the Palestinians, adding support of the Zionists to the mix. The British Mandate over Palestine recognized the Zionists making their way into this land with Palestine "the grounds for reconstituting their national home in that country." Several of the articles contained within the Palestine Mandate are relevant to the Zionists:

Article II: The Mandatory shall be responsible for placing the country under such political, administrative and economic conditions as will secure the establishment of the Jewish national home…and the development of self-governing institutions, and also for *safeguarding the civil and religious rights of all the inhabitants of Palestine, irrespective of race and religion* [author's emphasis].

Article V: The Mandatory shall be responsible for seeing that no Palestine territory shall be ceded or leased to, or in any way placed under the control of the Government of any foreign Power.

Article VI: The Administration of Palestine, while ensuring that the rights and position of other sections of the population are not prejudiced, shall facilitate Jewish immigration under suitable conditions and shall encourage…close settlement by Jews on the land, including State lands and waste lands not required for public purposes.

Article VII: The Administration of Palestine shall be responsible for enacting a nationality law. There shall be included in this law provisions framed so as to facilitate the acquisition of Palestinian citizenship by Jews who take up their permanent residence in Palestine.

Article XXII: English, Arabic and Hebrew shall be the official languages of Palestine. Any statement or inscription in Arabic on stamps or money in Palestine shall be repeated in Hebrew and any statement or inscription in Hebrew shall be repeated in Arabic.[37]

It seems the mandate turned into an utter failure; instead of a Palestine that was home to both Zionists and Arabs, it became one in which the Arabs were being dictated to concerning the newly arriving Zionists. It was true that the League of Nations was to see to the dissolution of the Ottoman Empire, but was it not also true that the Mandatory Powers were put in place to ensure a smooth, stable transition for these lands? Inviting outsiders into an area seems like anything but creating a smooth transition into a country with a viable government. Furthermore, Article V declared that no foreign power would gain control over the land, but that was precisely what the State of Israel was allowed to accomplish some three short decades beyond the establishment of the Mandate.

Whether the British knew exactly what they were creating is beyond the scope of this writing, but their presence certainly drew many more Zionists to the area, assured of safety and encouragement. In addition, Woodrow Wilson's Twelfth Point, which addressed the Arab lands of the former Ottoman Empire, was utilized to reinforce Jewish immigration into the region, despite the fact that it clearly stated that "…the other nationalities which are now under Turkish rule should be assured an undoubted security of life and an absolutely unmolested opportunity of autonomous development." This is not a statement supporting Zionist immigration into former Ottoman lands; rather a statement of support to the people already inhabiting the areas before the war. In any event, between 1919 and 1923, 35,000 Zionists made their way to Palestine with another 60,000 doing so between 1924 and 1932. The following year Adolf Hitler rose to prominence as Chancellor of Germany, prompting many to flee; throughout the remainder of the 1930s, 165,000 Zionists made it to Palestine, avoiding what nobody could have predicted at that time.

THE BRITISH AS MIDDLEMEN

Throughout the 1920s and 1930s, the Arabs of Palestine were steadily growing discontented as more and more Zionists found their way to the area. Arab anger was not so easily explained away by feelings of antisemitism. It was believed that, as late as 1913, only a small minority of Arab nationalists were opposed to Zionism or held the opinion that it threatened the Arab resistance to foreign rule.[38] But, not only did the Zionists bring themselves and their families to what the Arabs believed was Arab land, they implanted a feeling amongst the Arabs that the Zionists enjoyed somewhat of an audience in London, enabling the Jewish saga to unfold on sympathetic ears, and hence their encouragement to Zionists to emigrate. This led to a growing feeling of mistrust between the Arabs and the British (former allies in the fight against the Ottomans, after all), eventually boiling over into violence and the Arab Revolt of 1936. One Israeli historian, Benny Morris, believed that it was this revolt, lasting until 1939, that ultimately secured an Arab defeat in 1949, after the 1948 Arab-Israeli War began.[39] In any event, the Arab Revolt of 1936 was put down harshly by, primarily, British forces, through counterintelligence, destruction of property, raids, air supremacy, and a partnership with Jewish militias.

For the Zionists' part, a number of their successes could be measured through their creation and use of the Irgun, a Jewish militia and a precursor to the Israeli Defense Force (IDF). Of notable irony was the terror tactics employed by the Irgun during the fighting, escalating in scale from small ambushes and hit-and-run raids, to large-scale precursors to modern-era terror. According to Benny Morris,

...for the first time, massive bombs were placed in crowded Arab centers, and dozens of people were indiscriminately murdered and maimed-for the first time more or less matching the numbers of Jews murdered in the Arab pogroms and rioting of

25

1929 and 1936. This "innovation" soon found Arab imitators and became something of a "tradition"; during the coming decades Palestine's (and, later, Israel's) marketplaces, bus stations, movie theaters, and other public buildings became routine targets, lending a particularly brutal flavor to the conflict.[40]

As a result of this violence, a royal commission was established in Great Britain and sent to Palestine to investigate the problems and propose a solution. Headed by Lord Robert Peel, the Peel Commission concluded that the issue of increased Jewish immigration into Palestine was exacerbated by three global issues:

1. the United States' levying of restrictions on immigration as a result of the Great Depression and its terrible economic consequences,

2. the rise of the Nazi Party in Germany, and

3. economic strains experienced by Jews throughout Poland.

This of course ignored the fact, and seems to somewhat shift responsibility for the violence, that the British had been encouraging Zionist immigration into the area. As a result of these migrations into Palestine, the indigenous Arab populations became evermore adamant in their nationalism, with violent outbreaks in 1920, 1921, and 1929. But, according to the Peel Commission, Arab grievances towards Zionist immigration were unfounded, since the local economies were benefitting from the capital inflows, Arabs included. This seemed to justify the Zionist presence, undermine the Arab sentiment, and reinforce Britain's role in the entire episode.

One passage in particular warrants an in-depth look:

...the Mandatory has fully implemented this obligation to facilitate the establishment of a National Home for the Jewish people in Palestine, as [is] evidenced by the existence of a Jewish population of 400,000 persons. But this does not mean that the National Home should be crystallized at its present size. The Commission cannot accept the view that the Mandatory... would be justified in shutting its doors. Its economic life depends to a large extent on further immigration and a large amount of capital has been invested in it on the assumption that immigration would continue.[41]

So, it appeared that 400,000 Jews in Palestine was not enough; too much time and money had been thrown at the problem. In what seemed like a way to justify this British stance, the commission was sure to point out what it perceived to be benefits to the Arabs of the Zionist immigration: the increased capital brought by the immigrating Zionists as well as the social services that this expanding population and capital expenditure provided. Of course, the economic considerations were an effect of, and not the reason for, Zionist immigration. It failed to mention, however, the role that the Mandatory Powers might have played in increased social services and capital, particularly in the form of security. Most importantly, it failed to address the deleterious effects of allowing the growth of such a problem.

According to the Peel Commission report, their conclusions,

will not...remove the grievances nor prevent their recurrence. They are the best palliatives the Commission can devise for the disease from which Palestine is suffering, but they are only palliatives. They cannot cure the trouble. The disease is so deep-rooted that in the Commissioners' firm conviction the only hope of a cure lies in a surgical operation.[42]

The commission had no real solution to the unrest, only that limiting Zionist immigration was not the answer, and Arab unrest would continue. A "surgical operation" could be taken to mean that either the Zionists or the Arabs should be removed. As the commission was justifying Zionist immigration, clearly removing them was not the solution. It should, therefore, be taken that it would be best to remove the Arabs; perhaps this was foreshadowing the creation of the State of Israel. The British had the bull simultaneously by the tail and the horns, and could not safely let it go. This seemed to be the result of awful foreign policy and political pandering, promising two opposing parties the very same land. It seemed only afterwards, after the unrest and violence, did the British perhaps begin to doubt their double-dealing. The following, quoted from the Peel Commission report, is worth noting at length:

> The application to Palestine of the Mandate System in general and of the specific Mandate in particular implies the belief that the obligations thus undertaken towards the Arabs and the Jews respectively would prove in course of time to be mutually compatible owing to the conciliatory effect on the Palestinian Arabs of the material prosperity which Jewish immigration would bring in Palestine as a whole. That belief has not been justified, and there seems to be no hope of its being justified in the future. But the British people cannot on that account repudiate their obligations, and, apart from obligations, the existing circumstances in Palestine would still require the most strenuous efforts on the part of the Government which is responsible for the welfare of the country.[43]

With this, it seemed the British were attempting to justify their own underhanded actions towards the Arabs by taking credit for the Arabs' "gained economic advantage." This would not have been possible without the assistance of the British Mandatory Powers. Furthermore, their obligations to the Arabs seemed okay to repudiate but not that aimed at the Zionists.

While the Peel Commission failed to recommend a stop to all Zionist immigration, it did propose an end to the British Mandate, an end the commission concluded was necessary in order to avoid any further chasms between the Zionists and Arabs. It did not, however, issue a mea culpa in the damage it had wrought to that point. In ending the Mandate, the commission believed in drawing up a Partition, composed of a Jewish State, an Arab State, and a strip of land from Jaffa on the Mediterranean coast, eastward into and around Jerusalem. The Peel Commission Plan was endorsed by the British government but opposed by the League of Nations. Evidently Great Britain wanted to rid itself of the problem it had helped create.

Later, in 1937, in an effort to appeal to the Arabs and not further antagonize their former allies, the British government rejected the Peel Commission's conclusions. This prompted the creation of the Woodhead Commission, which published its findings in October

1938. Throughout the work of the Woodhead Commission, it was found that the findings of the Peel Commission were not feasible; partitioning Palestine as recommended by the Peel Commission would leave a minority Arab population within a Jewish state that would be surrounded by Arab states. Was this concern due to unfairness that might be extended towards those minority Arabs or a fear that those minority Arabs would potentially undermine a Jewish state? Today, the State of Israel is constantly reminded of its Arab minority; in 2018, the Israeli Knesset passed the Jewish Nation State Law, which, among other things, declared Israel "the nation-state of the Jewish people."

Naturally, the Zionists took issue with the Peel Commission as well. During the 20th Zionist Congress, held in Zurich in August 1937, the attendees debated the findings of the Peel Commission. For the Zionists, this gathering "solemnly reaffirms the historic connection of the Jewish people with Palestine and its inalienable right to its homeland."[44] Clearly any partition was opposed by the Zionists, which were adamant in drawing attention to the following points:

1. "...that the primary purpose of the Mandate, as expressed in its preamble and in its articles, is to promote the establishment of the Jewish National Home...,"

2. "...that the field in which the Jewish National Home was to be established was understood, at the time of the Balfour Declaration, to be the whole of historic Palestine, including Trans-Jordan,"

3. "...that inherent in the Balfour Declaration was the possibility of the evolution of Palestine into a Jewish State," and

4. "...that Jewish settlement in Palestine has conferred substantial benefits on the Arab population and has been to the economic advantage of the Arabs as a whole."[45]

Furthermore, the 20th Zionist Congress wished it be known that it reserved,

its strongest protest against the decision of His Majesty's Government to fix a political maximum for Jewish immigration of all categories for the next eight months, thus sweeping away

the principle of economic absorptive capacity, in violation of
Jewish rights and of the undertakings repeatedly given in this
regard by His Majesty's Government and confirmed by the
League of Nations.[46]

It should come as no surprise that the Zionists were unhappy, but
what about the Arabs, and most importantly, what about the conflicting promises made by the British to the Zionists and the Arabs? The
Woodhead Commission attempted to underplay the large numbers
of Jewish immigrants into the area, claiming that their birth rates
were higher, and death rates lower, than that of the native Arabs. This,
however, ignores the numbers that were most important; between
1922 (the start of the British Mandate) and 1938 (around the time
of the Woodhead Commission), the Jewish population increased
exponentially. In that period of a decade-and-a-half, the Arab population increased by 68%, from 589,177 to 989,500, while the Jewish
population increased from 83,790 to 401,600, an increase of 379%.
While it is true that the Arab population grew to a larger number
(989,500 versus 401,600), its growth rate was much lower than that
of the Zionists. More importantly, the vast majority of Arab growth
was due to natural births, while Zionist immigration accounted for
the greater number of Jews.[47]

In addition, the British attempted to point out that the Zionist
population of Palestine had inadvertently increased the quality-of-life
of the native Arabs. There is some truth to this in the sense that the
British Mandatory authorities were not economically subsidizing the
Zionist population and had very little oversight over the local economies. This, therefore, meant that any Jewish immigrants to the area had
to come to the area with enough resources to be self-sustaining (at least
initially), quickly become self-sufficient, or give into or take from the
socialist practices of the early Zionist populations. Scientifically, however, it is hard to conclude exactly how much worse off the Arabs would
have been economically had it not been for this large Zionist migration.
While the peoples of Palestine were largely located in rural areas, there
is nothing to say that the area would not have become urbanized and
evolved into a technologically sustainable economy, especially since
the fall of their Ottoman overlords. It also failed to take into account
the security and stability provided by British security forces.

While the Industrial Revolution swept through Europe and North America from about 1760 to around the first few decades of the nineteenth century, it did not make it to the Ottoman Empire at the same time. Perhaps this was due to the vast differences in agricultural output between the two. The Agricultural Revolution made the Industrial Revolution possible by freeing up workers from the fields to work in other economic sectors. According to British historian and anthropologist Alan Macfarlane, the Middle East, "started off in an arid area with difficulties, and the difficulties grew greater because the grazing, the eroding, meant that the tax base shrunk. You got an impoverished peasantry, and so the whole civilization declined on its agricultural side, while the West and its rich soils, great forests, deep plowing, new crops, particularly in Holland and England later on, had an agrarian revolution.[48] So, while the Agricultural and Industrial Revolutions did not root themselves in the Middle East at the same time that Western Europe and the United States were experiencing them, it is not to say that development ceased in the area. It is difficult to surmise what would have transpired had the area been free to development in a post Ottoman world, free of overbearing influences.

Despite the plans of partition set forth by the Woodhead Commission, fervor of the Arab Revolt continued; neither the Zionists nor the Arabs were pleased with the British solutions, eventually leading to the St. James Palace Conference from February 7 to March 17, 1939. The British Colonial Secretary, Malcolm MacDonald, held separate meetings between the Zionist and Arab representatives, as neither party wished to be in the same room as the other. In addition, the British-appointed Mufti of Jerusalem, Haj Amin al-Huseini, was refused permission to attend.

Ultimately the St. James Palace Conference failed and the British government subsequently published the White Paper in May 1939, months before Adolf Hitler's armies invaded Poland and ignited the Second World War. Hoping to restore Arab faith in British intentions, the White Paper addressed two main areas of concern: Zionist immigration into Palestine and land transfers. While immigration was a major sticking point for the Arabs, the British did not want to snuff it out completely. Doing so, the British believed, would undermine the local economies, hampering the standard-of-living enjoyed by both Zionists and Arabs, and also undermine Zionist efforts in establishing a home. The British solution was to allow immigration to continue for another five years, but severely limit the entries; a total of 75,000 would be allowed throughout that period. At the expiration of the five years, all Zionist immigration would cease (or at least become illegal) unless the Arabs agreed to its continuation. The British realized that such a statement would require enforcement and adopted measures to curb illegal immigration. If any illegal immigrants into Palestine were arrested, or otherwise caught, the individuals would be deported from the area; failing this, those numbers of illegals would be deducted from the overall total migrants. Some believed that this restriction on immigration made Great Britain partly responsible for Jews that were not able to escape the Nazi stranglehold over Europe. That seems unfair.

While enforcing immigration proved difficult, putting a stop to the purchase and transfer of Palestinian land by Zionists was much more successful. As the local Arabs were largely agrarian, it was of vital importance to limit Zionist land in order to ensure that the Arab standard-of-living, although improving, was at least maintained. The White Paper concluded by telling the Arabs and Zionists to get along:

> His Majesty's Government cannot hope to satisfy the partisans of one party or the other in such controversy as the Mandate has aroused. Their purpose is to be just as between the two people in Palestine whose destinies in that country have been affected by the great events of recent years, and who, since they live side by side, must learn to practice mutual tolerance, goodwill and cooperation.[49]

While the British had made conflicting promises to both parties, they were now realizing that their position within Palestine was untenable (especially with mounting tensions in Europe about to erupt in war) and forcing two feuding parties to face-off against the other. They used the Arabs to topple Ottoman power once-and-for-all, and seemingly protected the Zionists in Palestine against an Arab population that felt betrayed and cast aside, and attempted to, unsuccessfully, utilize protests and violence to reassert their natural rights over the area. Despite this, the British were still willing to admonish the two sides to live with "mutual tolerance." Furthermore, the British believed that an independent Palestine was feasible within 10 years, one in which Zionists and Arabs equally shared the political powers within one state.

The White Paper of 1939 was approved by the British House of Lords, but vehemently rejected by both the Zionists and the Arabs. The Arabs felt it did not go far enough, demanding an end to all immigration immediately while also an evaluation of all immigrants who had arrived following the First World War. The Zionists, for their part, believed it went too far, with the British going back on their word set forth in the Balfour Declaration.

WORLD WAR II

Ultimately, the White Paper was a failure, primarily because Zionists continued immigrating into Palestine, many illegally. Throughout the following years until the end of World War II in 1945, another 600,000 Zionists would find their way to Palestine. The British came to realize that their position in Palestine was untenable due to the disorganization of the Arab populations throughout Palestine, stiff Zionist opposition to a continued British presence, and the British opposition to the Arab's affiliation with Axis forces. The Arabs who had felt British and French imperialism prior to World War II, especially in Palestine and Syria, were very much eager to throw their support to the Nazi forces if it meant the end to the Mandates and the beginning of self-rule (sounds similar to what they did during World War I). The British-appointed Mufti of Jerusalem, Haj Amin al-Huseini (the same Mufti who was denied attendance to the St. James Palace Conference), contacted the German consul and pledged to help, being given assurances in return that, upon the defeat of Great Britain, the Arab peoples would have their freedom.

In 1940, with the Chamberlin-led government failing to curtail the rise of Hitler and quench the animosities brewing in the Middle East, the British transitioned into a government led by Winston Churchill. The pro-Zionist Churchill did not believe the British owed anything to the Arabs and evidently did not look favorably on the Arab desire to side with Britain's enemy. Despite the Irgun's attacks against British positions after the unpopular White Paper, the Zionists of Palestine saw a common enemy in Nazi Germany, and quickly allied themselves with the British, putting aside any differences over land, immigration, and Arab feelings. In the end, this went a long way in endearing the British mind to the plight of the Palestinian Jews and the Jews throughout Europe.

The British, however, had to balance these forces as they were not yet willing to completely sever their relationship with the Arabs. The British, despite their poor track record with their Mandates in Iraq and Palestine still held sway in Egypt, where control of the Suez Canal was still upheld; the British were successful in shutting off access to the Axis Powers while defending the canal during the North Africa Campaign. The British were also trying to think strategically, as oil reserves in the region would play a crucial role in the war, and lead to enormous potential after the war through expansion of trade. With this in mind, the British were reluctant to share the spoils with its new partners, the United States and the Soviet Union. The Zionists, on the other hand, were very much eager to acquire support from the United States and Jews within the US as well.

In May 1942, while the United States was ramping up its efforts in the war, the Biltmore Conference was being held in New York City. By the end of the conference, the attendees had published the Biltmore Program, an 8-point declaration of Zionist demands to see Palestine morphed into a Jewish State and the unrestricted flow of Jewish migrants, without which, a Jewish State would be impossible. In particular, the declaration declared the support of the American Zionists, who would "give expression to their faith in the ultimate victory of humanity and justice over lawlessness and brute force." The overriding sentiment of the declaration was resolving "the problem of Jewish homelessness." The only solution, in their view, was creating a Jewish State from Palestine, and vesting in the Jews, the authorities necessary to build and maintain such a country, including control of the immigration of world Jewry.

The intent of the Balfour Declaration was cited, and so too was President Woodrow Wilson's 14 Points, no doubt referencing Point XII, which stated, in brief, that "…other nationalities which are now under Turkish rule should be assured an undoubted security of life and an absolutely unmolested opportunity of autonomous development…" If the Biltmore Program were reading this point literally, then it would of course have realized that Point XII precluded all Jews who had immigrated to Palestine after the fall of the Ottoman Empire from being granted an "unmolested opportunity." It was clearly undermined and abused to fit the agenda of the Zionists to usurp Palestine. In order to secure this for themselves, the Zionists needed a means of defense "against the forces of aggression and tyranny, of which Jews were the earliest victims, and which now menace the Jewish National Home."[50] This force would not only fight for the Jewish State, but also, it claimed, the United Nations. The claim to Jewish homelessness was of course the means by which to justify the Zionists' end goal of establishing a nation state.

In any event, the conference questioned the "moral or legal validity" of the White Paper of 1939, decrying it as "cruel and indefensible" in not allowing Jews to flee Nazi Germany, and agreeing with Churchill's belief that it was "a breach and repudiation of the Balfour Declaration." To this point, it went so far as to declare that the White Paper was a nullification of "Jewish rights to immigration and settlement in Palestine." While hindsight is always 20/20, nobody at the time could have foreseen the shocks such that Hitler's Nazi Reich delivered. As horrible as the Holocaust was, it provided the Jews with the sympathy necessary in order for their plan to be carried out to fruition. They did not have the right to the land simply because they may have inhabited it 2,000 years ago. The British promised the Arabs and the Zionists the same stick, but the Jews were better able to foster widespread appeal in order to obtain a larger chunk, first with the British, and then with the Americans with the release of the Biltmore Program. The declaration ended with: "Then and only then will the age old wrong to the Jewish people be righted."[51] It seems they were digging deep for justification for their actions.

Throughout World War II, sides had been picked and the Zionists cast their lot with the British. Doing so provided them combat experiences that they could not have readily obtained otherwise. Despite their partnership with British forces, after the war, the relationship soon soured; with the war over, and the common enemy of the Jews and British defeated, the Jews could turn their attention back to securing Palestine for themselves. The British Mandate, however, still remained, along with a British presence. The Irgun and other Jewish militias began targeting British forces and their leadership.

The British intelligence apparatus, however, was functioning in Palestine, and in June 1946, British security forces launched Operation Agatha, arresting 2,700 individuals and seizing a large quantity of documents from the Jewish Agency office in Jerusalem. These documents helped the British Mandate better understand the role that was being taken by Jewish militias in undermining the British presence. Jewish operations did not cease, but instead, culminated in the bombing of the King David Hotel in Jerusalem on July 22, 1946, which was being utilized as the main office of the British Mandate government. The explosion killed 91 people in total: 41 Arabs, 28 British, 17 Jews, and 5 others. Menachem Begin, the leader of the Irgun who was responsible for planning but not executing the operation, claimed to have made three phone calls in an effort to limit civilian casualties. Like most terror attacks, the numbers are not so much important as how much resolve was weakened; for the British, it was fairly significant. So much so, that worries began running rampant of groups infiltrating Europe and England and continuing such operations. British intelligence even began marking Jews arriving in England as receiving additional security scrutiny, much like a "terror watch list" might function in the United States today, and also not unlike the fear of Muslims after 9/11.

ISRAEL CREATED

Following World War II, the British Empire was waning and its position throughout Palestine was growing precarious. The British left it to the United Nations General Assembly to vote over the status of Palestine and the fate of the British Mandate. The Zionists were not blindly gambling on a UN decision, however, because the Haganah had eyes and ears in New York at the time of the vote, routing intelligence to Jewish officials. Described in *The Friends: Britain's Post-War Secret Intelligence Operations*, author Nigel West described Jewish efforts to ensure a "yes" vote:

> It was discovered, for example, that the limousine company supplying the British delegation to the United Nations with transport was Jewish owned. As a result, every journey made by the delegates from their office in New York to the UN General

Assembly's special session at Lake Success on Long Island was bugged…Indeed, Jewish businessmen were also allocated rooms in hotels directly under or adjoining those of the debate's main participants.[52]

On November 29, 1947 the votes were cast: 33 voted yes, 13 voted no, and 10 abstained (one of which was Great Britain). The mandate would effectively end on May 15, 1948.

The creation of Israel would effectively split Palestine into two, a move that US President Harry Truman supported. According to President Truman, "…Jewish leaders in the United States were putting all sorts of pressure on me to commit American power and forces on behalf of the Jewish aspirations in Palestine."[53] Even after the UN vote, President Truman continued receiving pressure from Jews in the US, in the form of "[i]ndividuals and groups…, usually in rather quarrelsome and emotional ways," pleading for the US and the President "to stop the Arabs, to keep the British from supporting the Arabs, to furnish American soldiers, to do this, that, and the other."[54]

Middle Eastern specialists within the US State Department at this time typically sided with the Arab position. The mentality was, according to President Truman, that "Great Britain has maintained her position in the area by cultivating the Arabs; now that she seems no longer able to hold this position, the United States must take over, and it must be done by exactly the same formula; if the Arabs are antagonized, they will go over into the Soviet camp" (which did happen).[55] Some of these same State Department officials believed that carrying out the letter of the Balfour Declaration had turned into a zero-sum proposition, and that the true losers would be the Arabs. They believed that the Arabs should be mollified, in part, due to their possession of oil.[56] US President Franklin D Roosevelt had met with Saudi King Ibn Saud in the early months of 1945, assuring him that he would not undermine the Arab position vis-à-vis the Jews, nor be hostile in any way towards the Arabs. Furthermore, he believed that the creation and maintenance of Israel could only be done through the use-of-force.[57]

In a Central Intelligence Agency report from 1947 on the consequences of a Palestinian Partition, the CIA's assessment was that "[w]hatever the official position of the Arab governments may be, attacks on US property, installations, and personnel by irresponsible groups or individuals can be expected." This became reality on October 13, 1947 in which the US Consulate General in Jerusalem was bombed, "evidence of Arab resentment against US support of the majority plan."[58] Furthermore, the CIA believed that Jewish boundaries would be overstated, and Arab retaliation would ensue, leading to an Israeli propaganda campaign to cast such retaliatory actions in the light of terrorism and antisemitism. "This propaganda campaign will doubtless continue to influence the US public, and the US government may, consequently, be forced into actions which will further complicate and embitter its relations with the entire Arab world."[59] No truer statement could have been made in 1947 and yet today, it almost seems like ancient history; what 70 years can do to collective memories.

During a British cabinet meeting held in September 1948, Prime Minister Clement Attlee and his staff discussed the inevitability of the creation of a Jewish State. They made clear that the Arabs,

> were naturally apprehensive that the new Jewish State would later seek to expand at their expense; but it should be possible to allay this anxiety by making the United Nations responsible for guaranteeing the new frontiers. It was to be hoped that the Mediator's proposal for merging the Arab territory of Palestine with Transjordan would be accepted, since it had always been clear that a separate Arab State would not be viable.[60]

If this had always been clear, then why was there such a strong push for the Zionist cause? Without it, a "separate Arab State" would have had no meaning. In any event, the British went on to discuss oil and how, with a partnership with the US government, the possibility existed for a Middle East pipeline terminal in Gaza, and also the reopening of a refinery in Haifa. They did not want to undermine any agreements being reached and wanted to reach such an agreement before any assets and liabilities were distributed.

Anglo-American concessions and talks of oil came to little in 1948. On May 14, 1948, the last British troops departed from the port of Haifa, officially ending the British Mandate, resulting in the creation of the State of Israel. Eleven minutes later, despite the assessments of State Department and CIA officials, President Truman's press secretary announced that the US was to recognize Israel as a Jewish state. After the founding of the State of Israel, many Palestinians fled to neighboring countries, including Syria, and with the subsequent rage throughout the Arab World, resulted in the 1948 Arab-Israeli War.

CHAPTER 3
SYRIAN NATIONALISM

1948 ARAB-ISRAELI WAR

Syria, Jordan, Egypt, Lebanon, and Iraq (augmented by Sudan, Yemen, and Saudi Arabia) endeavored to drive the newly proclaimed Israelis into the sea. Opposing them was the Israeli Defense Forces (IDF), formed on June 1, 1948 from an underground paramilitary organization called the Haganah. Numerically outnumbered and completely surrounded by hostile forces (with the Mediterranean Sea to their backs), the Israelis fought a brutal campaign that saw the capture of large tracts of land and resulted in Jerusalem being effectively split in two.

The newly formed United Nations Security Council (UNSC) was put to the test by the conflict and encouraged both sides to a truce, selecting Count Folke Bernadotte as a mediator. The United Nations (UN) was formed in 1945 in the wake of World War II. Composed of many bodies and committees, the UN was tasked with addressing issues confronting humanity, such as: peace and security, terrorism, disarmament, humanitarian assistance, and much more. To assist with these measures, the UNSC was formed, holding its first meeting in London on January 17, 1946, and subsequently relocating its headquarters to New York City. The Security Council is composed of 15-member states: the United States, United Kingdom, France, Russia, and China, all comprise the five permanent members (P5), while another ten members are elected by the General Assembly for two-year terms, made up of three from Africa, two from Latin

America, one Arab country, one Asian, one Eastern and two Western European. According to its charter, only the Security Council can pass resolutions that member states are then obligated to implement.

UN Member States may participate in UNSC discussions, but cannot vote, while the 15-member states above hold one vote each. Regarding matters of procedure, nine members must cast an affirmative vote in order to obtain a majority. All other decisions must also obtain nine affirmative votes; however, members may dispute any decision by abstaining, at which point the resolution could still pass with nine affirmative votes. The P5 holds the distinction of an added veto power, which, if exercised, results in a disapproval of the resolution.

The Israelis could not be bothered with UNSC resolutions, however, as they needed the room to consolidate, reorganize, and obtain much needed supplies. The Arab forces, for their part, recognized this, and balked at a truce. The first truce, however, was agreed upon by all parties and took effect on June 11, 1948. Against the terms of the truce, the Israelis used this lull in the fighting to secretly funnel military material into the country for the inevitable resumption of combat. Believing that the truce would not hold, the Israelis struck first, resuming hostilities on July 9. This second stage of fighting was fierce, with Israel capturing towns, but unable to completely dislodge the Arab forces. Again, Count Folke Bernadotte pushed aggressively for a truce with the full backing of the UNSC and the international community. Israel was reluctant to come to such an agreement, due to its relative successes against a numerically superior foe, and the remaining Arab League countries, particularly Egypt and Syria, were opposed as well (King Abdullah of Jordan was the exception). Count Bernadotte was successful in his efforts, however, and a second truce was reached on July 19, 1948.

The second truce held the promise of permanence, with Bernadotte focusing on concluding the details that would turn into a concrete conclusion. Three seemingly unpopular points found their way into the agreement: recognition of Israel as a state; UN oversight of Jerusalem, as opposed to handing it back to the Arabs, which the Israelis opposed; and the acquisition of the Galilee region by the Israelis (acquired during the fighting), while abdicating any claims over the Negev, which the UN had originally mandated as Israeli land. The Negev, a swath of fertile, yet desert land running south towards the Gulf of Aqaba and then the Red Sea, was an important area for Israel, as it provided a means of access to those waterways, and the logistics that would come with it (not to mention arable land). President Truman stated that he "deplore[d] any attempt to take it away from Israel."[61] Not content to lose this land, the Israelis resumed hostilities on October 15. The Israelis, however, did not want to be responsible for resuming the fighting unmolested, and sought a means with which to accomplish a provocation. Years afterwards, Yitzhak Rabin would recollect that, as the Israelis had "taken full advantage of the respite, we were ready and eager for action. But there was one catch. To avoid the political handicap of taking the blame for breaking the truce, we had to find some pretext for renewing the fighting."[62]

The second truce permitted Israeli convoys to move through Egyptian lines en route to Israeli settlements; oftentimes, however, these convoys were attacked by Egyptian forces. So, to avoid that "political handicap" of renewing the fighting, the Israelis planned to send a convoy through the Egyptian lines and then launch their attack following the inevitable Egyptian aggression against the convoy. Surprisingly, to the Israelis, this did not come about. According to Rabin, "[e]very additional mile the convoy covered unmolested, the nearer our nerves stretched to breaking point. The excuse for our attack was slipping out of our grasp. In the end, with the aid of a random shot here, another there, we had our pretext."[63]

Led by Yigal Allon, with Yitzhak Rabin as his chief-of-staff, four brigades from the IDF launched an offensive to capture the city of Beersheeba (capturing it October 21), thereby facilitating Israeli forces into the Negev. After a little over a week of fighting, a large portion of the Egyptian force had retreated westward, yet Israeli forces had encircled a 5,000 strong pocket of Egyptian resistance, a quarter of the Egyptian force. David Ben-Gurion, the Israeli prime minister, would later write that Israel would benefit from this fighting when it came to negotiations in the UN concerning possession of the Negev.[64]

Fighting would continue in the Negev, Jerusalem, and northern Israel, but foreign pressure was mounting for the two sides to agree to a ceasefire. Fighting ended in January 1949, but was officially concluded until each individual Arab government signed an agreement with Israel. With 200 killed in the fighting, the Syrians were the last to enter into negotiations, not signing an armistice agreement until July 20, 1949. Despite his efforts at a short-term peace, it was Count Bernadotte's efforts at the long-term peace that both Arabs and Israelis took issue with. Despite saving thousands of Jews from concentration camps during World War II, his efforts to alter the Palestinian partition led to his assassination on September 17, 1948 by an Israeli nationalist group, led, in part, by future Israeli prime minister Yitzhak Shamir. This makes some sense, as the Israelis came out on top of the fighting and the partition plan: Israel captured 80% of the territory that was planned on being split between them and the Palestinians.[65]

During the fighting, 700,000 Palestinians had fled Israeli-occupied areas, while an equal number of Jews living in surrounding Arab countries fled into Israel. The Israeli government would grant these newly arrived citizenship; however, with the exception of those settling in Jordan, the Palestinians did not receive such a welcome from their Arab brethren, creating a great deal of hostility that persists into the present. These Palestinians, and the many Arab countries participating in the fighting, believed that quick work would be made of the Israelis, allowing the Palestinians to return to their homes. This was not to be, creating refugees of these Palestinians, either refusing to return or unable to return by the Israelis. A US intelligence summary from 1948 foresaw the problems of the region, stating that "[t]he Arab refugee problem is straining the economic and political resources of Syria, Lebanon, and Transjordan to such an extent as to endanger the stability of the whole area."[66] In another, produced weeks later, the analysis was equally dire, believing that "the refugee situation is producing an economic and political strain so severe that the Arab peoples, not yet realizing the hopelessness of further military action, may demand that their governments solve the problem by force."[67] This would inevitably lead to many problems for the Syrian people.

Israeli officials often cite their own open-handedness and hospitality at welcoming these Israeli refugees and, in turn, question the Arabs at not granting the same concessions to Palestinian refugees. Of course, Israel needed fresh citizens to bolster its position (it needed bodies for defense forces primarily), while the Arab countries were adamant that the Palestinians would be returning home. Furthermore, it seems to point to the fact, that the situation was more than just a Jewish-Muslim conflict, but very much a nationalist struggle. To the Israelis, it was about strengthening its own numbers, and to the Arabs it was about justice.

TURN FROM THE WEST

In the words of noted Middle Eastern scholar, Bernard Lewis, the years following World War II and the dissolution of the French mandate gave rise to the state of Israel and Arab nationalism:

> The failure of the combined Arab forces to prevent the birth of Israel gave rise to profound heart-searching in the Arab countries and, within a few years, to the violent removal of the rulers and sometimes even of the regimes that were held responsible...In March 1949, Colonel Husni Za'im, in a bloodless coup, terminated the presidential and parliamentary order and inaugurated a series of military coups d'état. This period of army government ended in 1954 with the restoration of the parliamentary regime and the holding of elections. This restoration was of brief duration.[68]

Between 1946 and 1970 (roughly the time of independence to the reign of Hafez al-Assad) the CIA estimated that Syria had undergone perhaps 21 coups or attempted coups.[69] No doubt the CIA took part in a number of these themselves. It is difficult to state unequivocally just how many of Syria's 21 or so coups were orchestrated with CIA-backing, since the agency rarely admits guilt. They of course control the history in a sense, since files related to "national security" can be kept in the shadows, and those that are brought out, can be redacted at the agency's discretion. Miles Copeland, Jr., a former CIA officer, claimed that the 1949 coup in Syria was orchestrated, in part at least, with CIA assistance. This was the first of Syria's many coups, and brought down a democratically-elected government (albeit a government that lost the war). The CIA's belief at the time of the coup was that US-Syrian relations would survive intact, due to the pro-Western stance of the new leader, Husni Za'im (who would only be in power for a few short months). The CIA believed that Za'im and his conspirators "will probably be able to consolidate their control over the

[g]overnment and, by ruling with a strong hand, may be able to solve many of Syria's internal difficulties."There will be adverse effects with any coup, and with this particular coup came the "inevitable delays in the ratification of the agreement for the Trans-Arabian petroleum pipeline…"[70] There is little to doubt that a connection existed between the coup and this pipeline.

It seemed the CIA was somewhat optimistic over the coup, calling the power grab "one of the dullest revolutions in recorded history." It was further added that "[t]he complete absence of any opposition to [Za'im] would seem to indicate that the population at large has few regrets over the ouster of President Quwatli…"This, however, might not be entirely accurate, for while Quwatli presided over Syria during its loss to Israel, he refused to enter into a truce with Israel (this was only done after his removal), no doubt endearing many to his side. The CIA optimism for Za'im seemed to quickly fade, however, for within a month of the coup, the CIA's assessment changed: "he does not appear prepared to risk subverting the constitution in order to retain power over the long run, and by deciding to deal with Israel he has discarded one obvious means of whipping up popular support. Vacillation over Tapline…is further specific evidence that his regime may well become as colorless and ineffective as the one it replaced."[71] Per these statements, it seems the CIA was betting on anti-Israel sentiment within the Syrian populace in order to strengthen the position of the pipeline.

In an interview with BBC, Copeland admitted that the US interfered with the internal workings of sovereign nations. In the interview, he expressed that this was not the right approach, and that if a country were to get a tough leader, or they just did not like one, the people of that country should "stew in its own juice."[72] Many agree. This is not black-hearted, simply a way of allowing a sovereign nation to dictate its own domestic issues. It is an altogether different perspective, however, if the United States were to directly interfere with that country's internal workings. This might make the US culpable for any issues later down the line, and since it no doubt utilizes taxpayer dollars, US citizens might be indirectly responsible as well.

Charles Yost was a US diplomat assigned to Damascus, Syria from 1957 to 1958. Years later, he gave an interview in which he described Syria upon his arrival:

In fact, in Syria, before I arrived, the CIA had tried to pull off a coup, support[ing] its military people who were planning a coup. The local CIA station chief strongly advised against this. They said they were quite sure that it was penetrated by Syrian intelligence. But nevertheless, orders came from Washington to support it, which we [the US] did. Of course, it was penetrated, and it was broken up. As a result, they told our ambassador, who happened to be home on leave at the time, he would not be welcome to return...But, we were trying rather clumsily to get into some of their domestic affairs.[73]

Ambassador Yost might have been referring above to the coup in 1957 in which it is largely understood that the CIA orchestrated a coup in order to undermine communist activities in Syria. According to a CIA memorandum from 1973, "...Syrian leaders have lively memories of efforts sponsored by the West in 1956 and 1957 to overthrow the left-leaning government in Damascus. *The US took particular blame for its sponsorship of the 1957 attempt* [author's emphasis]. Three diplomats were expelled, and evidence presented in the trials of the accused plotters severely incriminated the US along with some neighboring states."[74] It seems from the italicized statement above that the US did take some part in the attempted overthrow, however indirect it might have been. While Cold War tensions in and of themselves could have been to blame, no doubt of great importance to the US was the Soviet Union's persistent efforts to sabotage and otherwise undermine the Tapline; a cold war within a cold war.

This time period also coincided with the beginning of Syrian acceptance of military assistance from Czechoslovakia in the amount of $37 million and also from the Soviet Union for $42 million.[75] As of 1950, the people of the Middle East wanted the Arab League to disassociate itself from the British and Americans. This partly came about, according to the CIA, due to the "military and political support for Israel," while the "large investments of US oil companies in the Middle East have evoked charges of exploitation of Arab resources."[76] With the Cold War gaining momentum between the US and Soviet Union, if relations were to sour between the Arabs and Americans, then the Arabs could always turn to the East, thus undermining the West. The Arabs had wished to avoid that, however, due to the Soviet Union's lack of religion and ethics. For the Syrians, and the Arabs as a whole, the larger issue was Israel, but also the perceived Western interference in Arab resources, and thus, ultimately, their turning away.

TAPLINE

Nineteen fifty-six also saw the nationalization of the Suez Canal. Nationalizing infrastructure was significant at the period in Syria due to the recent construction of the Trans-Arabian Oil Pipeline, referred to as Tapline. The pipeline was constructed in the effort of moving Saudi oil to the eastern Mediterranean, thereby bypassing the Strait of Hormuz. Construction of the pipeline began in 1947 and was completed in 1950, becoming one of world's first long-distance pipelines capable of great quantities of product. It stretched over 750 miles through Saudi Arabia, Jordan, the Golan Heights of Syria (and later Israel), and ending in Sidon, Lebanon; it was capable of moving 500,000 barrels of oil per day. It was operated by ARAMCO, which was in turn owned by: Standard Oil Company of New Jersey with a 30% stake, Standard Oil Company of California maintaining a 30% stake, Texaco with 30%, and Secony Mobil Oil Company had 10% ownership. All of these companies were American.

The Chief of the Petroleum Division in the US State Department from 1944-1956, Robert Eakens, had this to say about the pipeline:

> I know one problem that we sat on and probably made a mistake on was getting an allocation of steel to build the trans-Arabian pipeline from the Persian Gulf to the Mediterranean. In retrospect, I think that was a serious mistake because of the political problems which have been encountered by the pipeline. The pipeline not only went through Saudi Arabia, but it went through Syria and Lebanon. Either one of these countries could cut off the flow of oil through the line—and did. If the same amount of steel had gone for the construction of tankers, our entire relationship would have been solely with Saudi Arabia. During this time we were naturally trying to protect investments in oil and trying to—once the pipeline was built—insure [sic] the continued flow of the oil.[77]

While communism was present in Syria and a "threat" to the West, the pipeline, as an American product, was no doubt seen as a national security interest that was worth safeguarding; this no doubt had a role in CIA activities in Syria and the region at the time. While the pipeline was generating transit fees for these Arab governments, Tapline was largely unpopular throughout Syrian society. The communists in Syria spread propaganda that some Tapline employees were US military personnel attempting to extend US influence outside of its presence already being maintained in Saudi Arabia (the CIA could very well have established its own personnel as Tapline workers).[78] Furthermore, Syrians were upset that ARAMCO was hiring too many foreigners to run the pipeline operations and not making the effort at hiring local Syrians.

In 1953, Syria, Lebanon, and Jordan began pushing for higher fees for ARAMCO's use of their territories. No doubt the instability in Syria postponed these fee negotiations; however, in 1960, Syria (part of the United Arab Republic with Egypt at the time) was again demanding higher transit fees from ARAMCO. The UAR wanted to increase the rate by 250%, a move that, if accepted by ARAMCO, would have forced the company to increase the fees to Lebanon, Jordan, and Saudi Arabia as well. ARAMCO could not possibly accept, however, as the higher fees were far too high and would cause financial losses for the company. The UAR threatened to increase the taxes on ARAMCO if this new rate formula was not met, and if ARAMCO refused, it would provide the UAR an excuse to close the pipeline. This was a win-win for the United Arab Republic as it would show that it was standing up against a perceived imperialist entity if it was able to extract higher fees. In addition, if the line was closed, the UAR would also benefit financially as the oil would then need to be diverted to tankers in the Persian Gulf, tankers that would then need to traverse the Suez Canal, providing revenue to the UAR that was 10 times what the pipeline fees generated. Also, at this time, Syria owed ARAMCO $4 million, due to the contractual obligation requiring ARAMCO to supply, through Tapline, oil for the government refineries, half of which had to be provided on credit. ARAMCO was threatening to withhold future shipments if debt was not paid.[79] As these Arab countries were pushing for higher fees in 1953, is it any coincidence that Syria experienced a coup the following year? Not likely.

Despite these issues, the CIA assessed that a pipeline shutdown "would not materially affect [the] oil situation in the West, since arrangements could be made easily for supplies from alternate sources."[80] Furthermore, had this been the case, resources would have been put to better use before Tapline had ever been constructed; clearly, profits were to be made, and interests protected. Given the CIA's role in Iran it seems highly likely this assessment would have been ignored anyway. After being democratically-elected as the prime minister of Iran, Mohammed Mossadegh was overthrown in a CIA-backed coup for nationalizing the oil industry in Iran, which was largely controlled by British companies. Despite Mossadegh's willingness to receive British proposals and his desire to sell Iranian oil to the US, there would not have appeared to be any significant impact to Western imports.[81] Despite this, the CIA staged the coup anyhow that continues to affect US-Iranian relations over 65 years later. If the US was willing to subvert a foreign government on behalf of British interests, it would most certainly do so for the interests of an American company like ARAMCO.

After the summer of 1956, and the Suez Crisis, the Syrian Military Intelligence Chief, Lieutenant Colonel Abdel Hamid al-Sarraj, threatened to sabotage Tapline. He gave the company two days to meet the "entire requirements of fuel oil" demanded by Syria, or the line would be blown up. Lieutenant Colonel al-Sarraj believed he controlled the fate of Tapline; to this end, there were mines laid over the underground portions of Tapline in a suspected effort to thwart any Israeli aggressions.[82] A second pipeline running from Iraq through Syria to Lebanon was in fact sabotaged following the Suez Crisis, but was reopened the following year.

Throughout nine months of 1970, Tapline had been closed, but operations renewed in January 1971, after ARAMCO agreed to pay higher transit fees to the countries involved. Israel, too, began efforts to acquire transit fees. After 1967, and Israel's capture of the Golan Heights, the portion of the pipeline that had traversed Syria, was then part of Israel. ARAMCO was unwilling to pay out to Israel, due to the fact that Israel had just captured the land and did not possess sovereignty. The CIA assessment of the situation was that "[t]he financial claim may be designed subtly to reinforce Israel's position that it will retain the Golan Heights in any peace negotiations." The

Israeli Deputy Finance Minister stated that the Golan was "part of Israel" and must be considered as such.[83] This question of ownership over the Golan is an issue that still plagues the region and Israeli-Syrian relations.

It would seem that geo-political contests would make running the pipeline incredibly costly, but it was the economies of scale of the supertankers from the Persian Gulf that made the line obsolete by 1975. It continued minimal operations in order to supply the refineries in Jordan and Lebanon, but ceased operations beyond Jordan in 1976 after the start of the Lebanese Civil War. Saudi Arabia continued exporting to Jordan until 1990 and the Persian Gulf War.

CHAPTER 4

LOSS OF GOLAN HEIGHTS & RISE OF HAFEZ AL-ASSAD

The repeated coups in Syria created further instability and unrest, due to the fact that nobody within Syria was able to effectively exploit the confusion to gain complete control. The US, through CIA actions, helped contribute to this. With this internal unrest, came the continued hostilities with Israel. Following the Arab-Israeli War in 1948, Israel had successfully survived its baptismal by fire, but the armistice with Syria was little more than an act of "kicking the can". Hostilities resumed along the two countries' mutual border in the form of Palestinian incursions into Israel (supported by Syria), access to water, and the Syrian-Israeli demilitarized zone (DMZ). In an effort to retake their homes from the Israelis, the Palestinian Liberation Organization (PLO) had been created in 1964 and began conducting cross-border operations into Israel from within its neighboring countries. By 1967, Israel had been experiencing increased cross-border penetrations of Palestinians from Syria, Jordan, and Lebanon; raising the issue only exacerbated tensions between these states. According to famed Israeli general, Moshe Dayan, these saboteurs "found hiding places in the homes of their relatives and in their former villages. From time to time local residents of the administered territories joined the terror organizations and took part in their operations." He added that Israel was effective in deterring such actions by destroying the homes where fighters were found hiding or ones utilized as weapons and explosives caches. For those "leaders who had taken an active part in incitement to terror or in helping saboteurs," exile was a preferred method.[84] Then-Israeli Prime Minister Levi Eshkol, growing tired of the growing failure of such measures, threatened military action against Syria if the country did not do its part to tamper such forays. This led, in April, to a dogfight between the French-supplied Israeli air force and the Soviet-supplied Syrian air force, in which six Soviet MiG fighters were lost. According to King Hussein of Jordan, this dogfight led to "a massive concentration of Israeli forces along the Syrian border. From this moment on, events moved inexorably toward war.[85]

Concerning the excursions across the border, Israel could do little more than patrol its borders, oftentimes engaging Syrian troops in minor engagements. Water, on the other hand, was a tool the Arabs were intent on utilizing in an effort to undermine Israeli prosperity and security. Israel had attempted to divert water from the Jordan River in 1953 in an effort to provide irrigation to its newly won Negev region. The UN, however, shot this down, forcing the Israelis to utilize the Sea of Galilee for this purpose. The Jordan River runs straight through the Sea of Galilee, and in the early years of Israel, was a natural border, in some parts, between Jordan and Syria, on one side, and Israel on the other. In 1964, Syria began major efforts at diverting the Jordan River itself, thus depriving Israel of an all-too important source of water. The Soviets, in the spring of 1967, utilized the escalating hostilities to leak false information concerning Israeli troop concentrations along the border with Syria.

Given the Cold War realities, were the Soviets bitter over the fact that their equipment had been bested by Western hardware in this dogfight? Were they intent on strengthening their position in the Middle East and their relations with Syria and Egypt? According to Ahron Bregman, in his book, *A History of Israel*, the Soviet Union presented false intelligence to the Syrians in order to entice the United States into a war in the Middle East, as it was already finding itself further embroiled in Southeast Asia. Bregman cited a document that recorded a conversation between a Soviet official and a CIA officer, where the Soviet official claimed that

> the USSR wanted to create another trouble spot for the United States in addition to that already existing in Vietnam. The Soviet aim was to create a situation in which the US would become seriously involved economically, politically and possibly even

militarily, and would suffer serious political reverses as a result of siding [with the Israelis] against the Arabs.[86]

In a 1973 memorandum to then-Secretary of State Henry Kissinger from the Director of Central Intelligence James Schlesinger, it was stated that, while "the Soviets have long maintained an overt policy against terrorism, we now believe they are covertly inciting hostility against US interests and personnel in the Arab world...We are unable to determine the extent to which these Soviet covert activities have high level approval in the Kremlin. On the surface at least, their timing would seem inopportune in view of the forthcoming summit talks...." These talks referred to the weeklong discussions held in June 1973 between US President Richard Nixon and Soviet General Secretary Leonid Brezhnev, in which the two agreed to steer their respective countries away from force or threats of force, whether towards each other or other nations. It seems unlikely that high level Soviet officials would not have signed off on such efforts to undermine the US in the Middle East at a strategic level at least, even if they were not aware of specific tactical-level functions. In addition, it seems unlikely that such activities had not been ongoing for some years.

Obviously nuclear war was an imminent threat to every nation's national security (at this time and presently), but was the use of proxies covered in this agreement? In the late-1960s, the US was still very much involved in combat operations in Southeast Asia. As it seemed the Soviet Union harbored no ill feelings towards the Israelis, it is likely that the Soviet's were interested in keeping the Americans busy.

Despite the United States' present-day support for Israel, it was not always so. After Israel was formed and throughout the 1950s, the United States maintained a standoffish policy towards the nascent nation. According to President Dwight Eisenhower, writing on March 13, 1956, "Of course, they [the Israelis] could get arms at lower prices from almost any European nation, but they want the arms from us [the US] because they feel that in this case they have made us a virtual ally in any trouble they might get into in the region."[87]

At the time, the United States was not overtly engaged in Middle East politics, although the CIA certainly was covertly involved. At this time, Great Britain, while no doubt experiencing a declining empire, was still seen as an empire, and was certainly attempting to continue its influence in the region. In 1955, Great Britain joined together with Turkey, Iraq, Iran, and Pakistan to form the Baghdad Pact (the United States was involved in the talks, but did not officially join), in a Cold War ploy of Soviet "containment". Egyptian President Gamal Abdel Nasser, and many Arab extremists, were outraged at such an agreement, with Britain's efforts at carving up the Middle East still fresh on Arab minds. In addition, like contemporary commentators on American Middle Eastern policy, there was the belief that the British were still stretching their might in an effort to secure oil concessions (this is certainly true concerning the situation with Mossadegh in Iran). For Nasser, however, it was somewhat personal, as he envisioned himself as the leader of the Arab world, a position potentially undermined by this pact. To this end, on September 25, 1955, Nasser formed a partnership with the Soviet Union to acquire weapons, which effectively ended any relationship between Israel and the Soviets. In its attempts to contain the Soviets, it seems the British had inadvertently contained themselves in the Middle East.

At this time, the Egyptian President Gamal Abdel Nasser nationalized the Suez Canal, offering fair compensation to those companies affected. This, of course, upset Great Britain, believing that its national security was in jeopardy and undermining relations between the countries (much like in Iran with Mossadegh). The French were troubled by this as well, and both were concerned with their waning empires; the French, in particular, did not want Nasser stirring up dissension in its own North African colonies. The Israelis, for their part, were concerned with Nasser's warming relationship with the Soviet Union and his procurement of Soviet arms and weapons systems on behalf of Egypt. This all came to a head when this tripartite alliance of Great Britain, France, and Israel invaded Egypt. In retaliation, the Egyptians sank several vessels in the canal in order to impede its flow of traffic, while the Syrians destroyed three pipelines carrying 500,000 barrels of oil per day from Kirkuk, Iraq through Syria to Mediterranean ports. This represented 25% of Europe's oil imported from the Middle East.[88]

The United States was very much opposed to the aggression of Israel and came out strongly opposed to such, and worked for the withdrawal of these forces from Egypt. This United States had come out strongly against the Soviets for their recent invasion of Hungary, and did not want to appear in support of aggressive, colonialist actions.

While the US was successful in its efforts, the result undermined British and French influence throughout the region. Fearing that this loss would encourage further Soviet encroachment and influence in the Arab world, as well as further inspire pan-Arabism, the United States launched the Eisenhower Doctrine. To this end, any country could request assistance from the United States, in order "to secure and protect the territorial integrity and political independence of such nations, requesting such aid against overt armed aggression from any nation controlled by international communism."[89] This strengthened the US position in the region and while sending a message that Israel was not fully supported by the US.

This US commitment did not stop Soviet partnerships, nor did tensions cease between Israel and its neighbors. According to Moshe Dayan, "[t]he heightened tension that developed between Israel and Syria in the period preceding the Six Day War sprang from the extremist character of Syria's regime; a fanatical hatred of Israel; attempts to divert from Israel the water sources of the Jordan River; and the Syrian army's sponsorship of terrorist action.[90] All of this was due, at least from the Syrian's perspective, to Israel's occupation of what once had been Arab lands.

This left unresolved issues smoldering and both the Israelis and Arabs were not shy about acquiring armaments for the inevitable renewal of fighting. Both parties wanted a fight: the Israelis wanted to expand their territory in order to afford themselves more defensible borders, while the Arabs wanted redemption for their previous losses and for the perceived treatment of the Palestinians. As the Soviets were supplying the Syrian and Egyptian forces more and more, the United States began increasing its shipments to Israel; Cold War geopolitics at work, a sort of cheerleading for their respective "teams."

By 1967, the penetrations across the Israeli border from Syria, along with Syria's other attempts at undermining Israel, caused Israel to place some troops along this corridor. Whether or not this was an actual troop buildup for offensive purposes is debatable; suffice it to say, Egyptian President Gamal Abdel Nasser did not seem to be under the illusion of Israeli troop buildup, but he did attempt to utilize the opportunity for Egypt's gain. In May, he began moving large forces into the Sinai Peninsula, which was being occupied by a UN peacekeeping force, deployed there following the 1956 Suez

War. The UN Secretary General, U Thant, not wishing to undermine Egypt's sovereignty, ordered the withdrawal of the UN force at Nasser's request. Part of the UN force's mandate was the facilitation of open access to the Strait of Tiran for both Arabs and Israelis, which the latter took full advantage of through its port city of Eilat. Now, with freedom-of-movement, and pressure from his Arab allies, Nasser ordered the closure of the strait, which then, with the UN's departure, reverted to Egyptian territory. With Egypt massing troops and the closure of this waterway spelling a commercial nightmare for Israel (and thus undermining its fragile security), Israel launched a military strike against Egypt on June 5. Leaving few fighters to defend Israeli airspace, nearly the entire Israeli air force was launched against Egypt, catching its forces almost completely by surprise. In two waves of attacks, the Israeli forces killed a third of Egypt's pilots, rendered 13 of its bases inoperable, destroyed nearly two dozen radar and anti-aircraft sites, and most importantly to the Israelis, destroyed 400 of Egypt's planes, granting Israel nearly complete air superiority for the duration of the fighting. The next day, Israel reopened the Strait of Tiran to shipping and went on to seize the entire Sinai Peninsula in just four days of fighting.[iv]

Israel's attack against Egyptian positions triggered the activation of Syria's mutual defense pact with Egypt, causing Syrian batteries to begin firing into Israel. The Golan Heights provided the Syrians with a commanding position over Israel, one in which they had used to shell Israeli towns since they had begun fighting in 1948. The Israelis were intent to capture these heights to gain a commanding position over the Syrians, and in the last days of the war, succeeded in driving the Syrian forces away. Through the years, the Golan Heights would prove, not only to be a strategic military position, but also a valuable stretch of fertile land and supply of one-third of Israel's water needs (rainwater runs down from these heights into the Jordan River). In addition, Israelis are able to enjoy the Golan Heights for skiing, no doubt adding to the popular sentiment that the Golan Heights should remain in Israeli possession. In December 1981, the Israeli government took

---

iv   In 1979, the Sinai reverted to Egyptian control, in exchange for peace and a normalization of diplomatic relations; Egypt became the first Arab country to enter into peace with Israel.

steps to ensure just that by unilaterally annexing the land and placing it under civilian control. This angered the entire international community, particularly Syria, but also the United States at the time. In March 2019, US President Donald Trump officially recognized Israeli sovereignty over the Golan Heights, prompting a vow from Israeli Prime Minister Benjamin Netanyahu that an Israeli settlement on the Golan would be named after President Trump. Yousef Jabareen, an Arab-Israeli with a seat in the Israeli Knesset, tweeted,

> It's fitting for US President Trump to have a settlement named after him that's illegal and contravenes international law. Trump's recognition of Israel's sovereignty in the Golan Heights is spitting in the world's face. Transferring Israeli citizens to the Golan is a war crime under the Rome Statute of the International Criminal Court. A war crime named after Trump.[91]

In the early 1990s, US President Bill Clinton met with Hafez al-Assad in Geneva, Switzerland, in their very first meeting. During this encounter, President Clinton described Hafez as making the "first explicit statement that he was willing to make peace and establish normal relations with Israel." He understood Syria's previous reliance on the Soviet Union for support, but with its collapse in 1991, Syria was more willing to turn to the West for economic assistance and regaining the Golan Heights. "To do that, he had to stop supporting terrorism in the region, which would be easy to do if he made an agreement with Israel that succeeded in giving back to Syria the Golan Heights…"[92] The only way for Syria and Israel to have a viable peace is for Syria to regain this land peacefully, action for which Israel has made difficult. While Israel was once willing to cede control of the Golan back to Syria, the Syrian Civil War and Iran's role in it, has convinced Israel of potential security concerns in doing so.

According to Bernard Lewis, "[t]he Soviet leader [Nikita] Khrushchev, who had remained cautiously silent in the earlier stages of the Six-Day War, realized that a pro-Arab statement brought no danger of a collision with the United States and then—and only then—came out strongly on the Arab side."[93] So it was that the US was not yet fully supporting Israel prior to the war. Had it been, perhaps it could have urged caution on the part of Israel, and thereby limited the Arabs' willingness to turn to the Soviet Union for support, thereby further alienating Israel and the Arab States. This might then have limited the Soviet's influence in the region and also limited the eventual role of the US in the region.

UN RESOLUTION 242

Concerned over the fighting throughout the summer of 1967, the persistent tensions in the Middle East, and the "inadmissibility of the acquisition of territory by war," the United Nations adopted Resolution 242 in November 1967. Drafted by Lord Caradon of Great Britain, it called for peace in the region by means of Israeli withdrawal from territories captured during the Six Day War and every nation's right to maintain secure and recognized borders without threats or force. In addition, it called for:

1. guarantees of freedom of movement through international waterways in the region,

2. settling the issue of refugees [caused not just by the recent fighting], and

3. a guarantee of "territorial inviolability and political independence" of all regional states.

In order to establish such a peace, the UN believed it necessary to call for the adherence of two principles, one being the end of hostilities and respect to every neighboring nation's sovereignty. The other principle has been the center of much disagreement over the years, and reads in full: "Withdrawal of Israel armed forces *from territories occupied* in the recent conflict" [author's italics].[94] As there is no definite article preceding "territories" in the text, the question remains open as to which territories must be vacated. The word "the" (or any word of quantity for that matter) was clearly not utilized and therefore seemed to give Israel discretion as to how much and which territories it would cede back to the Arab states. This is in direct contradiction to the French text (which stated "des territoires occupés"), which clearly utilized the definite "des," which then should have required Israel to return "the occupied territories" (read: all). The Arabs, of course, hold that the Israelis must cede ALL territory occupied during the fighting, essentially a return to Israel's original borders, while Israel maintains that returning the Sinai Peninsula to Egypt was more than enough to satisfy the terms of the agreement.[95] This persists into the present and has no doubt contributed to continued tension and animosity in the region. Syria, of course, maintains that the Golan should be returned.

Further contention revolves around the "just settlement of the refugee problem." Obviously, the Palestinians were understood to be a part of such a "refugee problem;" however, the text does not mention the Palestinians by name. The understanding being (perhaps better understood in 1967 than the present) that while the Palestinians were refugees from their homes in Israel, the state of Israel had settled a proportionate number of Jews that had previously had homes in Arab countries. It has been argued that while Israel has failed to compensate the Palestinians for their flight (whether voluntary or forced), the Jews fleeing Arab countries had not been compensated by those respective Arab countries either. Was UN Resolution 242 a deliberately misleading document or just poorly written? It is hard to believe that all the collective minds working on this small document could have been so intentionally careless, and yet, the absence of a seemingly innocuous word such as "the" has in fact caused some bit of harm.

After the 1967 war, in a National Intelligence Estimate from 1968, the CIA was under the impression that the Soviet Union was not looking to undermine Israel to any significant level. Despite Soviet assistance to Syria and Egypt, the Soviets recognized the right to exist of the Israelis and were pushing the Arabs to adopt a more peaceful stance towards their neighbor. Despite this, Israel remained wary of the relationship and continued to view the US as the appropriate balance.[96] It seems that perhaps the Soviets were using the Arabs to draw the United States into a wasteful Middle Eastern foreign policy, while the Israelis were using the United States to protect them from the Arabs (and their Soviet protector).

HAFEZ AL-ASSAD

With the military's solid backing, Hafez al-Assad staged a bloodless coup d'état, seizing power in November 1970. In what came to be known as the Corrective Movement, Hafez quickly consolidated his influence and position within Syria and the Ba'ath Party. He increased the military, which he could justify by Israel's continued occupation of the Golan Heights, as well as Syrian internal security services, which grew to 15 competing intelligence organizations targeting the Syrian people. He took a page from the Soviet Union, establishing a single-party police state that limited high-speed or mass communications, like fax machines and newspapers, and later, the internet. While the internet was in its infancy in the later years of Hafez al-Assad's rule, it would be utilized effectively in organizing resistance to his son, Bashar, during the Arab Spring and the Syrian civil war.

The senior Assad was born and grew up during the French mandate and also during a time of increasing Zionist aspirations. He was born in 1930 in the predominantly Alawite village of Qardaha, Syria, near the historic port city of Latakia, approximately 200 miles northwest of Damascus. He did not come from a great deal of money, and as a member of the minority Alawites, was ostracized by the majority Sunnis, which undoubtedly led him to see something worthwhile in the Ba'ath Party, which he joined while still a student in high school.

The Ba'ath Party, a secular, revolutionary, socialist organization, sought to undermine imperialism, and promote Arabism. With pan-Arabism at its core, the Ba'ath Party in Assad's time wanted a resurrection of the Arab World, a day when the Arabs were once again on top and the days of Ottoman and European imperialism were forgotten; and in this sense Ba'ath derives its meaning in Arabic, "resurrection" or "renaissance". In April 1941, an Iraqi politician named Rashid Ali al-Gaylani, with military backing, seized power in Iraq, establishing a government friendly to the Axis powers during World War II. A committee was formed in Syria to aid al-Gaylani, but he was eventually removed by British forces, but not before elements of the Ba'ath Party were formed within Syria, leading to conflicting branches governing separately in Syria and Iraq.[97] While the Ba'athists were not necessarily opposed to the various ethnic identities present in Syria, it was through the Ba'ath Party that the country's religious minority were able to gather support of the other minority classes, thereby undermining the strength of the predominant Sunnis. It was for this reason that the Shi'a (particularly the Alawites), Christians, Ismailis, and Druze, found a certain privilege in Syria that might not have been possible elsewhere in the Middle East.[98] Due to their lower socio-economic standing in society, Alawites tended to hold prestigious positions throughout the military and intelligence circles. Their role to this end would increase after France ended its mandate over Syria, with the proportion of Alawite officers reaching 42% by 1970, and by extension, growing the Alawite proportion of senior Ba'ath officials, reaching 25% by 1970.[99] This no doubt caused a great deal of resentment and hostility, particularly throughout the majority Sunni population.[100]

Following high school, Hafez al-Assad entered the Air Force College in Aleppo, graduating with the rank of lieutenant in 1955. In 1958, Syria and Egypt joined together to form the politically short-lived United Arab Republic, hoping that this pan-Arab sentiment would sweep through the Middle East. During this time, Hafez al-Assad was stationed in Egypt; however, by 1960, disillusioned with Egypt's attempts to bolster its own position at the expense of Syria, he joined a Ba'athist committee in Cairo composed of his fellow military officers. In 1961, Ba'athist military officers staged a coup back in Syria, leaving Hafez temporarily without work, but also leading to the dissolution of the United Arab Republic. He was soon transferred to the Syrian Ministry of Economics, which would give him a front row seat to the end of democracy in Syria with the 1963 coup. Called the 8th of March Revolution, Hafez was the leader of a five-man committee operating underground, utilizing their extensive network of contacts to ensure the movement's success.

In the aftermath of this revolution, the Ba'athists quickly moved to consolidate their control over the country by announcing an emergency law, a move that would not be reversed until 2011. During this time, constitutional rights were undermined; the government conducted preventative arrests, threw out statutes of the penal code, barred court complaints, and even prevented a lawyer's presence during interrogations. Worst of all, the mukhabarat, the Syrian secret police, were not given to oversight and possessed little, if any, accountability, leading to the potential for suspects to be detained for unspecified lengths, tortured, and in extreme cases, outright killed. This led to a great deal of corruption throughout the mukhabarat (absolute power corrupts absolutely, according to Lord Acton), and a somewhat equal level of fear and uncertainty throughout the populace.

This was also true of the Ba'ath Party, which had not quite solidified its position throughout Syria. Thanks to the many coups throughout the '50s and '60s, the party had room to grow, and during the 23 February Movement in 1966, in which Hafez al-Assad played a part, the Ba'ath Party was able to secure relative stability, enough so that Assad could take complete control of the country and the party by the '70s.

The frustration over Resolution 242 coupled with the Arabs' failure to recover Palestinian lands was too much for most to accept. Hafez al-Assad, for his part, was distraught over the loss of the Golan Heights to Israel during the fighting in the Six-Day War in 1967, as were many Syrians and Ba'athists alike. During this time, Hafez had been the Minister of Defense and no doubt felt some responsibility in its loss, and a burning desire to reclaim it. In September 1970 (Black September), Palestinians living in Jordan launched an offensive to unseat Jordan's then-King Hussein. Looking to aid the Palestinians' efforts, Syria sent an armored column into Jordan, but was repulsed by Jordanian air power. King Hussein of Jordan described the situation:

> Here, in Jordan, we had not authorized such an army's [PLO] formation. Even more, we had refused to let them [PLO] send us troops. The Palestinians living in Jordan had become Jordanian citizens without restrictions of any kind, and under no conditions did we wish to offer up the Hashemite kingdom to the divisions which existed elsewhere. Therein lay one of the reasons for our misunderstandings with Cairo and Damascus.[101]

For his part, as Minister of Defense, Hafez refused the use of Syria's air force as he did not approve of attacking Syria's Muslim neighbor. The PLO was soundly defeated in Jordan and, with their base of operations no more, they settled in Lebanon to continue their fight against Israel.

After coming to power, Hafez also needed to ensure that he had the control of the Ba'ath Party and went about reforming and consolidating it into a newer, more responsive party (at least as benefited himself).[102] In a multiethnic state, the Ba'ath Party's secular ideology could become a unifying element for the Syrian people; however, Hafez used it to unify supporters who would strengthen his own position, and theirs' through the subsequent cronyism. He appointed and promoted members of his own religious group, the Alawites, into influential positions in the military and security services, particularly intelligence, special forces, and armored units. While this undoubtedly benefitted Hafez, it also provided a great many opportunities for the underrepresented and underprivileged Alawites that had been looked down upon throughout Syria in years past.

Syria's continued military losses to the Israelis, and especially its loss of the Golan Heights, served to justify, in the eyes of Hafez al-Assad, the continuation of the Emergency Laws enacted in 1963. Through them, Hafez was able to consolidate his power throughout Syria, and retain his power until his death in 2001. Because of this, Hafez was unwilling to undermine the Emergency Law without serious concessions from the Israelis, and most certainly not without regaining the Golan.[103] It seems, with this, that Assad was able to shift attention from his own tyranny unto the tyranny of the Israelis. With Syria and Israel in a constant state of militarization, with the former hoping against hope that they would be victorious in reclaiming their lost land, and the latter defending this land so that in could not be utilized against them, it seems the Syrian people were willing to tolerate such tyranny for the sake of the country and national pride.

Despite the growing bureaucracy and limiting of freedoms under Hafez al-Assad's rule, there were improvements made in the overall standard of living amongst Syrians of all classes and ethnicities: access to education, running water, and electricity; a reduction in infant mortality rates; an increase in life expectancy rates and literacy; and infrastructure improvements through the laying of railroad tracks and roads. No doubt these were instruments utilized to satisfy and control a population, lest it become unwieldy and discontented, rather than a benevolent ruler showing concern for his people. They also contributed to Syria's national security and state of readiness for the inevitable next round against Israel. However, a country ramping up its military spending while simultaneously ramping up social spending could not financially sustain itself for long.

THE ECONOMY

By 1973, according to a US National Intelligence Analytical Memorandum of that year, it was determined that "Syria is no longer the erratic, coup-prone cockpit of inter-Arab politics that it was in the 1950s and the early 1960s. Multiple upheavals have helped to produce, and to mask, a thoroughgoing revolution in national institutions and attitudes. The new pattern that has developed in the past decade appears to have a number of durable elements."[104] It seemed, even the CIA recognized the "stabilizing" policies of Hafez al-Assad.

This state of readiness, while having an effect on the people's rights, also had an effect on Syria's economy; preparing for war presented an opportunity cost for Syria. During the Six-Day War in 1967, Syria's military expenditures were just over 8% of its Gross Domestic Product (GDP). When Hafez al-Assad seized power in 1971, it was 8.5%, shooting up to 15% in 1973 during the Yom Kippur War. Three years later, when Syria invaded Lebanon, it was still hovering at nearly 15%, peaking at 17.7% in 1984 during its occupation of Lebanon. From there it steadily declined to nearly 7% in 1990. Since Syria was dependent on Soviet largesse, the decline in its military expenditure could likely be due to the Soviet Union's waning influence during its invasion and occupation of Afghanistan. In 1991, Syria's expenditure peaked again at 10.4%, likely due to the Gulf War, and since 1991 also witnessed the fall of the Soviet Union, Syria's military spending declined to 5.2% by 2002, increased a percentage point the following year (likely due to the US invasion of Iraq), and then declined from there. Israel spent even more, peaking at nearly 26% in 1975, before gradually declining to 6.7% in 2007. To put things into perspective, the United States spent 8.7% of its GDP on military spending at the height of the Vietnam War in 1967.[105] Spending such an enormous percentage of its GDP on its military forces, meant that Syria was forgoing spending in other areas or just simply wasting a great deal of money.

The changes brought about by Hafez al-Assad's consolidation of power throughout the 1960s and 1970s did not include democratic freedoms or the repeal of the 1963 emergency laws. The loss of the Golan, in addition to the huge burden of military spending, no doubt took its toll on Syrian society, with some elements within Syria organizing resistance and assassinating Ba'ath officials in an attempt to regain control of the government.

As Ba'ath Party members dominated Syrian politics, so too did they dominate matters of the economy, forming business leagues rife with cronyism. This level of corruption stifles innovation and competitiveness by limiting the barriers-to-entry, making business creation difficult, and limiting employment possibilities for all. In addition, the Ba'ath Party's socialist policies were affecting large land-owners and merchants who were forced to surrender large spoils of their labor to the government for redistribution. While the masses suffered under such corrupt cronyism, a small but powerful core of individuals retained commercial, banking, and landholding interests, clearly exploiting their privileges.[106] In the early years after Bashar's assumption of the presidency, one-in-five Syrians were unemployed and nearly half of the population was considered in poverty.[107] Clearly the Ba'ath Party's socialist agenda had failed the people of Syria, but so too was the political suppression, corruption, and economic instability.

From the 1970s, Syria had strong trading ties with Europe and eventually the European Union (EU). At the peak of this relation-ship, two-thirds of Syria's global exports landed in Europe, with between 30%-40% of Syria's imports originating from the same.[108] The European Union was Syria's largest contributor of foreign direct investment (FDI), a necessary multiplier on top of its trade, due to its weak economy. Syria's trade with Europe fell off in the later years of Hafez's presidency; it continued to export large quantities of oil, while turning more and more to imports from China and Southeast Asia. As capitalism was not a strong component of its economy, competi-tion was never much present, and exporting was viewed in a negative light, contributing to a larger mess of its economy.[109]

Adding to the weak economic numbers, there was the growing concern caused by water shortages in the country and the region. According to research conducted by the National Aeronautics and Space Administration (NASA) and its German counterpart, between 2003 and 2009, the Tigris-Euphrates River Basin (Turkey, Syria, Iraq, and parts of Iran) lost water at the greatest global rates, with the excep-tion of northern India. As both the Tigris and Euphrates originate in Turkey, Turkish damming and hydroelectric activity along these rivers adversely impacts Iraq and Syria; since 1975, Syria has experienced a

40% reduction of its Euphrates levels. In 2006, a drought developed in Syria so severe that farmers were forced to abdicate their lands and search out employment in urban centers. This no doubt led to growing discontent in a country feeling largely marginalized, and possibly added fuel to the intellectual movement to remedy the nation's ills.[110] Prior to the drought, agriculture was responsible for one-quarter of Syria's GDP and one-quarter of its labor force; two years later, it amounted to just 17% of its GDP.[111]

Also, of some concern for Syria's economy was its oil production. In a 2006 analysis conducted by the International Monetary Fund (IMF), it concluded that Syrian oil revenues were falling, partly due to its declining oil reserves, although solid, global oil prices were keeping Syria afloat.[112] These high oil prices were negatively affecting the Syrian people (as they could not afford the commodity for their own personal uses), and the government had begun introducing petroleum subsidies by 2008. These subsidies covered 4.4 million tons of diesel fuel at an unsustainable rate[113] for the Syrian government as the costs incurred by the government were ultimately incurred by the people through taxation; governments do not themselves produce like a business produces. To further complicate Syria's economic woes, the IMF was predicting the exhaustion of its oil resources by the 2020s.[114] While new techniques are always being adopted to increase the reaches with which oil can be extracted, it is unlikely that Syria would have the resources to conduct such exploration and would likely require greater levels of FDI or a reduction in the state-control of the economy, allowing the promotion of free enterprise. In any event, by 2009, Syria had become a net oil importer, drastically undermining its fragile economy.[115]

YOM KIPPUR WAR

After the 21 coup d'états that swept through Syria, the country finally found stability in the form of Hafez al-Assad in 1971. For this reason, neither Israel nor the United States confidently believed a war would be forthcoming from Syria. As Egypt's air force had been all but destroyed in 1967, it was confidently felt that Egypt's efforts at rebuilding would sideline it for many years, leaving Israel's borders relatively quiet. Furthermore, in regards to

Egypt, intelligence assessments concluded that "the whole thrust of President [Anwar] Sadat's activities since last spring has been in the direction of bringing moral, political, and economic force to bear on Israel in tacit acknowledgement of Arab un-readiness to make war."[116]

The CIA was aware of Egyptian and Syrian military buildups, but believed any attack was "dubious." On October 5, 1973, the day before the war, the CIA was aware of large military activities in Egypt, concluding that it did "not appear to be preparing for a military offensive against Israel," and that there were no indications "that any party intends to initiate hostilities." The CIA continued the next day, believing "[f]or the Syrian president, a military adventure now would be suicidal."[117] Clearly, the CIA failed in accurately assessing their intentions and capabilities, for on October 6, the Egyptian and Syrian military launched a coordinated assault into the Sinai and Golan Heights, respectively, catching the international community by surprise. October 6, 1973 happened to be the Jewish holiday of Yom Kippur, the holiest day in Judaism, and also happened to fall during the Muslim holy month of Ramadan.

On Israeli's Northern Front, the Syrian military had overwhelming superiority: in its initial assault into the Golan, Syria fielded 500 tanks and 690 artillery pieces, ultimately bringing to bear 1,700 tanks, 1,300 pieces of artillery, 350 aircraft, and 4,500 infantrymen. Also, unbeknownst to Israeli intelligence, the Syrian military outfitted its infantry troops with devastating anti-tank weapons that could significantly weaken Israel's defenses.

Israel, for its part, was wholly unprepared. Although it commanded the high ground along defensive positions throughout the Golan, it possessed just 177 tanks, 44 artillery pieces, and very few infantry troops dispersed along its lines. The Syrians attacked along two fronts, one attacking north of the city of Kuneitra, and the second south of the city. Although the Syrian offensive had stalled by around midnight on the morning of October 7, that southern thrust had succeeded in breaking through Israel's primary defensive line. While the majority of Israeli's air force was tied up in heavy fighting along its Southern Front near the Suez Canal, there were enough planes to slow Syrian forces enough to keep them from making an all-out breakthrough. With reservists en route to the Golan, the situation was dire for Israel. According to Moshe Dayan, Israel's defense minister during the fighting:

> The depth of the Golan Heights is altogether not more than fifteen miles. If the Syrian forces reached the descent to the Jordan River, it would be very difficult to repel them, particularly when they possessed such powerful quantities of weapons and manpower, and we also had to fight on the Egyptian front. It was evident that we had to stop the Syrians near the point of the breakthrough, even if it meant investing all our strength.[118]

This defensive, delaying fight worked well enough for Israeli reservists to slowly stream into the area, and by the evening of the second day, October 8, the Syrian advance had completely stalled. Intent on regaining the initiative, Syrian forces launched a counterattack on the 9th, but were checked by the Israelis, by then heavily complemented with its reserve forces. With fighting so intense and desperate throughout the Golan during the first few days of fighting, Syria sustained 900 disabled tanks, well beyond its initial commitments.[119]

With Syrian forces stalled, Israeli forces began their own offensive; however, on the Kuneitra-Damascus road, Israeli units encountered stubborn resistance. With such stubborn fighting ongoing along the Suez Canal as well, the Israelis needed more than a stalemate along the Northern Front. By moving into Syria and threatening Damascus, the Israelis could capture additional territory while seeing further expenditures of Syrian resources. As Syria had already lost the Golan Heights, the thought of further humiliation might resolve Assad to keeping distance from Israel, or so the Israelis had hoped.

After learning of the surprise attack after several hours of fighting, US Secretary of State Henry Kissinger (himself a Jew having fled from Nazi Germany) placed a call to the British Ambassador to the US, Lord Cromer. Kissinger apologized for the US having interfered during the Suez Crisis of 1956. Lord Cromer responded: "And a little late, it was a mistake."[120] Was this the official US position or simply the US mollifying the British with roles ironically reversed? In any event, the US was reluctant to assist the Israelis for fear of a Soviet response, but the US had to make the effort to intercede or risk the appearance of scheming with the Israelis. Later during the day of the 6th, Kissinger expressed to Lord Cromer, in another conversation, that calling a ceasefire too soon would be short-sighted, as the Israelis were likely to beat back the Arab offensive, and then themselves cross the Suez Canal while simultaneously entering Syria. He then added: "And we may then find such a resolution extremely handy on getting them back." He expressed the idea that once the resolution was put forth at the UN Security Council, the whole process could be stonewalled by ongoing debates within the General Assembly. Lord Cromer conceded that a return to the status quo was ideal for all parties, but timing was crucial, as they risked alienating the Arab countries.[121] This reinforced comments made by Kissinger in the earlier conversation in which Kissinger stated that the US would be accused of colluding with the Israelis if efforts were not forthcoming to stop the fighting. He confided to Lord Cromer that officials within the Department of Defense wanted "to drop the Israelis" because "[w]e don't want to lose Arab oil."[122] So, the US wanted the best of both sides: the Israelis recapturing the land it was losing on the first day, so that land-for-peace could become a potential bargaining position, while also sympathizing with the Arab position in order to continue receiving economical oil.

In an effort to sustain such operations, the Israelis were in dire need of supplies, getting little help from many European countries, who were withholding such supplies or delaying shipments. As Minister of Defense, Moshe Dayan,

> raised the question of arms from the United States. [Israeli Prime Minister] Golda [Meir] made several suggestions, the main one being that she fly to Washington for a secret meeting with…[US President Richard Nixon]. She though it important to explain our [Israeli] situation to the president in a face-to-face talk, tell him about the vast quantities of Soviet arms in the hands of the Arabs, their huge numerical superiority, and what was happening on the fronts. It was not only weapons we needed. She also wanted President Nixon to know what had happened in this war, and why.[123]

Throughout the fighting, the United Nations had been hard at work, passing Resolution 338, calling for the cessation of fighting in positions occupied at that time, and a subsequent return to the status quo as outlined in Resolution 242. On October 25, 1973, the Israelis and Egyptians signed a ceasefire agreement, thereby forcing Syria into a cessation of fighting as well. However, Syria did not officially sign such an agreement until May 31, 1974, due to an impasse developing over when prisoner-of-war (POW) lists would be exchanged. Although the two sides finally reached an agreement over their respective POWs, as well as the positioning of UN troops in a buffer zone between the two countries, Hafez al-Assad felt that Egypt's unilateral move to negotiate with Israel, undermined Syria's position, forcing it to negotiate from a weakened position. Therefore, in 1979, Syria would vote to expel Egypt from the Arab League (Syria won its case, but Egypt was readmitted after about 10 years).

Although the Yom Kippur War had been a tactical and strategic defeat for the Arab armies, there was a certain level of pride redeemed by their performance. The Syrians had lost two-thirds of its attacking force,[124] and yet, they fought valiantly. Even Moshe Dayan recognized this by writing, "[a]s for the fighting standard of the Arab soldiers, I can sum it up in one sentence: they did not run away...Furthermore, the standard of combat of the Arab soldier had improved.[125] If they had earned respect from their enemy, certainly they had earned it from their friends and countrymen as well. There is little doubt that the Soviet assistance that began flowing to the Arabs after 1967 helped contribute to the rise in quality; morale is a powerful tool. In the six years between the two wars, the Arab armies tripled their strength, with troop levels rising from 300,000 to 1,000,000; tanks increasing to 5,000 from 1,700; over 1,000 planes from just 350; and bringing artillery pieces up to 4,800 from 1,350.[126] The overwhelming success during the Six-Day War attributed to Israel's air force, was drastically undermined during the Yom Kippur fighting by Soviet supplied anti-aircraft batteries and their respective technicians and advisors. The fighting in 1973 showed the Arabs that the Israelis were beatable, and it showed the Israelis that they needed their own superpower support in order to stand a chance.

It was this bipolar balancing act that brought the United States into full support of Israel. During one discussion with Henry Kissinger, Moshe Dayan "happened to remark that the United States was the only country that was ready to stand by us [the Israelis], my silent reflection was that the United States would really rather support the Arabs."[127] Despite this uneasy feeling, the US did indeed make a friend out of Israel. After Israel's desperate initial days, with the Arabs attacking, the Soviets supplying the Arabs, and the Europeans reluctant to assist in supplying the Israelis, the US began a month-long airlift of supplies beginning on October 14. There is little doubt that this greatly helped the Israelis turn the tide, and again, according to Dayan,

> The American government has helped us a great deal, with the supply of arms, economic assistance, and political support. I hate to think what our situation would have been if the United States had withheld its aid, or what we would do if Washington were to turn its back on Israel one of these days.[128]

To help secure future support, Israel began simultaneous talks with the US. Not only was financial aid and a steady supply of military equipment vital, but so too was "confirmation that the United States would not demand from us [the Israelis] further withdrawals from the Golan Heights."[129]

Following the end to the Yom Kippur War, Syria did not allow itself much of a respite, as Lebanon was inching towards civil war. As Syria believed Lebanon was rightly a portion of Syrian territory rather than an independent country, as per the Sykes-Picot Agreement, Syria invaded and occupied its neighbor in 1976, following Lebanon's civil war in 1975. A multiethnic country, political power in Lebanon was shared between the Christians, Sunni Muslims, and Shi'a Muslims, but with the mass exodus of Palestinians from Israel into Lebanon, and the subsequent immigration of the PLO from Jordan after Black September, the fabric of Lebanese society had shifted by 1975. Militias formed, typically along demographic lines, and fighting intensified into an all-out civil war, racking and destabilizing the country until 1990. Following Syria's intervention, tensions continued mounting until 1978, when, after Palestinian guerillas attacked an Israeli bus in northern Israel, Israel itself invaded southern Lebanon. In these early years of fighting in Lebanon, Syria maintained 40,000 troops inside its neighbor's territory, but still had no interest in getting mixed up in another war with Israel, largely keeping its forces north of the

Litani River, while the Israelis predominantly maintained a presence south of the same river.

While the Syrian military lost 12,000 troops in its nearly three decades long occupation of Lebanon, advantages were stacked in its favor as well: over 1 million Syrians were employed throughout Lebanon, creating jobs and remittances for the Syrian economy; Lebanese banks provided loans to Syrian government cronies; and smuggling increased, flooding Syrian goods onto Lebanese markets and cheap Lebanese goods into Syria. It was little surprise that Syria was so willing to sacrifice to keep its reach over Lebanon throughout the years, but the international community grew concerned over Syria's occupation. The United Nations Security Council passed Resolution 1559 in 2004, calling for the disarming and disbanding of militias and the removal of foreign troops in support of the "sovereignty, territorial integrity, unity, and political independence" of Lebanon, so that free and fair presidential elections could be held.[130] Unperturbed, Syria carried on until the assassination in 2005 of Lebanese businessman and politician, Hafiq Hariri. Investigations later revealed the possibility of Hezbollah involvement in his death, but regardless, many suspected Syrian manipulation. Outrage formed and calls for Syria's withdrawal reached fever pitch both within and without Lebanon, culminating in Lebanon's Cedar Revolution, and leading to Syria's withdrawal in April 2005.[v]

After Israel's invasion of Lebanon, Iran saw the need to defend Islamic principles, therefore Iranian officials began meeting in Damascus on how best to combat these perceived aggressions, staging Islamic Revolution Guard Corp (IRGC) forces in Syria for an eventual fight in Lebanon. The IRGC was established in Iran following the 1979 revolution in order to protect Iran's Islamic system and values; as a majority Shi'a Muslim country, it is these Shi'a ideals that Iran sought to uphold. Composed of 125,000 recruits, the IRGC operates independently of the Iranian armed forces, and maintains its own ground, naval, and air forces. The IRGC also operates a 15,000-strong

---

v   While Syria withdrew its military forces and hardware, many believed that Syrian intelligence apparatus stayed behind, guaranteeing Syrian influence in Lebanon in the subsequent years.

unit for all its operations taking place outside Iran, known as the Quds Force.[131]

A special relationship soon formed between Iran and Syria following the Israeli invasion of Lebanon. The IRGC were willing and motivated to support Syrian forces deployed in Lebanon in a fight against Israeli forces. The Syrians had lost the motivation to do so; however, an agreement was reached between the two nations for building a resistance force within Lebanon, which came to be known as Hezbollah (Arabic for "Party of God"). The IRGC established a base within the Beqa'a Valley of Lebanon and began building a force that could then be unleashed against Israel, but also utilized to win the "hearts and minds" of Lebanon's Shi'a through various social programs. Iran could then easily funnel trainers, money, and equipment into Lebanon via Syria, to maintain this new proxy army.

HAMA

One of the biggest threats and tests of Hafez's rule in Syria was the uprising in Hama in 1982. After Syria invaded Lebanon in 1976, animosity once again culminated in large-scale demonstrations in Hama. Attempting to arrest an opposition leader, government forces raided a building in Hama, but were ambushed and killed. These actions directly challenged the legitimacy of Hafez al-Assad and the Ba'ath rule (and by extension, minority oversight). The opposition was able to maintain control of Hama for four days; government forces responded with 12,000 soldiers. Hama was cordoned off and shelled for nearly a month, resulting in the destruction of half the city and many dead (the exact count is disputed, with figures ranging from several thousand, to perhaps 40,000). This effectively silenced, albeit temporarily, an opposition that had slowly been brewing.

Throughout the 1990s, Hafez al-Assad began to consolidate power for the eventuality of one of his sons assuming the presidency. Bassel, Hafez's eldest son, was believed to be the heir-apparent, but his death in an automobile accident in 1994 forced Hafez to begin grooming another son, Bashar. Training in London to be an ophthalmologist, Bashar al-Assad, "The Hope," as he came to be known by many within Syria, was announced to be the next-in-line, bringing with the pronouncement a great deal of optimism for those yearning for democracy and freedom. Hafez al-Assad died in Damascus on June 10, 2000 at 69 years old; the following day, Bashar al-Assad was unanimously elected the new president of Syria. Despite the younger Assad being too young for the presidency under the Syrian constitution, the national assembly amended Article 83, changing the age from 40 years to 34 years, Bashar's age. Syria's parliament voted in favor of Assad's nomination and, in a nationwide referendum, he received over 97% of the vote.[132]

SYRIAN ACCOUNTABILITY AND LEBANESE SOVEREIGNTY RESTORATION ACT OF 2003

According to former-US President George W Bush, his administration's "strategy was to isolate Iran and Syria as a way to reduce their influence and encourage change from within" the countries.[133] Isolation is a long-term policy, one that only works when the international community supports it. On the part of the United States, the US 108th Congress passed House Resolution (HR) 828, the Syrian Accountability and Lebanese Sovereignty Restoration Act of 2003 to encourage Syria in halting any and all support of terrorist operations, including the facilitation of fighters into Iraq, where the United States had recently invaded. It further sought to halt Syria's development and utilization of surface-to-surface missiles (both medium- and long-range), its research and development of chemical and biological weapons, and an encouragement for bilateral negotiations with Israel. Until Syria followed through with such actions, the act further authorized the Department of State to continue listing Syria as a state sponsor of terror. To enforce the terms of the act, Congress granted the president the ability to: exclude all US products from entering Syria (excluding food and medicine, which negates the concept of isolation), forbid US business operations and investments in Syria, and limit US-Syria diplomatic activities. To couple the carrot with the stick, if Syria were to comply with all terms of the act, the US government was willing to provide developmental assistance. It seems Syria only began sponsoring terrorism to undermine Israel, particularly after it lost the Golan Heights. Would the US have been willing to facilitate its return if there was a significant reduction in terrorism?

At that time, Syria was still occupying parts of Lebanon, utilizing its military presence to support Hezbollah fighters who were then launching harassing attacks against Israel's northern border. More than this though, Hezbollah, under the leadership of Imad Mugniya, was credited with a role in the USS Cole blast in 2000. It was Mugniya's group, protected by occupying Syrian forces, that had made the explosives for the al-Qaeda terrorist in Yemen. Furthermore, it was also believed that the CIA had learned the names of Syrian army officers who were directly involved in the 1983 truck bombing of the Marine barracks in Lebanon, an operation handled by Syrian officials utilizing Syrian militias.[134] The US did have a national security concern for stopping terrorism emanating from Syria, but to call for Syria to enter negotiations with Israel, and then punish it if it did not, was quite another. Money cannot always buy cooperation, especially when that same money is viewed as supporting one's enemy. By demanding Syria enter into negotiations with Israel, the US must have known that the effort would fall short. Furthermore, by allowing fighters to move through Syria into Iraq, Bashar al-Assad (whether he publicly allowed it or not, he certainly knew it was ongoing) clearly felt threatened by an invading US Army next door to his country. Would the US act differently if Russia or China were to invade Mexico? A stable Iraq is in Syria's best interest, but not one occupied with US forces, seen as staunch allies of Israel.

The only aspect of HR 828 that could possibly make any sense, but which accomplished nothing, was attempting to halt Syria's efforts at furthering its chemical weapons, either in quantity or quality. These could definitely prove harmful to US national security, although attempting to halt surface-to-surface missile development would not, as they would not have the capability of striking the United States from such a distance.

However, in 2009, as the new Administration of Barack Obama was taking over the helm in the US, there were signs pointing to reconciliation between Washington and Damascus, with American officials being sent to Syria even before the inauguration. In an interview, Assad was quoted as saying "[w]e have positive signs from the new administration, but we have learned to be cautious and not to count on such signs as long as there is nothing tangible. If there are conditions, then there will be no dialogue. They know that."[135] The

American ambassador had been pulled from Syria following Bashar al-Assad's continued support of terrorism, specifically the transnational succor being provided for insurgents battling US and Iraqi forces following the US invasion of Iraq in 2003.

CHAPTER 5

BASHAR AL-ASSAD &
RENEWED DISSENT

Following the election of the new Assad and into the initial months of 2001, Bashar began the implementation of a series of liberal policies throughout the country. During his inaugural speech, Bashar al-Assad looked to the future:

> ...thus society will not develop, improve or prosper if it were to depend only on one sect or one party or one group; rather, it has to depend on the work of all citizens in the entire society. That is why I find it absolutely necessary to call upon every single citizen to participate in the process of development and modernization if we are truly honest in attaining the desired results in the very near future.[136]

It sounded inclusive and it was looking like "the Hope" was living up to the Syrian people's expectations of him.

Bashar was born on September 11, 1965. He was educated at al-Hurriya in Damascus, where he learned French and English before graduating in 1985. He studied medicine at the University of Damascus, followed by residency at a military hospital, and, in 1992, attended the Western Eye Hospital in London, England for post-graduate studies. Following his brother's death in 1994, he was recalled to Syria where he attended the military academy, reaching the rank of colonel and becoming an advisor to Hafez al-Assad. In this role, Bashar involved himself in citizens' appeals as well as stamping out corruption. After his election, Bashar noted that the economy was "a priority for us all to improve its performance and improve the life of our citizens. So is corruption."[137]

In reaction to such rhetoric, several informal political forums began appearing throughout the capital, such as the National Dialogue Forum and the Jamal al-Atassi Forum, while committees began forming along with intellectual discussions, increasing demand for political, judicial, and civil reform. In September 2000, 99 individuals made formal such demands with their aptly named Statement of 99, followed by the Statement of 1,000 in January 2001. The former called for "political and intellectual pluralism" while the latter sought an end to the 1963 Emergency Law and democratic representation, composed of multiple parties throughout the government.

The new regime took notice, but was not moved by the enthusiasm and failed to recognize the demands. The Assad government did take steps at reform by allowing constituent parties to be established (or at least did not prevent their establishment) along with office locations and newspaper printings. Several human rights organizations also began appearing, hoping to urge the government towards more reforms. Assad ordered hundreds of political prisoners released from incarceration and even, in November 2000, closed the infamous Mezze Prison, the site of brutal interrogations and deaths. It seemed, however, that this was the high-point of Bashar's reforms.

Following this, through the summer of 2001, political freedoms began gradually disappearing. Through discussions with his mukhabarat chiefs, who told him his presidency would certainly be undermined through continued reforms, Bashar al-Assad began efforts to reestablish stability and to force a sense of nationalism. Many remnants of Hafez al-Assad's regime still remained through the changeover, and it seemed likely that this old-guard was very much pushing for a dialing down of reforms. At this time, Riad Seif, businessman and former Syrian parliamentarian, began forming the Movement for Social Peace to rival the Ba'athists on the political front. The political forums were quickly closed, however, and Riad Seif, along with several others were arrested for "attempting to change the constitution by illegal means." By the summer of 2002, the regime's efforts at discrediting such actions proved successful and the entire movement died.[138] These crackdowns shattered the apparent intellectual climate throughout the Damascus Spring, as this period of attempted reform came to be known, which saw eight civil society leaders arrested and all but one civil society forum forcibly closed.[139]

DAMASCUS DECLARATION

The subsequent crackdowns, following the Damascus Spring, became known as the Damascus Winter, and despite the regime's efforts, the people had evidently appreciated the freedom. The desire for political reform and government transparency remained alive, and in October 2005, the Damascus Declaration was issued. Drafted by Michel Kilo, the Damascus Declaration came about from a group of pro-democracy supporters, most of whom had been active during the Damascus Spring. Several of these members had also been jailed for their commitments and many would go on to serve key roles in the opposition following the outbreak of the Syrian Civil War in 2011.

The Damascus Declaration was more than just a statement however, it was an embodiment of various factions throughout Syrian society, which also became an inherent weakness of the body. Due to the conflicting ideologies of these various groups (leftists, secularists, Islamists), there was no real unity, aside from the desire to establish a multi-party democracy through non-violence (this of course had to be changed after armed opposition ensued). They were of course all committed to change, but the means with which to achieve it were varied, as were the thoughts behind actions after change was achieved.[140] While a noble effort, according to Kilo, the Declaration had not created unification: "Instead of becoming stronger, the opposition became weaker because of the Declaration. Now, the Damascus Declaration will need a lot of work to achieve its original goals."[141]

In 2006, in an effort to curb any influence that might have sparked from the Damascus Declaration, the Syrian government began blocking political activists from leaving the country. The following year, and again in 2011, social media sites were censored and blocked, while activists were reportedly detained and tortured, some disappearing or being killed. Naturally, the Syrian government did not like the Damascus Declaration, while the State Department in Washington tried to "donate" $5 million dollars, which was turned down, with the group declaring that all foreign funding would not be accepted. Kilo stated that "[w]e are not toys in the West's hands. We will make a democratic state in this country no matter the cost."[142] This more than likely stemmed from the US's frustration over fighters streaming into Iraq from Syria, rather than any goodwill towards democracy or the people of Syria. The relationship between the United States and Syria was also a sticking point for the Declaration group, as the US was trying to pressure Syria to reconcile its relationship with Israel and pullout of its occupation of Lebanon. While the Syrian people would no doubt support a Lebanese withdrawal, giving up on the Golan Heights would be another matter entirely.

Following the US invasion of Iraq in 2003, the Kurds in Syria began agitating for a national sense of their own.[vi] Feeling internal pressure from the Kurds and the Damascus Declaration, as well as externally from the US and Israel, the Assad regime began blaming the internal discontent on these external actors. The regime was successful in scapegoating the Kurds, thus driving a wedge between the Kurds and the various opposition elements that made up the Damascus Declaration.[143] Added to this, was the US's economic pressure on Syria for its support of terrorism and its occupation of Lebanon (Syrian Accountability and Lebanese Sovereignty Restoration Act of 2003), a plight that no doubt proved irritating to the Syrian people, if not an outright hardship.

THE ARAB SPRING SWEEPS INTO SYRIA

What came to be known as the Arab Spring began in Tunisia in December 2010 when a local fruit vendor, Mohammed Bouazizi, set himself on fire in front of city hall after several seemingly unprovoked encounters with the local police. The police in Tunisia were not trusted by the locals, they lacked accountability for their actions, and they conducted arbitrary investigations against the populace, fueling resentment and anger that had been festering for many years. After this statement of protest by Bouazizi, demonstrators took to the streets in his hometown and outrage quickly spread throughout the country. Security forces arrested many and futilely attempted to restore civil

---

vi   Prior to the invasion, the US had sent clandestine teams into Kurdistan, and with Saddam Hussein's impending downfall, the Kurds of Iraq began agitating for more autonomy themselves.

order, even going so far as to shut down the internet; however, after 23 years, the repressive government of President Zine al-Abedin Ben Ali ended when he and his family fled the country on January 14, 2011. The Muslim world had not seen an uprising to this extent since the Iranian Revolution in 1979, and the repressed populations throughout the region were emboldened after years of heavy restrictions.[144]

Heartened by the successful demonstrations and ouster of a repressive leader, enthusiasm spread to Egypt where the "January 25 Revolution" began, with protestors calling for an end to corruption and injustice, and improvements in economic conditions. Syria faced much of the same conditions experienced by Egyptians: poverty, high unemployment, and corruption. While Egypt was able to amass demonstrations relatively quickly and in large numbers through social media, particularly Facebook, the social networking site had been banned in Syria again, although some were able to bypass this government restriction in order to fully engage with protestors.[145]

The Arab Spring swept into Syria on January 26, 2011, albeit with relatively minor and peaceful protests. This changed, however, when several children were arrested in Dara'a, Syria in February 2011, after they were accused of spray-painting anti-government slogans on a school wall. While the graffiti itself was hardly shocking (graffiti was becoming such a nuisance that IDs were required to buy spray paint), and their anti-government stance was relatively mild ("the people want to topple the regime"), it was the reported beatings and torture after the students' arrest that caused the most outrage.[146]

This outrage burst into protests throughout Dara'a in March 2011. With these demonstrations came the government crackdown and repression, culminating in the military laying siege to the city on April 25, 2011. One witness described the scene as such: "Dara'a is completely surrounded by tanks and armed troops. There are snipers on the roofs of government...and tall buildings. They are hiding behind water tanks and some even hiding in the minarets of mosques." Another described the scene in this way: "We are totally besieged. It is a tragedy. Many houses are levelled by shelling from the army. For the past six days we haven't seen an ambulance." Villagers from surrounding areas attempted to break the siege, but without communications equipment or other supplies, coordination and sustainment made any effort a fruitless endeavor.[147] The episode in Dara'a sparked renewed tensions throughout the country, and a "Day of Rage" was organized to show support for freedom and to protest government repression. Protestors demanded sweeping political reform and ultimately, the removal of President Bashar al-Assad. The Kurds were welcomed in such efforts as well, joining in to seek equal protections under the law.

The government responded with an almost simultaneous stick and carrot. On April 21, 2011, the government formally declared an end to the 1963 Emergency Law, which was viewed as a panicked response to the protests and did little to quiet the growing dissent. The same month, the government initiated its countrywide crackdowns, utilizing tanks and snipers (which were granted the use of deadly force), and shutting off utilities and confiscating food in some areas of protest. Demonstrators appeared in most major cities and several dozen were reportedly killed by government security forces who claimed to be in conflict with "extremist and terrorist groups".[148] In order to expose the uprisings in this light, Bashar al-Assad intentionally released jihadists from Syrian jails, further hoping to win over the Alawites, Christians, Druze, and other Syrian minorities who might become fearful of sectarian fighting, and their own tenuous socio-political positions throughout Syrian society.[149]

According to then-US Secretary of Defense Robert Gates, the US Ambassador to Syria from 2010-2014, Robert Ford, in a White House meeting, stated that "Assad is no Qaddafi. There is little likelihood of mass atrocities. The Syrian regime will answer challenges aggressively but will try to minimize the use of lethal force.[150] Whether or not this was a sentiment shared by the Central Intelligence Agency (whose fact-finding and analyses are presented to policymakers), it had clearly failed to forecast events on the ground in Syria and throughout the Middle East. But, as events were playing out on the ground, Bashar al-Assad was showing himself unafraid to use lethal methods necessary to retain his power base.

FREE SYRIAN ARMY & SYRIAN NATIONAL COUNCIL

Throughout this period, and into the summer of 2011, Syrian soldiers grew increasingly uncomfortable with orders to shoot demonstrators and began defecting and forming into units to resist the regime. On

July 29, 2011, these defectors, and many others, formally announced the creation of the Free Syrian Army (FSA).[151] With all levels of the Syrian Army ranks joining the FSA, including a brigadier general, a great deal of resilience, sophistication, credibility, and experience were affixed to this armed opposition. The United States, Turkey, Saudi Arabia, and Qatar were quick to back the FSA, with the US State Department handing over $15 million in non-lethal aid, although some believed it might have been much more.[152] Despite the largesse that the United States could rain down on the opposition, America's reputation certainly preceded any aid, with one civil-society activist remarking "Libya will have a new dictator. We don't want another dictator with American backing."[153] The US's role in overthrowing Saddam Hussein in Iraq and Gaddafi in Libya were no secrets, and neither was the aftermath in both countries as the US attempted to oversee the formation of stable, democratic governments (or in the case of Libya, maintained a small presence with which to buy up left-over arms).

The following month, the Syrian National Council (SNC) was formed, bringing together members of the Damascus Declaration, the Muslim Brotherhood, Kurdish groups, Local Coordination Committees (groups that had been helping to organize and document the protests), and other tribal and independent leaders. All of this made it appear that the Free Syrian Army would become the armed section to the Syrian National Council and the opposition as a whole. That was the aim of the FSA, in any event.[154]

The FSA and the SNC did not maintain consistent communications, however, and with the SNC headquartered in Turkey, away from the fighting, it became viewed as ineffective and out-of-touch with the struggle within Syria. While the SNC was the largest of the opposition groups, there were many throughout Syria, and international pressure began mounting for a more unified group, allowing for an ease of support from regional neighbors and western governments, including "new channels of funding."[155] After months of infighting and negotiations, these disparate groups came to consensus on November 8, 2012, merging to form the National Coalition for Syrian Revolutionary and Opposition Forces, known simply as the Syrian Coalition. The group quickly outlined its goals, setting out to:

1. unify support between the military council, revolutionary council, and the FSA; generate funds;

2. create a Syrian National Legal Committee; and

3. establish a transitional government.

In May 2017, Riad Seif, the former businessman and Syrian parliamentarian responsible for the Movement for Social Peace and then subsequent political prisoner, was elected president of the National Coalition for Syrian Revolutionary and Opposition Forces,[156] although Abdurrahman Mustafa has been at the helm as of May 2018.

According to the Syrian Coalition, the FSA had been utilized to carry out its political objectives, while protecting the rights of Syrian civilians, chiefly by denouncing terrorism and the use of chemical weapons. In order to facilitate collaboration between the two, the FSA established a Supreme Joint Military Command Council in December 2012. This military command council had been responsible for the planning and execution of tactical operations, as well as strategic-level planning. Salim Idriss headed the council as Chief-of-Staff, but was later replaced by Brigadier General Abdel-ilah Albashir in 2014. Ultimately, this council would be overseen by civilian authorities, but until an interim government could be established, a civil ministry acted in its place.

In November 2011, the Arab League had attempted to work out a settlement with the Assad regime that would bring an end to the fighting. The plan would have required the withdrawal of government forces from urban centers; a release of all political prisoners; and access for the media, human rights groups, and Arab monitors. There was disagreement over where discussions should be held; the Arab League plan suggested talks take place in Cairo, while the regime wanted to remain in Damascus. This plan did not come to fruition and, in December, the Arab League proposed referring the Syria issue to United Nations Security Council, although Russia and China threatened to veto any sanctions leveled against Syria and the Assad government.[157] Syria, however, did allow Arab monitors into Syria, bowing to pressure from Russia. Led by the Head of Mission Lieutenant General Mohammed Ahmed Mustapha al-Dabi of Sudan, some 500 monitors entered Syria, traveling throughout the country in December and into January 2012.

GENEVA I CONFERENCE ON SYRIA (2012)

In April 2012, after a year of violence in Syria, the UN adopted Resolutions 2042 and 2043, calling for the cessation of hostilities and authorizing monitors to deploy to the country. Fighting had been raging for over a year, claiming 10,000 lives in the process.[158] UN Resolution 2042 outlined a six-point plan, challenging all parties in the conflict to:

1. commit to work with the envoy [Staffan de Mistura] in an inclusive Syrian-led political process to address the legitimate aspirations and concerns of the Syrian people,

2. commit to stop the fighting and achieve urgently an effective United Nations supervised cessation of armed violence in all its forms by all parties,

3. ensure timely provision of humanitarian assistance to all areas affected by the fighting,

4. intensify the pace and scale of release of arbitrarily detained persons,

5. ensure freedom of movement throughout the country for journalists and a non-discriminatory visa policy for them, and

6. respect freedom of association and the right to demonstrate peacefully as legally guaranteed.[159]

Representatives were also meeting in Geneva from the United Nations, the Arab League, China, France, Russia, Great Britain, the United States, Turkey, Iraq, Kuwait, Qatar, and the European Union to discuss the growing violence in Syria; surprisingly absent were representatives from within Syria. The members of the meeting agreed that a transnational element of the fighting existed and required an international focus in order to alleviate. On June 30, a communique was issued calling for the implementation of the above six-point plan and the steps necessary for a transition within Syria. To meet these goals, the represented parties agreed "to offer significant support for the implementation of an agreement reached by the parties.

This may include an international assistance presence under a United Nations Mandate if requested. Significant funds will be available to support reconstruction and rehabilitation." However, this was to be done with "joint and sustained pressure" and an opposition "to any further militarization of the conflict" (see Appendix). Just what specifically this entailed and from where it would originate was not specifically outlined.

HOULA

Just as soon as these UN resolutions were passed, they ultimately broke-down after the Houla massacres took place the following month. According to UN observers that were present on the ground, 108 civilians were killed, 83 of which were women and children. Despite the initial reports, it appeared that, while the majority of the victims had been shot, they were not shot execution-style, but rather were apparently shot as a result of rooms having being sprayed with automatic weapons fire. However, it was concluded in a report generated by an independent body, working under the auspices of the UN Human Rights Council, that government forces were responsible for these deaths. It furthermore concluded,

> that war crimes, including murder, extrajudicial killings and torture, and gross violation of international human rights, including unlawful killing[s], attacks against civilians and acts of sexual violence, have been committed in line with State policy, with indications of the involvement at the highest levels of the Government, as well as security and armed forces.

In addition, the group found that "brutal tactics' and new military capabilities have been employed in recent months by both sides of the conflict."[160] The one sure thing that could be concluded was that both sides were desperate and conducting atrocities. The government benefitted by causing fear in the populace, perhaps dissuading some from joining the opposition, while the opposition could take the same approach, with the addition that such atrocities would bring international attention to their plight. If Bashar al-Assad was being viewed as a responsible party, so too, would opposition leaders need to be.

ALEPPO

Despite the "Houla Massacre" and the 18-month conflict, the catalyst that brought the conflict widely to the international arena (at least within the United States) was the fighting in and around the city of Aleppo. The Syrian government appeared to be waning by the summer and fall of 2012: Syrian generals were defecting; rebels were capturing territory, including border crossings into Turkey and Iraq, and large swaths of rural Syria. Since the beginning of the fighting in the country, Aleppo had been nearly divided equally between the government-controlled west and rebel-held east, although it had been spared from relatively heavy fighting. Located approximately 30 miles from the Turkish border, Aleppo, in 2012, was the second largest city in Syria and home to nearly 3 million people.[161]

Aleppo was a strategically significant city: opposition fighters were near the Turkish border, able to receive supplies to continue the fight, while the Syrian government, by controlling Aleppo, could cut that main supply artery of the opposition and utilize it for its own commercial purposes. Fighting began increasing in Aleppo in 2012; from July to December, 5,684 people were killed in the city and its environs, of which three-quarters were civilians.[162] By the end of the year, the opposition fighters had carved out a significant chunk of northern Syria and large parts of Aleppo. This, however, did not include the Kurdish areas of northern Syria, which the Syrian government affectively ceded to the Kurds in July 2012.[163] This Kurdish region, known as Western Kurdistan, was the location of talks amongst the Democratic Union Party (PYD) and other Kurdish groups, who would assume administrative responsibilities as well as security, important in an area that was flanked by a concerned Turkey and, eventually, a hostile Islamic State (IS).[164]

As 2013 dawned, the opposition was keeping up the pressure, focused on pushing government forces out of Aleppo, and very nearly cut off the government's supply route from Damascus. The increased fighting led to desperate acts on both sides and amplified the humanitarian crisis felt by the civilian population within the besieged city. With the city cutoff, basic goods could not get through, leading to sharp spikes in prices, relative to the rest of the country. With transportation affected and untenable security, international aid workers could not get through to provide humanitarian assistance to the populace. By the end of the summer, the situation proved dire for the civilians, but the opposition had made gains, cutting off the route to Damascus, compelling government forces to find a secondary supply route. After securing an alternate route, government forces and other militias began pushing opposition forces back, albeit slowly. September and October of 2013 began showing signs of a turnaround for government forces, while the opposition elements began undermining their advances with disastrous disagreements, resulting in poor coordination and loss of battlefield tempo.

With the slow progress at best, and even a stalemate at worst, on November 22, 2013, government forces began circumventing military targets, instead utilizing barrel bombs seemingly over civilian areas, killing hundreds of civilians and only a fraction of opposition fighters. Barrel bombs are crude instruments of war, particularly for a nation-state to use, in which an oil drum (or other such container) is packed with explosives and fragmentation (nails or pieces of jagged metal) and then dropped from a hovering helicopter. The archaic weapon is reminiscent of World War II and prior, when weapons systems lacked guidance and advanced navigation, relying on munitions to be dropped in large quantities over large areas, resulting in many civilian casualties and destruction of property. It seems such weapons were intended to inflict fear rather than serve any strategic purposes. However, this period also witnessed opposition fighters disregarding their own civility; launching rockets and mortars into government-controlled areas, killing and wounding dozens of civilians as well.[165]

TERRORISM AND US AID

Throughout the chaos in Syria and the focused fighting in Aleppo, terrorist groups began sprouting up within Aleppo and Syria as a whole, notably al-Nusra Front and the Islamic State (IS). IS saw its beginnings in Iraq, with Sunnis seething under the minority-control of Saddam Hussein's Shi'a government. Founded by the Jordanian Abu Musab al-Zarqawi in the late-1990s, the group was originally known as Jama'at al-Tawhid wal-Jihad. After the US invasion of Iraq in 2003, the group had a new purpose, and the following year, swore allegiance to Osama bin Laden, becoming al-Qaeda in Iraq (AQI). In 2006, Zarqawi was successful in bringing together several Sunni groups under a single umbrella called the Mujahedeen Shura Council (MSC), and was the beginnings of establishing an Islamic state. Soon afterwards, Zarqawi was killed in a US airstrike, but the group remained. More groups fell under the fold, and a new name emerged, the Islamic State in Iraq (ISI), with a new leader, Abu Bakr al-Baghdadi.

When violence began to peak in Iraq in 2007, the Bush Administration ordered an additional 20,000 troops to the country. This "surge" of American troops, coupled with the recruitment of Sunni tribes (the Sons of Iraq) to assist in the fight, successfully tampered down the violence, so much so, that an American withdrawal was agreed upon for 2011. US forces officially withdrew from Iraq in December 2011 after nearly nine years of occupation. While this should have been a momentous occasion, the sectarian fault lines had already begun to appear in Iraq, with Shi'a Prime Minister Nuri al-Malicki at the helm. His apparent lack of respect and consideration for the Sunnis and the Kurds fueled a great deal of hostility and resentment, thereby further validating ISI's existence. The point being that the US should not, nor any country, pick demographic winners and losers; self-determination should best be left to the people. The people should make decisions that affect their own lives.

As the fighting in Syria began developing throughout the early months of 2012, and US forces all but gone from Iraq, Abu Bakr al-Baghdadi saw the confusion in Syria for what it was: turmoil leading up to a failed state, and an opportunity. To ascertain just how bad the situation was and potentially grow the group beyond Iraq's borders, he dispatched a small team into Syria. While the government and opposition were concentrating on fighting one another, ISI was free to grow with relative ease, especially without American-backed security forces interfering. Abu Mohammed al-Julani, the leader of this small group, stated that, "Syria would not have been ready for us if not for the Syrian revolution. The revolution removed many of the obstacles and paved the way for us to enter this blessed land.[166] Julani's small group would form what would come to be known as al-Nusra Front or Jabhat al-Nusra. While initially a front-group for ISI, al-Nusra was known for its affiliation with al-Qaeda as well. ISI persisted in Iraq due mostly to the sectarian fault lines established by the US-backed Iraqi government, while the formation and expansion of IS grew out of the fighting in Syria. While placing US troops in the region might have created some of the issues, its withdrawal certainly did not.

Al-Nusra Front grew rapidly, mainly through the ignorance and complicity of Bashar al-Assad. Attempting to lend credibility to his claim that he was fighting against extremists and terrorists, Assad had released many Islamists from prisons, who promptly rejoined their factions in order to take part in the fighting. Once fighting commenced, it was perhaps Assad's desire to see the Islamic State and resistance groups fight one another to their own ends, or even to force the international community to choose the lesser of these evils in the fight (which would be him and his regime, of course).

Just as ISI had grown thanks to prison escapes in Iraq, so too was al-Nusra nourished, and it grew quickly in power and influence, shielding its presence through the early violence afflicting Syria. Its use of Sharia law and suicide bombings did not endear all to its side, but it was relatively successful in cannibalizing recruits from the Free Syrian Army. Al-Nusra's growth also allowed the Syrian government to continue to undermine all opposition forces' efforts against the regime, erroneously citing that the FSA was not a tangible force within Syria, only a front for al-Qaeda operations.[167] This, no doubt, led to a great deal of confusion for Western governments attempting to make sense of the military landscape within Syria.

Al-Nusra Front naturally found itself on the receiving end of the US's attention. In July 2016, the group claimed that it would be severing ties with al-Qaeda in order to "expose the deception of the international community, namely the US and Russia, in their relentless bombardment and displacement of the Muslim masses of Syria under the pretext of bombing al-Nusra Front." Then al-Qaeda second-in-command, Ahmed Hassan Abu al-Khayr, stated that instructions were sent for "the leadership of Nusra Front to go ahead with what protects the interests of Islam and Muslims and what protects jihad" within Syria. Ayman al-Zawahiri, who took over al-Qaeda following the death of Osama bin-Laden in 2011, further stated that "[t]he brotherhood of Islam is stronger than any organizational links that change and go away."[168] Such statements certainly do not lend credibility to al-Nusra's claim of dissolving its ties with al-Qaeda; western governments persisted in their skepticism of al-Nusra Front and continued in their belief that it remained a terrorist organization.

By December 2012, the US Department of State had recognized al-Nusra Front as an alias for al-Qaeda in Iraq. However, al-Baghdadi had been sending funds and fighters to al-Julani in Syria and wanted full control. In early 2013, the two began a feud that even al-Qaeda could not successfully mediate. Soon after, an official split took place, with al-Nusra Front retaining half the resources and manpower, and ISI taking the rest. With a presence now in Syria and Iraq, ISI quickly morphed into the Islamic State.[vii]

The many factions fighting within Syria were composed of varying ideologies, ethnicities, religions, leaders of varying effectiveness and support, and varying levels of effectiveness on the battlefield. Added to this were the differing missions: some were fighting to overthrow the government, some were fighting in support of the government, some were fighting extremist groups, and some were fighting one another for influence and control. The United States and other western governments became hesitant to provide lethal aid to the FSA for fear of inadvertently supporting any one of a number of extremist groups, or even still, handing over weapons and supplies which might then be captured by extremist groups during the fighting. Some believed Bashar al-Assad was successful in using the extremist groups to his advantage, using IS to destroy the secular groups supported by western governments; after all, western governments were trying to support moderate groups to bring stability. To this end, it was Bashar's hope that the world would then be forced, with the moderate groups sidelined by fighting on two fronts (against IS and Bashar's forces), to make the tough decision of supporting the extremists or keeping him in power. While IS and Bashar were not exactly allied, that did not mean that they did not have beneficial ties, as Bashar was known to have bought oil from the Islamic State.[169]

---

vii   Although known as the Islamic State in Iraq and Syria (ISIS), the Islamic State of Iraq and the Levant (ISIL), and its Arabic name of al-Dawlah al-Islamiah fi al-Iraq wa al-Sham (Da'esh), throughout this text, they will be referred to simply as the Islamic State (IS).

The United States struggled with the best decision to alleviate problems in Syria. With so many American troops having been killed and maimed in Iraq and Afghanistan, there was little support for intervention in Syria. One poll conducted found that half of Americans opposed, and only 42% supported, becoming entangled in Syria, with 80% believing Congressional approval should be necessary before any U.S. forces were committed.[170] Leon Panetta, the U.S. Secretary of Defense at that time, described the situation in his book, Worthy Fights, as such:

> The problem with it was that Syria was not Libya. Assad was much more heavily armed, the country was far less accessible, and among the military's munitions were large storehouses of chemical weapons and modern air defense systems, the latter supplied by the Soviet Union and later Russia. The primary concern was locating Assad's chemical weapons and preparing to seize and secure them if the situation required it. The conclusion was that it would require more than seventy-five thousand soldiers, perhaps as many as ninety thousand, roughly what we had in all of Afghanistan.[171]

Despite this assessment, it appeared that the United States was providing Syrian rebels with more than just non-lethal munitions in the early years of fighting. With the American "success" in funneling arms to the Afghan groups fighting the Soviet Union in Afghanistan in the 1980s, this would no doubt be an attractive option for politicians. Providing lethal options to opposition groups, it could be conducted clandestinely, therefore granting US officials plausible deniability if need be, or the aura of action if so demanded, and all without committing conventional US forces. During fighting in Libya to oust Ghaddafi, most nations had closed up diplomatic shop in Benghazi due to the extreme violence; however, the United States maintained a secret annex located near the State Department's Special Mission Compound. The State Department wanted to maintain a diplomatic presence in order to send a message to the Libyan people that the United States was keeping a watchful eye on the new Libyan government and would not tolerate Gaddafi-style rule.[172] This, despite the fact that the US State Department had warned of the increase of "political violence in the form of assassinations and vehicle bombs…in both Benghazi and Tripoli" with the possibility of…"[i]nter-militia conflict" in the summer of 2012.[173]

The CIA presence, on the other hand, was an overall effort "to constantly plumb the depths of al-Qaeda sympathy and affiliation," despite being burdened with "…young, inexperienced case officers…"[174] More pressing than this, was the CIA program to gather "information on the proliferation of weaponry looted from Libyan government arsenals, including surface-to-air missiles (SAM)." It would seem that some of these heavy weapons were making their way into the hands of Syrian opposition fighters, via Turkey. Evidently, in September 2012, a Libyan ship, weighing 400 tons, docked in a Turkish port carrying a large quantity of armaments bound for Syria, including small arms and SA-7 SAMs. Undoubtedly, the CIA was supplying small-arms to various Syrian groups, and there seems little doubt that they would not have known of such shipments.[175] In addition, the very day that US Ambassador Chris Stevens was killed, he had met with the Turkish Consul General Ali Sait Akin; there is no record of what the two discussed. Coincidence? Possibly, but it seems highly unlikely.

Furthermore, Simon Chase, a pen-name used by a former British Special Forces soldier and private military contractor, stated in his book, *Zero Footprint*, that he was tasked to open a front company in Iraqi Kurdistan in order to import weapons that would then be smuggled to Syrian opposition fighters. He did this, he claimed, by first establishing a joint-venture security company, along with a local Kurdish company, who would then secure a contract to provide security services for an oil company. This relationship would then allow Chase's security company to obtain a firearms license and a legitimate end-user certificate with which to import arms. Of course, the arms were not to end-up with the company in Iraq, but were to be clandestinely shipped further on to Syria.[176]

With a location to ship weapons, Chase further described his part in acquiring the weapons. They could not simply materialize from the US government, which was why the end-user certificate was so important. This lets companies know to where they are to ships their products, lets countries know what products are traversing through their borders, and lets these countries know from where and whom the products are originating. With the logistical questions taken care of, Simon Chase described his role in acquiring weapons in Benghazi, Libya through al-Qaeda in the Islamic Maghreb (AQIM). According to his CIA facilitator, this was a perfectly natural business, due to the fact that AQIM's "friends in the al-Nusra Brigade are some of the FSA's best fighters, and the other anti-Assad groups are working together toward the same goal." Furthermore, he stated that "[t]his can be a win-win for us. We get the MANPADS, Stingers, and other weapons out of the hands of those f***ers in Libya, and help the FSA."[177] If this is all to be believed, then the CIA and US government were certainly responsible for the tragic events that transpired in Benghazi, along with proliferating small- and heavy-arms to groups within Syria (including, potentially, terrorist groups).

After the US draw down in Iraq, and no doubt before, the Iraqi military became plagued with corruption, ill-discipline, and poor leadership. When IS captured the northern Iraqi city of Mosul in June 2014, the Iraqi Army had been ill-prepared and ill-led, despite years of US training and assistance. Without a doubt there were many a brave and competent Iraqi soldier, but they were ultimately driven from the field, allowing IS to capture large tracts of territory, arms, equipment, money from looted banks, and, after capturing prisons and releasing the inhabitants, new recruits. Much of what was captured had once been US-supplied goods intended for Iraqi security forces.

The Islamic State had effectively captured such large swaths of land in little time due to their ability to coordinate indirect fire with lightly-armed ground units; part of their indirect fire came from mobile artillery, which they effectively utilized against static-defensive Iraqi positions. With Mosul under IS control, the approaches to Erbil were threatened; if Erbil capitulated to IS, the approaches to Kirkuk and then Baghdad would have been wide open. Mosul and Erbil were also considered pieces of Kurdistan, drawing the Kurds into the fight, and, as this region contained a great deal of Iraqi oil, endangered government coffers, while also providing revenue to the Islamic State. Nervousness and downright fear prevailed in Iraq, while embarrassment was felt in the United States; the same soldiers throwing down their arms and retreating from the advance of IS, were the same troops trained by the United States.

Then-Senator Barack Obama had campaigned for the White House on a promise to pull US troops out of Iraq, and followed through with these promises a full year before his first term was set to expire. With a tough race out of the way and his reelection in January 2013, President Obama did not want to destroy his legacy by recommitting US troops to Iraq; doing nothing, however, could be viewed as weakness by his political opponents. With Erbil threatened, the US President ordered military assessment teams to evaluate both Kurdish and Iraqi security, linking up with both Iraqi and Kurdish Peshmerga forces, while stepping up Intelligence, Surveillance, Reconnaissance (ISR) assets over the area. On August 7, US and British air forces began dropping supplies in an effort to relieve areas cut off from Iraqi lines but not yet controlled by IS. In a combined effort, nearly 86,000 meals; 20,000 gallons of water; and over 500 shelters were dropped, primarily to the Iraqis trapped on Mount Sinjar.[178] The following day, airstrikes were conducted, officially beginning kinetic operations. According to General Lloyd Austin III, the ranking officer of Central Command: "As the president made clear, the United States military will continue to take direct action against [the Islamic State] when they threaten our personnel and facilities."[179] Thus began Operation Inherent Resolve.

The following month, September 2014, the US began operations inside Syrian territory.

CHAPTER 6

CHEMICAL WEAPONS & RUSSIAN ASSISTANCE

While conflicts can take extreme tolls on combatants, it is especially troubling when civilians become collateral damage, or worse yet, are specifically targeted. Conventional war is concerning enough without adding the risk of chemical, biological, or nuclear armaments to the equation. Throughout the spring and summer of 2013, rumors and reports had been circulating that chemical weapons were being perpetrated against soldiers and civilians within Syria. While there was "credible information that corroborates the allegations that chemical weapons were used" on several different occasions throughout Syria, the attacks were small in scale and the information could not be "independently verified," according to the UN.[180]

The dynamics within Syria changed on August 21, 2013 after several hundred civilians were killed in an apparent chemical weapons attack in the Damascus suburb of Ghouta, including over 400 children.[181] While there were other locations reportedly hit with chemical weapons, Ghouta presented the United Nations Mission "clear and convincing evidence that chemical weapons were used... against civilians, including children, on a relatively large scale." Based on testimony from medical staff treating the victims, and samples taken from the victims, it was concluded that this attack was executed utilizing sarin gas.

U.S. President Barack Obama called the chemical attack a "challenge to the world" and was considering a "limited, narrow act."[182] This of course, comes in direct contradiction to statements he had made the previous year, in which he had called chemical weapons use a "red line." In July 2012, President Obama stated that "they [Syrian government forces] will be held accountable by the international community and the United States should they make the tragic mistake of using those weapons." The following month, he went on to explain that,

> We cannot have a situation where chemical or biological weapons are falling into the hands of the wrong people. We have been very clear to the Assad regime –but also to other players on the ground—that a red line for us is we start seeing a whole bunch of chemical weapons moving around or being utilized. That would change my calculus; that would change my equation.[183]

He further added that,

> We're monitoring the situation very carefully. We have put together a range of contingency plans. We have communicated in no uncertain terms with every player in the region that that's a red line for us and that there would be enormous consequences if we start seeing movement on the chemical weapons front or the use of chemical weapons. That would change my calculations significantly.[184]

According to the then-Secretary of Defense Leon Panetta, it was the realization by the international community that chemical weapons had in fact been used, that the United States began reconsidering the option of arming the Syrian rebels.[185] However, despite President Obama's tough rhetoric and threat of "enormous consequences," no action was undertaken to hold Bashar al-Assad responsible, or anybody else for that matter.

The introduction of chemical weapons in the Middle East was a result of the ever-present tension between Israel and its Arab neighbors. Two weeks before the beginning of the Six-Day War in 1967, artillery shells in the Sinai Peninsula had been discovered by Israeli intelligence, loaded with Soviet nerve gas.[186] According to a 1985 paper produced by the CIA, Syria was likely spurred into its chemical weapons program as a result of Israel's own program. In the 1960s, the Soviets had begun training Syrian units on defensive chemical techniques. It is not clear as to where Syria acquired the equipment and material for such a program, but the paper was clear that no evidence existed of any "Soviet provision of the production facilities, chemical precursors, or scientific expertise that would aid nerve agent research."[187] As Syria became the fourth Middle Eastern power to acquire them (after Egypt, Iraq, and Israel) it seems likely that given their relationship, Egypt would most likely have assisted.

It was believed that Syria had purchased all the necessary equipment for its own chemical production capabilities in 1983, given that 1985 marked the start of full-scale production.[188] This timeframe is interesting due to the fact that Syria's military expenditure, as a percentage of its gross domestic product, decreased by just over 50% between 1984 and 1988. This could be taken to mean that its reliance on conventional forces was no longer necessary, as it possessed a powerful deterrent and offensive weapon, if needed. Clearly, its enemy in Israel remained with chemical weapons with which to defend itself, it seems likely that Syria felt confident enough to cut expenditures so drastically, despite occupying Lebanon.[189] In addition, the war that had been raging for most of the 1980s between Iran and Iraq, might also have given Syria the confidence to pursue its chemical weapons program aggressively. According to the above-mentioned CIA report, "Syria's development of a CW production capability and the absence of a major international outcry over Iraq's use of chemical weapons against Iran suggest a lower threshold for the use of chemical weapons in future Middle East conflicts."[190]

The document concluded that,

Syria's ability to manufacture chemical weapons will increase the tension between it and Israel, as well as moderate governments in the region, particularly its neighbor Jordan. Were Israel to launch a preemptive strike to destroy such facilities before substantial weapons could be developed, would likely result in Syrian retaliation, further escalating tensions.

Hafez al-Assad was determined to gain as many concessions as possible from Israel in any peace process. He found it necessary to build up a large, technically proficient military equipped with chemical weapons in order to exploit an Israeli desire for peace on its borders. This could benefit Assad by allowing him to forgo many serious concessions beneficial to Israel.[191] This was true of both father and son.

Assuming that Syria began production in 1985, it had nearly three decades of production capacity behind it when the attack in Ghouta came to light. Following these chemical attacks, US President Barack Obama and Russian President Vladimir Putin, during a G20 Summit in St. Petersburg, Russia in September 2013, discussed the need for international control over Syria's chemical weapons arsenal. US Secretary of State John Kerry and Russian Foreign Minister Sergei Lavrov met in Geneva to hash out a framework on the subject, coming to a consensus on a workable timetable, a need for the Syrian government to release a list of their weapons, and an assessment of the types and quantities of weapons within Syria, which the two countries believed could amount to 1,000 tons. President Obama was quick with stern warnings, declaring his intent to level "consequences should the Assad regime not comply with the framework agreed today. And, if diplomacy fails, the United States remains prepared to act." In what amounts to a great deal of foreshadowing, then-head of the Free Syrian Army, General Salim Idriss, expressed indignation over the deal, stating that chemical weapons were already being relocated outside the country in neighboring Lebanon and Iraq. He predicted that this would give the Syrian government the capacity for future chemical weapons deployments, while being empowered to deny such attacks. Furthermore, many in Syria, and elsewhere, derided the contradiction of government forces killing with impunity utilizing conventional weapons, but drawing international criticism only when it was done with chemical weapons.[192]

Finalizing preparations and discussing actions needed if the Syrian government failed to cooperate, the United Nations adopted Resolution 2118 the same month. In it,

> the Council prohibited Syria from using, developing, producing, otherwise acquiring, stockpiling or retaining chemical weapons, or transferring them to other States or non-State actors, and underscored also that no party in Syria should use, develop, produce, acquire, stockpile, retain or transfer such weapons.[193]

The oversight of this would be carried out by the Organization for the Prohibition of Chemical Weapons (OPCW) that would be responsible for inspecting Syrian chemical facilities, which began on October 6, 2013. The OPCW would be responsible for implementing plans to properly dispose of all chemical stockpiles and any means of further manufacturing of such weapons. If the Syrian authorities did not grant "immediate and unfettered access to—and the right to inspect—any and all chemical weapons sites," the United Nations reserved the right to implement measures outlined in Chapter VII.[194] Chapter VII of the United Nations Charter outlines measures for the UN Security Council to take should threats to international peace and security be breached. While soft actions might push for the "complete or partial interruption of economic relations…and the severance of diplomatic relations," such actions at times fail or prove insufficient. Chapter VII then grants authority to the Security Council to call upon its members to commit armed forces to conduct operations that "may be necessary to maintain or restore international peace and security."[195] Furthermore, the United Nations made clear its endorsement of the Geneva Communique from the previous June, and recommended an international conference to see to its implementation. It remained to be seen if the UN would intervene militarily in Syria; its charter did permit such an action.

In December 2013, the OPCW was awarded the Nobel Peace Prize for "its extensive efforts to eliminate chemical weapons."[196] By May 2014, 90% of Syria's chemical weapons had been removed or destroyed, although the entire process was to have been completed by June 30, 2014. The Assad regime was responsible for consolidating its chemicals and transferring them to the Mediterranean port city of Latakia, Syria. From there, UN member states would assume responsibility for transportation and destruction of the chemicals. The Syrians blamed the truncated timeline on its internal struggles: January 2014 witnessed the failure of the second round of Geneva discussion, the regime was making slow progress pushing back rebels in eastern Syria, and IS was gaining large swaths of land.

With the majority of the weapons transferred out of Syria in May, the UN Security Council proposed a resolution to refer the use of chemical weapons throughout Syria (among other war crimes and not just confined to Assad and the regime) to the International

Criminal Court (ICC) for prosecutions; however, this was vetoed both by China and Russia. While the regime in Damascus was the likely culprit for chemical weapons use, both sides have committed atrocities against one another, including torture, starvation, and inhumane treatment of detainees.[197] As regards the chemical weapons use, the Obama White House determined that these weapons had been controlled by the Syrian Scientific Studies and Research Center (SSRC), falling under the Syrian Ministry of Defense. As head of the country and the Ba'ath Party, Assad would have carefully selected workers involved in Syria's chemical weapons program to better ensure loyalty and discretion. Ultimately, all decisions involving this program would have been his alone.[198] By January 2016, all remaining chemical weapons that had been declared by Assad's regime were completely destroyed by the company that had been contracted by OPCW. This company had taken possession of 75 hydrogen fluoride cylinders that had deteriorated over the years, causing hazards to the disposal team, and ultimately delaying the disposal process.[199]

GENEVA II (2014)

While the UN and OPCW were trying to extract Syria's chemical weapons from the country, the threat caused by these chemical weapons initiated another round of talks in Geneva, beginning January 22, 2014. Taking place in two rounds (January 23-31 and again from February 10-15), the talks brought together representatives from some three dozen countries, including Syria and opposition members. The Assad government declared Assad's future as head-of-state would be respected and a non-negotiable element to the talks, while the opposition, represented by the Syrian National Council, fundamentally disagreed with such a sentiment, and only voted to attend the talks days right before they convened. Despite the preexisting conflict of interest, Geneva II marked the first time that the two sides had come together after nearly three years of fighting.

Despite the two sides coming together, the Syrian government still insisted that it was fighting terrorism, not a civil war. With such a sentiment, it would seem the government had no intention of substantial talks with the Syrian National Council, perhaps only seeking to reiterate to the international community this "terrorist" threat, and seek a greater level of support. By demanding the removal of Assad as an extreme in itself, perhaps the opposition had no intention of seeking success either; perhaps it too was merely seeking the international attention. Of course, with such tensions, the talks ultimately failed, although some hope was buoyed after an agreement was carved out to evacuate some residents of Homs and help alleviate some humanitarian issues.[200] Opposition fighters controlled large areas of Homs, which the Syrian government had besieged and bombarded since 2012. During the early months of 2011 when the uprising began, Homs became a hotbed for opposition, making it a particularly thorny issue for the government. It also granted internal lines-of-communication to the opposition, as Damascus to the south would be severed from Aleppo to the north and Latakia on the Mediterranean coast. During the discussion throughout Geneva II, 5,000 people had been killed in Syria, further highlighting the failures of the talks.[201]

To further reinforce the failure of the talks, elections were held in June 2014, in which Bashar al-Assad won election with nearly 90% of the vote, and a turn-out of nearly three-quarters of the population. Of course, few believed in the veracity of such numbers, pointing to Assad's grip on power and the opposition's claim that his tenure as head-of-state must be ended in order to transition Syria into a viable government. Despite the glaring falsehood that such numbers represented, the election marked the first-time the ballot contained multiple candidates, whereas the past elections with Bashar and his father, the voters were given the one name, and a choice between yes or no. This election will secure Bashar's tenure into 2021 for a seven-year term.[202]

RUSSIA TO THE RESCUE

Beginning in early September 2015, a year after the US began operating inside Syria, Russia began moving military hardware into the war-torn country, including anti-aircraft systems, citing a request from Damascus for its assistance. On September 30, 2015 Russia's parliament approved the launching of air strikes within Syria, initiated by President Putin, in order "to fight and destroy militants and terrorists on the territories that they already occupy, not wait for them to come to our house." This theory of just war has been utilized since the time of the Romans, positing that attacking one's enemy before they attack you is a preventative strike, and therefore a justified means of warfare. The US had been using this position as well to deploy larger numbers of its military to the Middle East and throughout the world. It seemed, however, that Russia had entered the fight in Syria for more than just defense of the Russian homeland. After Russia's airstrikes, US troops and allied forces noted a lack of IS positions targeted by the Russians, instead appearing to target opposition to Assad's government. Russia claimed justification as Damascus had requested Russian assistance from the beginning.[203] According to Jane's 360 Center for Terrorism and Insurgency, after Russia's intervention, airstrikes throughout Syria increased in 2015 by 150%, while only 14% of those strikes had targeted the Islamic State.[204] Russian President Vladimir Putin dismissed such rhetoric as "thoughtless" and vowed that "[t]he entire territory of Syria must be 'liberated.'" The Kremlin Press Secretary Dmitry Peskov further stated that keeping Assad in power was the only alternative to terrorist groups taking power, thus ensuring "a political settlement."[205]

Russia has had a special relationship with Syria, dating back to the Cold War when the Soviet Union began attempting to exert its influence on the region and selling military equipment to Hafez al-Assad. According to historian Bernard Lewis,

> certainly the Arabs had no special love for Russia, nor did Muslims in the Arab world or elsewhere desire to bring either Communist ideology or Soviet power to their lands. Nor was it a reward for Moscow's Israel policy, which had been rather friendly. What delighted the Arabs was that they saw the arms deal—no doubt correctly—as a slap in the face for the West. The slap, and the visibly disconcerted Western and more particularly American response, reinforced the mood of hate and spite toward the West and encouraged its exponents.[206]

When the Soviets begun supplying the Arabs in the 1970s, it prompted the US to view the Israelis as more of a buffer between the Soviets and their Arab allies. The notion that Israel is the oldest and dearest ally of the US in the Middle East does not tell the full geo-political story. In the early years of Israel, France was very much an important partner for the burgeoning state, years before the United States began its sponsorship. As described by Bernard Lewis,

> The spread of Soviet influence in the Middle East and the enthusiastic response to it encouraged the United States to look more favorably on Israel, now seen as a reliable and potentially useful ally in a largely hostile region. Today, it is often forgotten that the strategic relationship between the United States and Israel was a consequence, not a cause, of Soviet penetration.[207]

Despite the passing of the Syrian Accountability and Lebanese Sovereignty Restoration Act of 2003, Syria had been a sponsor of terrorism years before this, yet its Cold War-era relationship with the Soviet Union granted it protections that the US was not willing to test. According to Robert Gates, "Syria was not seriously considered as a target during the Cold War because such action would almost certainly bring a confrontation with the Soviets. Syria had the most effective military, would have to play a key role in any Middle East peace process, and was relatively invulnerable to U.S. economic pressures.[208]

The Soviets had been involved in supporting the Syrians since 1956. For the next 15 years, the Soviets supplied the Syrians $580 million in military aid in addition to infrastructure improvements. Despite this show of support, Syria was unwilling to reciprocate, refusing to sign a treaty of friendship, a step that was not taken until October 1980. It was this treaty of friendship that would prompt Russia to intercede 35 years afterwards. For the Soviets, this largesse was not charity, but rather a key to maintaining their position in the Middle East, particularly after 1972 when they were expelled from Egypt. It also put the Soviet Union in a position of keeping Israel on guard from undertaking any actions that might undermine Arab positions.[209] Throughout these years, the Soviets sent Syria aircraft, surface-to-air missiles, advanced tanks, and in 1972, just before the Yom Kippur War the following year, they sent 800 technicians and advisors. While this was vital to Syria's modernization efforts, Syria provided Russian naval vessels access to Latakia and Tartus as well, important Mediterranean Sea ports with which they could be utilized for ports-of-call and minor repair work.

After Syria's Soviet-supplied air force was bested by the Israelis during Syria and Israel's occupation of Lebanon, the Syrians began complaining to the Soviets. After this, the Syrians began receiving advanced air defense equipment from the Soviet Union, accompanied by advisors and technicians, and SA-5 surface-to-air missiles. By January 1983, these SAM sites were installed, casting the potential for Soviet forces to be directly involved in this Arab-Israeli conflict.[210]

The relationship between Moscow and Damascus can at least be partially explained by these Cold War ties. Russian President Vladimir Putin has been quoted as saying "the greatest geopolitical catastrophe of the twentieth century" was the collapse of the Soviet Union.[211] The Soviet economy could not maintain the demands of its military, and its authoritarian regime could not maintain the political demands for autonomy. If it is a return to Soviet aggression that Moscow is seeking, it clearly will not end well, if history is any judge. While the US and allied militaries might have hastened its fall, it was economics that was largely responsible. Things did not end well for the Soviet Union, and as one of its recipients of military and economic aid, Syria did not fare well either.

However, there was more. Former Russian President Dmitry Medvedev believed that "if Libya breaks up and al Qaeda takes root there, no one will benefit, including us [the Russians], because the extremists will end up in the north Caucasus" area of Russia.[212] However, this belief was replaced by a feeling of betrayal. According to former Secretary of Defense Robert Gates:

The Russians later firmly believed they had been deceived on Libya. They had been persuaded to abstain at the UN on the grounds that the resolution provided for a humanitarian mission to prevent the slaughter of civilians. Yet as the list of bombing targets steadily grew, it became clear that very few targets were off-limits and that NATO was intent on getting rid of Qaddafi. Convinced they had been tricked, the Russians would subsequently block any such future resolutions, including against President...Assad in Syria.[213]

In early October 2016, after its initial deployment and operations in Syria, Russia began moving S-300 anti-aircraft missiles into the port city of Tartus, a move that somewhat undermined, yet again, its claims to be battling terrorist groups.[214] Neither the Islamic State nor the Syrian opposition groups had aircraft of their own to necessitate an air defense system throughout Syria. This same month, Russia deployed nuclear-capable Iskander missiles to Kaliningrad in order to check NATO moves, which Moscow believed were aimed at Russia. The previous May the United States had setup its own missiles in Romania to, in Washington's view, counter any launches from Iran.[215] The whole episode stank of Cold War maneuvering; to end the Cuban Missile Crisis, then-US President John F Kennedy agreed to dismantle US missiles that had been established in Turkey in exchange for the Soviets removing their own hardware from Cuba.

INTERNATIONAL SYRIA SUPPORT GROUP AND THE VIENNA TALKS

The International Syria Support Group (ISSG) was formed in the fall of 2015, during the Vienna talks taking place at the time. It was co-chaired by the US and Russia, composed of 19 founding members: China, Egypt, the EU, France, Germany, Iran, Iraq, Italy, Jordan, Lebanon, Oman, Qatar, Russia, Saudi Arabia, Turkey, the United Arab Emirates (UAE), Great Britain, and the UN. Other states and organizations also joined, including: the Arab League, Australia, Canada, Japan, the Netherlands, the Organization of Islamic Cooperation, and Spain. According to the group, it was created with an unwavering commitment "to strengthen the Cessation of Hostilities, to ensure full and sustained humanitarian access in Syria, and to ensure progress toward a peaceful political transition," a transition upheld as "Syrian-owned and Syrian-led."[216]

To this end, the ISSG met in Vienna to restart the peace process in Syria. The failure of Geneva I & II highlighted the importance of consensus, and the first round of talks were held on October 30, 2015. While Geneva II brought opposition elements and government representatives to the table, they were absent from Vienna. The primary sticking point again was the question of Assad's status: should he be kept in power or be removed to allow for popular elections? Saudi Arabia, the Gulf States, and the US were pushing for removal, while

Russia and Iran were in support of their ally. There was agreement, however, on the best path forward, with agreements on the holding of elections and a rewriting of the Syrian constitution. No specifics were discussed or timelines formulated, however.

Despite enormous tension amongst the regional actors, particularly Saudi Arabia and Iran, the parties met again for a second round on November 14 in order to conclude their previous discussions. While many differences remained, the representatives were able to agree on nine points:

1. Syria's unity, independence, territorial integrity, and secular character are fundamental;

2. State institutions will remain intact;

3. The rights of all Syrians, regardless of ethnicity or religious denomination, must be protected;

4. It is imperative to accelerate all diplomatic efforts to end the war;

5. Humanitarian access will be ensured throughout the territory of Syria, and the participants will increase support for internally displaced persons, refugees, and their host countries;

6. [Islamic State], and other terrorist groups, as designated by the U.N. Security Council, and further, as agreed by the participants, must be defeated;

7. Pursuant to the 2012 Geneva Communique and U.N. Security Council Resolution 2118, the participants invited the U.N. to convene representatives of the Government of Syria and the Syrian opposition for a political process leading to credible, inclusive, non-sectarian governance, followed by a new constitution and elections. These elections must be administered under U.N. supervision to the satisfaction of the governance and to the highest international standards of transparency and accountability, free and fair, with all Syrians, including the diaspora, eligible to participate;

8. This political process will be Syrian-led and Syrian-owned, and the Syrian people will decide the future of Syria; and

9. The participants together with the United Nations will explore modalities for, and implementation of, a nation-wide ceasefire to be initiated on a certain date and in parallel with this renewed political process.[217]

While these nine points were a significant achievement, given the disparate and large numbers of parties in attendance, the fact remains that the two parties that would be responsible for its implementation were absent. While it is one thing to write out neat instructions, it is quite another to ensure all follow through with them. The parties agreed on a timeline for diplomatic negotiations between warring parties to begin in January 2016, with a political transition to begin within six months, and the holding of elections within 18 months; somewhat idealistic given that differences existed and fighting continued.

In response to the Vienna talks, the UN Security Council adopted Resolution 2254, acknowledging "the close linkage between a cease-fire and a parallel political process." To achieve these efforts, the UN was in support of the ISSG, but also called on UN member states to assist in any missions necessary in regards to a ceasefire while also combatting terrorist groups within Syria. With these in place, a return of refugees would be possible, but would further increase efforts at post-conflict rebuilding, with the UN expressing "its support to the post-conflict reconstruction and rehabilitation of Syria."[218]

HIGH NEGOTIATIONS COMMITTEE

The failure of the Geneva II talks in 2014 brought the realization that the numerous opposition groups were not in a significantly influential position to represent the opposition as a whole, and to therefore successfully negotiate on the behalf of all. With this in mind, Saudi Arabia, with the support of many other governments, organized and hosted the Riyadh Conference in December 2015, hoping to establish a representative body for all the opposition groups (with the exception of the Kurds), while simultaneously establishing an outline for the success of future talks. This representative body would come to be known as the High Negotiations Committee (HNC).

Due to its three-decades long conflict with the Kurdistan Workers' Party (PKK), Turkey threatened to withdrawal its support from the conference if PKK-affiliated Kurdish groups were given a voice. This move succeeded, forcing the Kurdish groups to establish a separate meeting in the city of Rumeilan, in Syrian Kurdish territory. Here it was hoped that the Syrian Democratic Forces could establish a political entity, give support to the Kurdish population and a stronger push for autonomy. While the United States was supporting the Riyadh Conference, so too it seems, it was supporting the exclusion of the Kurds, the very group that it had hinged its bets on in ousting the Islamic State from Iraq and Syria.

The Assad regime held its own conference in Damascus as well, hoping to "disrupt the Riyadh proceedings by pushing a rival 'internal opposition' into the limelight."[219] The hope here being that the regime could potentially water down opposition arguments and undermine their entire efforts in future negotiations.

In September 2016, the HNC released its proposals for ending the conflict and transitioning into a stable and democratic country. To be successful, Syria would need to be headed by a transitional government while ongoing negotiations took place between the opposition and Assad regime. At the end of those negotiations, Bashar al-Assad would be required to step down, at which point the transitional government would assume authority for 18 months, concluding in democratic elections. According to the HNC's chief negotiator, the opposition would not compromise on its fundamental issues: "[i]f what the Russians and the Americans agree upon is very much different from what the Syrians aspire to, then we shall not accept it." While peace and stability are the ultimate goals for all parties involved, the means by which to attain this are of course the sticking point. Past negotiations had failed to bring about any consensus, particularly on Assad's removal; however, getting both sides to sit down together would be challenging in itself. The chief negotiator continued by stating that the parties had,

> gone through rounds of talks and a political process in 2014 and unfortunately we failed. The political process failed because there was refusal to talk about the political transition

by [UN Special Envoy to Syria] Staffan de Mistura. He knows that over the past few months the regime has refused to talk about a political transition and, practically, we do not have any negotiating rounds happening in Geneva because the regime was very rigid and absent. We feel we have to move to a new phase, and the new phase cannot happen without a political transition and the political seriousness that will compel the regime and its allies.[220]

This could potentially create an inherent problem if the opposition is unwilling to accept even some responsibility for the situation in Syria. It goes without stating that the Assad regime and Ba'ath Party were overbearing on the Syrian people, and their frustrations culminated in a revolution against such tyranny. While the opposition's goal is transitional government and Bashar removed from power, Bashar's goal is to stabilize his position of power within the country, thus stabilizing the country, while the UN and international community desires an end to the conflict first and foremost. It is not wholly the UN's responsibility to compel Assad into a political transition; the only way possible for this would be the UN's use-of-force against Assad. The opposition must move itself into negotiations from the most advantageous position as possible. Thucydides still reverberates today when he wrote, "…the standard of justice depends on the equality of power to compel and that in fact the strong do what they have the power to do and the weak accept what they have to accept."[221] As long as the opposition was failing militarily in Syria, it could not hope to win diplomatically or politically.

CHAPTER 7

THE US RESPONSE TO THE ISLAMIC STATE

OPERATION INHERENT RESOLVE

Although Operation Inherent Resolve was initially confined to Iraq, where American efforts ramped up in order to protect Americans on the ground (US troops, principally), it would not stay confined to Iraq. According to the then-US Secretary of Defense Chuck Hagel, "Department of Defense personnel in Iraq…continue to assess opportunities to help train, advise, and assist Iraqi forces, and will provide increased support once Iraq has formed a new government."[222] This, coming nearly a dozen years after the US invaded Iraq, with the drain on resources and manpower, the feeling seemed to remain: Iraq was owed American nation-building efforts. More importantly than this: is 12 years not enough to forge Iraqi forces? And how many new governments did the Iraqis need to go through in order to satisfy the United States?

After conducting over 190 airstrikes against IS in Iraq, in September 2014, President Obama authorized strikes to begin within Syria. This of course, could be construed as an act of war. While the President, under Article II, Section II of the US Constitution "shall be Commander in Chief of the Army and Navy" it is Article I, Section VIII that grants Congress the authority "to declare War." Not only has the US Congress not declared war against IS or Syria, it has not so much as debated the increased spending and the decisions, sacrifices, and consequences that will befall servicemembers being asked to go into harm's way (not to mention consequences involving US soft power, regional security and destabilization, weapons proliferation, conflict escalation, the ever-expanding role of terrorist groups, and humanitarian crises).

Most presidents believe that it is within their power to conduct such operations, certainly Presidents Obama and Trump are no different in this respect. Once such operations have been launched, the Congress is reluctant to defund such situations, despite the legislature being a check and a balance to the executive. In an effort to curb this seemingly Executive prerogative, Congress adopted the War Powers Resolution (or War Powers Act) in 1973. As the US population was reeling from the escalation in Vietnam, the Congress was looking to curb Executive overreach, especially when committing armed forces. To some, "the exercise of power per se made the United States arrogant" and it had been demonstrated that "democracy and power politics were simply incompatible."[223]

To this end, the War Powers Resolution limited the Commander-in-Chief in engaging the military only with a declaration of war, a "specific statutory authorization," or any attack upon US soil (including territories) or military personnel. This, however, becomes more and more like quicksand: as US forces are deployed in ever-increasing numbers around the world, the President's authority to utilize force grows concurrently, as more forces are in harm's way.[224] In doing so, the President must consult with Congress prior to the introduction of forces, while continuing to consult members while those forces are deployed. This is not permission, merely a nod to the Congress. Once the President informs Congress, forces must be withdrawn within 60 days, unless Congress approves of operations beyond that period. Since the War Powers Resolution was adopted, Presidents have submitted 120 reports to the Congress.[225] Rarely is Congress capable of thinking beyond their next election, and with the War Powers Resolution, it seems the President was handed unintended carte blanche to continue deploying the military well into the future, and to continue spending US tax dollars for this and all its consequences. To this end, in the aftermath of the September 11th attacks, Congress granted:

> That the President is authorized to use all necessary and appropriate force against those nations, organizations, or

persons he determines planned, authorized, committed, or aided the terrorist attacks that occurred on September 11, 2001, or harbored such organizations or persons, in order to prevent any future acts of international terrorism against the United States by such nations, organizations or persons.[226]

Based on that statement, it becomes clear why the Bush administration was so adamant to link Saddam Hussein and the Ba'ath Party of Iraq to al-Qaeda; it justified war against Iraq. However, this does not authorize US armed forces to operate against IS or to operate within Syria. On the other hand, it would justify military action against Saudi Arabia for its part in aiding the 9/11 hijackers. Sixteen years after the events of that day, in a lawsuit filed against Saudi Arabia, evidence was submitted that may indicate Saudi employees from its embassy in Washington, DC aiding (funding) several of the hijackers in their efforts to conduct a "dry run" before the "live fire."[227] Will that evidence drive the United States to declare war against Saudi Arabia? Of course, it likely will not.

Along with the beginning of airstrikes in Syria, the US Congress also voted to begin arming "moderate" rebels. It was couched in the larger government funding bill, and it did not address funding for such an operation, nor did it limit these opposition forces to fighting only Islamic State forces. Perhaps most important of all, what did the term "moderate" rebel entail? And how would that be determined? When the US government vets its own personnel, it conducts extensive background checks, including: credit, residence, references, schools attended, employment history, and criminal history. In the US, this can be done fairly easily, even when people have similar information, such as names. However easy it might be, the process can take a considerable amount of time; case in point, the Trump Administration. One year after taking office, there were still individuals on President Trump's staff that had access to secret information, whose security clearances had not been completed.

If this sort of lapse is going on at the White House, one can only imagine the inherent problems in vetting Syrian opposition fighters. One added difficulty in this process in Arab countries, is maintaining consistency when transliterating an individual's name in a database. One name could be spelled multiple ways; for instance: Mohammed,

Mohamed, Muhamed, Muhammed or Mahmood, Mahmud, and so on. These spelling varieties can also add confusion to the naming conventions in the Arab world and the differences in the Arabic and English alphabets, not to mention shifting loyalties. In addition, the tribal, ethnic, religious, cultural differences create a terribly difficult, if not impossible, task when looking into one's background.

The program set the audacious deadline of December 2015 to have 3,000 fighters vetted, trained, outfitted, and deployed in the fight against the Islamic State. However, the program earmarked a budget of $500 million annually, yet it only achieved a fraction of its intended goal with 150 fighters; the program was scrapped on October 9, 2015. Coming on the heels of this failure was the announcement, on October 30, that not more than 50 special operations troops were being sent to northern Syria to link up with and assist local forces' efforts against the Islamic State. Even if their mission had not been to directly engage IS fighters (and the White House was adamant in pointing out that these forces had not been given a combat mission), their mere presence put them in harm, facilitating the requirement for self-defense from time-to-time. Putting "boots-on-the-ground" was contrary to what President Obama had declared in 2013: "I will not put American boots on the ground in Syria."[228] Combat mission or not, boots-on-the-ground was just that, boots-on-the-ground.

US troops have experienced an escalation of force at least twice in the Middle East, once in Lebanon and the other in Somalia, by their mere presence.[viii] Deployed to Beirut, Lebanon in 1982 as part of a multi-national peacekeeping force, US troops were to oversee the withdrawal of the Palestine Liberation Organization (PLO) following fighting in the country. The situation had grown dire in Lebanon following the outbreak of their own civil war in April 1975. The violence was largely sectarian, pitting militias of various demographics. Assessments from the CIA at the time believed that US positions could be targeted in an effort to provoke a larger US response, thereby undermining US-Arab relations. It was believed that such a reaction from the US would catalyze a unification of the Druze, Shi'a, and Palestinians behind Syria in a drive to topple the Lebanese

---

viii Somalia, although technically not Arab nor located in the Middle East, is predominantly Muslim and a haven for terrorists.

government, allowing Syrian forces to install a pro-Syrian government. This was further aggravated by claims, no doubt perpetrated by Syria, that the US's presence in Lebanon was an effort to bolster the Maronite (Christian) political position.[229] This appeared to be true after US forces became directly involved in the fighting by shelling the positions of opponents to the Maronite militias, subsequently leading to the bombing of the US Marines and the US embassy.

Beginning in December 1992, US forces again deployed as part of a multi-national peacekeeping force, this time to Mogadishu, Somalia. After a civil war that left the country ravaged, and without a viable government, the United Nations stepped in to distribute aid to the locals. Local warlords, attempting to fill this power vacuum, vied for control of the city. UN-mandated troops were brought in to safeguard the supplies in order to prevent these warlords from hijacking them or the distribution process and thereby exerting their will over the locals. After two dozen Pakistani peacekeepers were killed by the minions of one warlord, Mohammad Aidid, the passive peacekeeping efforts turned into active raids, centered on finding Aidid. A series of raids in 1993 culminated into a deadly engagement with US troops, resulting in 18 killed and another 84 wounded US soldiers. Although George H W Bush ordered the peacekeepers to Somalia, President Bill Clinton oversaw the combat phase and had this to say:

> I was sick about the loss of our troops and I wanted Aidid to pay. If getting him was worth eighteen dead and eighty-four wounded Americans, wasn't it worth finishing the job? The problem with that line of reasoning was that if we went back in and nabbed Aidid, dead or alive, then we, not the UN, would own Somalia, and there was no guarantee that we could put it together politically any better than the UN had. Subsequent events proved the validity of that view: after Aidid died of natural causes in 1996, Somalia remained divided.[230]

Essentially, he was stating that if the US took it upon itself to fix the problems of Somalia, then the US would be responsible for the consequences. There was a larger problem in Somalia than these warlords, it was the lack of solid governance. Introducing US troops into the mix, even with the best of intentions, did little to alleviate any of the issues, but did cost the US lives and resources. The same potential existed for the US in regards to Syria, the Islamic State, and the Middle East as a whole.

OPERATION INHERENT RESOLVE: PHASE I - DEGRADE

When Iraqi forces had begun pushing Islamic State from the northern Iraqi city of Mosul, a push to retake Raqqa, Syria, the capital of IS, was being formulated by the US under Operation Inherent Resolve. President Trump supported plans to arm the Kurdish Peoples' Protection Units (YPG), a Syrian-Kurdish faction within the Syrian Democratic Forces. The US was intent on distributing heavy weapons that the Syrian Kurds could utilize against IS, such as machine guns and mortars.[231] Overall, the Syrian Democratic Forces were made up of 50,000 fighters, about evenly split between Kurds and Arabs.[232] While the United States has generally had amiable relations with the Kurds, despite some setbacks in Iraq, Ankara has had no such relationship, within Syria, Iraq, or its own borders.

Ankara has declared the YPG as an arm of the Kurdistan Workers' Party (PKK), which has been labeled as a terrorist organization by the Turks, European Union, and the US. The PKK, formed in 1974, is a socialist organization representing Kurdish nationalism with the intent, at least initially, of carving out land for an independent Kurdish country. Kurdistan, as this area is known, is composed of the world's largest stateless population, numbering roughly 30 million people. In its early years, the PKK relied on guerilla warfare, kidnappings, suicide bombings, and attacks against Turkish diplomatic offices. While they concentrated attacks mainly against Turkish security forces, they also attacked uncooperative civilians and kidnapped foreign tourists. Except for a brief ceasefire from 2004 to 2007, the fighting has taken its toll on both sides, with an estimated 37,000 people having been killed.

After the US-led invasion of Iraq, the security along the Iraqi-Turkish border weakened to such an extent that the PKK was able to stage cross-border attacks into Turkey from Iraq, leading to parliamentarian-approval of Turkish operations in 2007 to route out these elements. In recent years, the PKK has refocused its efforts from undermining Turkish security, to promoting civil rights coupled with an autonomous Kurdish state within Turkey. It is possible that the PKK is truly committed to a peaceful resolution after three decades of fighting, but Ankara is not about to let its guard down. Some believe the US-led invasion of Iraq encouraged those fighting for Kurdish freedom, as they have seen the autonomy offered to the Kurdish region within Iraq.[233] In any event, the PKK has not renounced terrorism as a means to garner recognition from the international community and political recognition from Ankara.

While the US was covertly arming the opposition to Assad, after Operation Inherent Resolve officially began conducting operations against IS, the US began arming its partners in the fight. The Pentagon initially attempted to field and train a fresh unit of vetted fighters, but the program ended in terrible failure. Instead, they turned to the fighters that had already been in the fight. This program was begun by President Obama in September 2015 and cost the US taxpayers $700 million. When the Trump Administration took over, another $600 million was requested; contracts are expected to run through 2022 for another $900 million. Logistics routes were established to Syria through Turkey, Jordan, and Kuwait, originating from the Balkan countries, Georgia, Ukraine, and Kazakhstan. End-user certificates were falsified, which could put the originating countries in jeopardy of international law violations and raise questions that could prove harmful to all involved.[234] Proliferation (whether it is small-arms or nuclear weapons) is not necessarily the best solution to the problems plaguing Syria.

The first major operation to be launched inside of Syria was the fighting in and around Kobani, near the Turkish border; Kobani was not of particularly strategic importance, but it was important for the Kurds. After the Syrian Civil War began, the Assad regime entered into a deal with the Democratic Union Party (PYD), in which the Syrian government would cede parts of northern Syria to the PYD in exchange for quelling anti-government dissent. It was this that prompted the PYD to form the YPG. This collusion between the PYD and the Assad government undermined PYD efforts, as government opposition groups, coalition countries wanting Bashar's removal, and some Kurdish groups were opposed to such an agreement.[235] In any event, the PYD and YPG set up Kobani to be a model of Kurdish autonomy within Syria, along with Afrin and Jazirah; for the Kurds, if Kobani were to fall, the other two would be defensively vulnerable to IS fighters.

Beginning in September 2014, Islamic State fighters began an offensive to take Kobani, creating hundreds of thousands of refugees. YPG and FSA fighters fended off this IS offensive, but after a month of fighting, it looked as if Kobani might fall to IS. Despite the fact that the city was not all-too strategically important, its capture would have been a public relations coup for the Islamic State, particularly as it concerned American airpower. Not wanting to grant this to the Islamic State, the US began to increase the intensity of its airstrikes against IS targets while dropping supplies to Kurdish positions.

These sorties were being conducted near the Turkish border, causing much distress in Ankara; nobody wanted sustained military operations by Turkish forces. Turkey initially began operations against Syria in October 2012, after the Turkish city of Akçakale received indirect fire from within Syria. While the Turkish parliament authorized strikes within Syria, Turkey did not commit ground forces to the unrest, instead responding with artillery strikes and air force sorties. As an ally of the United States, and largely at odds with Russia, Turkey was convinced not to complicate matters in Syria by entangling its forces on the ground, at least initially.

Turkey, aside from this, was reluctant to assist in any way, given that the fighting was being handled largely by Kurdish units. The US convinced the Turks that an IS-dominated Kobani would not be good for Turkish security and the Turks, six weeks into the fighting, allowed Iraqi-Kurdish Peshmerga to cross into Syria from Turkey. These reinforcements brought much needed supplies and bolstered the spirits of those exhausted from fighting. Turkey agreed to the passage of 2,000 fighters, although only 150 entered Kobani. The Syrian-Kurds were just as worried as Turkey in allowing Iraqi-Kurds to enter Syria, perhaps not wanting Syrian-Kurdish aspirations for an autonomous area within Syria undermined, much as the Iraqi-Kurds had had done in Iraq. After four months of fighting, victory was declared on January 26, 2015, although fighting continued as IS fighters still maintained a presence in outlying areas of the city.

The FSA seemed none too happy about the US support afforded to the Kurds in the defense of Kobani. One FSA commander stated that,

> It is disgusting politics for the U.S. to deliver weapons to the Kurds who have been fighting [the Islamic State] for only a month in a small town, while depriving the mainstream opposition for more than three years from any military and strategic aid while resisting the Assad regime that commits any kind of war crime...Airdropping weapons to the Kurds shows the hypocrisy of the Washington administration.[236]

Some Arab fighters were further discouraged after some Kurdish peshmerga refused to share US-supplied rifles and ammunition. In addition, the FSA believed that much more importance should have been placed on operations in and around Aleppo specifically.

Turkish President Recep Tayyip Erdogan also questioned coalition efforts aimed at assisting in the operations around Kobani. "Why Kobani and not otherwise towns like Idlib, Hama or Homs...while Iraqi territory is 40 percent controlled by the Islamic State? There are only 2,000 fighters in Kobani. It is difficult to understand this approach. Why has the coalition not acted in other zones?"[237]

In any event, Kobani was taken as a victory for Operation Inherent Resolve and the first major defeat suffered by IS in Syria. The Islamic State lost approximately 1,200 fighters, showing its resolve in holding onto its territory. Such destruction is not created in a vacuum, however, as collateral damage throughout the city was staggering. Kobani suffered from 3,200 buildings being severely damaged or destroyed, forcing the people and the local governments into the harsh task of cleaning-up and rebuilding.

Following on the heels of this success in Kobani, the Western al-Hasakah Offensive was launched in May 2015, quickly capturing the area. In order to establish a link between it and Kobani, it became necessary to capture Tal Abyad, an important supply route for the Islamic State, especially for fighters coming through Turkey. Closing the border crossing would allow coalition forces to contain IS at one more point before the drive to the IS capital of Raqqa could begin. Lasting from late-May to July 2015, the Tal Abyad Offensive succeeded in uniting this part of northern Syria under coalition and Kurdish control, while depriving the Islamic State of a major supply route. Coupled with the ongoing fighting in Iraq, the Islamic State was slowly losing ground, but not necessarily influence or potency.

Turkey, on the other hand, did not see the same results. Turkish President Erdogan was quoted as saying "All they [Kurds] want is to seize northern Syria entirely. We will under no circumstances allow northern Syria to become a victim of their scheming. Because this constitutes a threat for us, and it is not possible for us as Turkey to say 'yes' to this threat."[238] The situation along the Syrian-Turkish border is complicated by history. When the border was formed by the modern Turkish state after the fall of the Ottoman Empire, a railroad was utilized in some parts as the border, forcing some towns to be divided up. This has given Syrian Kurds cause for sympathy with the PKK in Turkey; a significant portion of PKK fights are made up of Syrian Kurds. In addition, the Syrian and Turkish Kurds both speak Kurmanji, a dialect of the Kurdish language, giving the two sides common ground culturally.

Turkey was also concerned with the demographics of Tal Abyad, which is largely Arab and Turkomen, with the Kurds not in the majority. While the residents were no doubt enthusiastic over the departure of the Islamic State, living within a Kurdish enclave might not sit well with them; they are more culturally aligned with the members of IS than with the Kurdish YPG. The Kurds were predominately united in their sentiment towards IS, while the Arabs and Turkomen, mainly Sunni Muslims, remained divided. Ankara, believing that PKK-sympathies existed within these groups, was concerned about cross-border spillover in its attempts to limit its own internal struggles with the PKK. US-support of the Kurds could lead to increased tension and violence throughout Turkey, not to mention Syria.

While operating alongside the YPG, the United States was attempting a balancing act with Turkey. To appeal to Ankara, the US State Department refused to issue a visa to the leader of the Democratic Union Party (PYD) leader, no doubt stirring up some confusion. This sort of behavior sends a message to the international community, where reluctance to fully support the YPG becomes embedded, necessitating the YPG to maintain or strengthen ties with Tehran and the Assad government.[239]

OPERATION INHERENT RESOLVE:
PHASE II - COUNTERATTACK

On December 2, 2015, 14 people were killed, and another 21 injured, following an attack in San Bernardino, California, perpetrated by Syed Rizwan Farook and his wife, Tashfeen Malik. Syed Rizwan Farook was born in Illinois to Pakistan-born parents. Tashfeen Malik was born in Pakistan, grew up in Saudi Arabia, and returned to Pakistan for university studies. There was no evidence linking the couple to a terrorist network, but they had evidently been planning several attacks and both were sympathetic to terrorist ideologies. When police entered their home after the attack, they found 12 completed pipe bombs and a magazine published by al-Qaeda, open to an article on how to construct timed hand grenades. Farook had also been planning an attack in 2012, with the help of a Muslim-convert, Enrique Marquez, Jr. Ultimately, heavy police activity had dissuaded him from carrying out any plans, but the husband and wife used these intervening years to reach out to terror groups, obtaining contacts at least in al-Nusra Front in Syria and al-Shabab in Somalia. In 2012, Malik had expressed support for Islamic jihad as early as 2012, and had pledged fealty to the Islamic State on Facebook the same day as the attack in San Bernardino.[240] The Islamic State was evidently pleased, broadcasting news of the attack and claiming the couple as members of the group. They were both killed by police in a shootout, ending their "jihad".

The end of 2015 brought some successes against IS, clearing the way for the transition into Phase II. In January 2016, US Secretary of Defense Ash Carter outlined upcoming objectives against IS: continue to apply pressure on Raqqa and Mosul, target IS and allied groups internationally, and defend against their attacks internationally. The United States and coalition partners had been providing support to ground forces in their fight against IS, and in April 2016, the Pentagon announced the initiation of Phase II, which would seek to "blunt [the] expansion and reduce [the] combat effectiveness" of IS, while also reinitiating the program to train Syrian groups to operate against the Islamic State. Perhaps starting and stopping such programs would lead to increased efficiency from lessons learned, but the cost/benefit certainly did not seem to be there.

After the successful completion of the Tal Abyad Offensive, SDF elements had begun a slow advance towards Raqqa, meeting resistance and seizing areas along the way, eventually establishing themselves around Raqqa. This move south towards Raqqa corresponded with the offensive by Iraqi forces into Mosul, Iraq. The successful completion of both offensives would serve to deprive IS of its two biggest urban centers and the corresponding finance, recruitment, propaganda, and internal lines-of-communication that they afforded to the group.

GENEVA III & CEASEFIRE (FEBRUARY 2016)

With the last round of Geneva talks having taken place in 2014, there was renewed interest in peace in 2016, coupled by Syrian opposition forces desperately holding onto ground in Aleppo. Aleppo had been a city effectively divided since 2012 with neither side making significant progress in capturing it. This began to change with the intervention of Russian forces in 2015. Anticipating a major offensive, government forces began moving to reinforce their positions in and around the city. With Russian air power and pro-government forces (including Syrian Democratic Forces), an operation began in February 2016 with the apparent objectives of: cutting off opposition supply routes via Turkey, bolstering the territorial gains of Kurdish forces, and effectively encircling the city of Aleppo.[241] The SDF and YPG were more than happy to accept assistance from Russia, even while simultaneously fighting alongside the US and coalition partners.

With Russia increasing its bombing runs in Aleppo, and Kurdish forces making gains in northern Syria, Ankara was feeling the pressure. Russia's air campaign was creating refugees that were then, given the proximity of the border, attempting to flee into Turkey. The progress of Kurdish forces was depriving territory to opposition forces, but creating in Turkey the notion that a Kurdish autonomous area was growing. Not wanting to commit ground forces to this fight with the threat of direct confrontation with Russia a possibility, Turkey began shelling Kurdish positions.

In this atmosphere, the third round of peace talks began in Geneva. UN envoy Staffan de Mistura invited the belligerents for mediation talks in which he agreed to shuttle between Syrian government representatives and representatives from the High Negotiations Committee.

The opposition, however, attached terms to their attendance: a bombing freeze, the lifting of sieges, and the release of prisoners. The Syrian government agreed to consider such items, but not as preconditions to be met, but rather as issues to discuss; little doubt Assad was unwilling to give up gains being made in and around Aleppo. The talks resulted in yet another failure on February 3, 2016, after only three days of discussions. The government believed the opposition had placed premature and all-too demanding conditions on the potential for peace, while the opposition accused the government of insincere motives and stalling tactics. With the failure of negotiations, and even during the talks, Syrian government forces continued operations, attempting to gain ground in Aleppo, eventually succeeding in cutting an opposition supply route.

During the G20 summit being held at the time, the United States and Russia met and reached an agreement to enforce the terms of a ceasefire, excluding terrorist elements, which would begin February 27. A previous ceasefire agreement had been abandoned in prior weeks due to the continued fighting, especially with the regime's advances in Aleppo. The fact that the ceasefire did not apply to terrorist groups complicated the ceasefire; while the Islamic State was relatively confined to its "caliphate" within Syria, and relatively straightforward in identifying, al-Nusra Front, for its part, was more difficult. It was typically operating within Syrian urban centers and often fought alongside FSA units, leading many to believe that Syrian government forces would use this as a means of continuing its targeting of opposition elements. With Turkey's growing unease, the US and Russia stepping up efforts in Syria, and Iran's proxies' continued presence, many hoped this ceasefire would appease the parties involved, and prevent further expansion of the conflict.[242]

GENEVA IV (APRIL 2016)

In March, Special Envoy Staffan de Mistura drafted a document based on common views shared by both parties on a way toward a unified and lasting peace in Syria. In summary, here are those 12 points (see Appendix II for full text):

1. Respect for the sovereignty, independence, unity, and territorial integrity of Syria…The people of Syria remain

committed to the restoration of the occupied Golan Heights by peaceful means;

2. The Syrian people alone shall determine the future of their country by democratic means;

3. Syria shall be a democratic, non-sectarian state;

4. Members of all communities…shall enjoy equal opportunities in social, economic, cultural and public life;

5. Women shall enjoy equality of rights and representation in all institutions and decision-making structures at a level of at least 30 percent during the transition and thereafter;

6. …the political transition in Syria shall include…credible, inclusive and non-sectarian governance,…drafting a news constitution and free and fair elections…;

7. Such governance shall ensure an environment of stability and calm during the transition;

8. Continuity and reform of state institutions and public services…;

9. Syria categorically rejects terrorism and strongly opposes terrorist organizations and individuals…;

10. Syrians are committed to rebuilding a strong and unified national army…;

11. All…displaced people wishing it shall be enabled to return safely to their homes with national and international support…; and

12. There shall be reparations, redress, care, and restitution of rights and properties lost…[by] the holding of a major donor conference to gain funds for compensation, reconstruction and development of the country…[243]

Added to this list could be the lasting ties with Israel; however, these points only seem possible in the long-term if the first one is acknowledged. From April 16—23, the two sides, through the mediation of the UN Special Envoy, attempted to move forward on political issues, utilizing these 12-points of commonality. While the ceasefire on the ground was proving shaking, the talks were shaping up in a similar fashion. Idlib Province was the site of some government targets, and while al-Nusra Front maintained a large presence in the province, the ceasefire did not apply. The HNC ended up leaving the talks in an effort "to highlight the cynicism of the regime in pretending to negotiate while escalating the violence." The talks were ultimately a failure, highlighting the waning influence of the opposition and the growing power of the Syrian government. The opposition was slowly losing its grip in and around Aleppo while the Islamic State was holding its own in eastern Syria.

At the beginning of April, the US military announced that it had again begun training Syrian opposition groups to combat the Islamic State, despite ending a similar program in October 2015. The US planned on fielding 5,000 soldiers in the opposition to Assad, but managed to train barely a fraction of this. The ones that were trained and equipped were an embarrassment. This first group of about 50 were trained in Turkey over the summer, and upon the completion of the program, moved south back into Syria, at which point they were ambushed by al-Nusra Front fighters. They fled, leaving arms and equipment on the field for al-Nusra to collect. The US was unable to account for these fighters or the equipment that was distributed. In September, another 70 were trained and pushed back into Syria, at which point they surrendered to al-Nusra Front in exchange for unmolested passage through al-Nusra-controlled territory. In the process, they relinquished US-supplied trucks, ammunition, and other equipment, bringing the program, in effect, to an end. The US government had expended $500 million for such efforts. The CIA had also renewed efforts to supply Syrian opposition groups with weapons, despite the lackluster results from its efforts in 2013. The efforts were ultimately scrapped in late summer of 2017, with an unbelievable price tag totaling $1 billion.[244]

OPERATIONS EUPHRATES SHIELD (AUGUST 2016)

The ceasefire ultimately failed: it did nothing to calm fears in Ankara, and operations around Aleppo continued as if there were no ceasefire.

Some hope had festered briefly when President Assad declared that parliamentary elections were to be held in April; the Syrian parliament is elected to four-year terms, carrying the country through to 2020. The Ba'ath Party won a clear majority; refugees could not cast a vote however, while many, nevertheless, were not surprised at such a victory, believing that such elections were geared heavily in favor of the ruling Ba'ath Party.

In August, Turkey began pulling the rebel fighters it backed out of Aleppo in order to take part in an offensive in a city called al-Bab, northeast of Aleppo. Part of Operation Euphrates Shield, the move was Ankara's effort to secure its border with Syria by taking the fight to IS and al-Nusra Front, and also denying operational centers from which the PKK could launch attacks into Turkey.[245] Lasting until March 2017, Turkish military forces, teamed up with Free Syrian Army units, had cleared a wide swath of Syrian territory along the Turkish border, effectively ending its operation. In total, the Turkish military had pushed south into 60 miles of Syrian territory, clearing the way of Islamic State fighters and also Kurdish YPG militia fighters.

Despite capturing al-Bab, Ankara did not immediately announce the cessation of Operation Euphrates Shield. As the Turks were deeply unsettled by American support of the Syrian Democratic Forces, it was perhaps hoped that American forces would reconsider such support, and turn to its long-time ally, Turkey, for assistance in driving towards Raqqa.[246] This did not pan out, adding to tensions on the ground.

US PRESIDENTIAL ELECTIONS & RUSSIAN INTERFERENCE

On June 12, 2016, 49 people were killed and another 53 wounded at the Pulse nightclub in Orlando, Florida. The shooter was a US citizen of Afghan parents named Omar Pateen. Pateen was interviewed twice by the Federal Bureau of Investigation (FBI), but was not deemed a threat. Despite initial claims, it was believed that Pateen's action was intended as a response to the US's international anti-terror policies; the target was chosen at random as the shooter's first choice contained too much security.[247] Omar Pateen was killed in a shootout with police. A website associated with Amaq, the Islamic State news agency, posted a message, stating "the armed attack that targeted a gay night club in the city of Orlando in the American state of Florida and that bore more than 100 killed and wounded was carried out by an Islamic State fighter."[248] Whether or not that was an authentic message seemed to be irrelevant as Pateen pledged his allegiance to the Islamic State in a 9-1-1 call during the siege at the nightclub.

Coupled with this attack, was the continued fighting around Aleppo, keeping Syria in the media. This necessitated the question of "what to do?" in Syria to the US presidential candidates in 2016.

Candidate Hillary Clinton took the typical Democrat stance by promising to establish no-fly zones to prevent the Syrian government from utilizing its air force to target civilian areas. Furthermore, she would call for the targeting of IS while supporting Kurdish allies, but she would also bring many more refugees into the United States. While no-fly zones might have proved successful in Iraq following the Gulf War and in Libya that helped bring down Ghaddafi (his air force was largely destroyed in 2011), Syria was a different situation, particularly after Russia entered the fray in late 2015. With Russia's extensive air-defense systems in place, and its and Syria's air forces conducting operations to subdue opposition in Aleppo, enforcing a no-fly zone would prove dangerous in escalating hostilities. It would needlessly endanger coalition aircraft (particularly American since it would no doubt supply the bulk of such efforts) and any downed pilots would become political fodder, with each side seeking to capture/rescue pilots in an effort to embarrass/glorify their respective countries. This would inevitably lead to the bolstering of forces, and further destabilize the situation. Furthermore, it would do nothing to pressure Assad or the opposition, only embolden Russian forces to test US forces, and put Syrian civilians in the crossfire. Bringing in larger groups of refugees from this conflict (and others like it for that matter), proved largely unpopular in the US, due to spikes of crime in many European countries by Arab immigrants, and in any event, it does nothing to solve the long-term events undermining Syrian society. Furthermore, her belief in supporting the Kurds showed a lack-of-understanding of the situation on the ground at best, and at worst, a misguided desire to continue dragging the US into a Middle Eastern quagmire.

Candidate Donald Trump proposed almost the complete oppo-
site approach: working with regional allies and curbing immigration
of people from countries with ties to terrorism, such as Syria, as well
as taking the fight to the Islamic State. For most, limiting immigration is not a matter of race, but rather culture and appropriate
levels of assimilation into the receiving society. For him, defeating
IS was a far more serious issue than forcing the removal of Bashar
al-Assad. He also believed that Hillary Clinton's proposed no-fly
zones, could potentially pull the United States into another global
conflict. Establishing a no-fly zone would have required the US
to actually defend and police such an area, potentially pitting US
forces directly against Russian forces, thereby exasperating tensions, not only in Syria, but around the world. Candidate Trump
was also critical of President Obama's handling of the fight against
IS, believing that committing only 50 soldiers to the fight in Syria
was an unnecessary half-measure. He believed that returning those
troops to Iraq was the way forward; however, he did not rule out
a ground fight in Syria, if full measures were taken to combat the
Islamic State.

On the other hand, the Libertarian candidate, Gary Johnson
(while not in any of the debates), undermined the movement he
represented in the presidential race. When asked "what would you
do if you were elected about Aleppo?" Johnson responded, "and what
is Aleppo?" Although he subsequently gave an answer that indicated
he was aware of the situation in Syria, after prompted, he did not
give a cogent enough argument to satisfy people of America's need
for relative isolationism, particularly as it pertained to Syria and the
Middle East. Subsequently, he stated: "I do understand Aleppo and I
understand the crisis that is going on. But when we involve ourselves
militarily…in these humanitarian issues…we end up with a situation that in most cases is not better, and in many cases ends up being
worse." He went on to add that American constituents seek solutions
to problems, and that U.S. "politicians are up against the wall…and
this is why we end up committing military force in areas that…at the
end of the day have an unintended consequence of making things
worse."[249] Although his statements were not entirely incorrect, his
somewhat vapid response "What is Aleppo?" no doubt undermined
Libertarian arguments for a reduced American military role in the

world, and hence the perception of Libertarians as isolationists with no understanding of the world, or the US's role in it.

The issue with the terrorist attacks taking place in the US was that they were overblown in 2016. While San Bernardino was the first major attack, and the Pulse nightclub was the most serious, there were only a handful of attacks inside the United States believed to be inspired by Islamic State propaganda. From the first attack in October 2014 for three years through December 2017, there were a total of 72 individuals killed and another 108 wounded. This is not meant to undermined the lives lost, or the mindset of the survivors, it is only meant to contribute to a pragmatic analysis of the cost/benefits of waging war inside a sovereign country in order to eradicate a group that posed no substantial threat to the sovereignty of the United States.

According to a Pew Research Center poll from October 27, 2016, 54% of Americans polled believed that the US should deal with its own problems before interceding in Syria, while 41% said it was okay to help out. The issue of refugees was also an issue throughout the debates in 2016, with 54% polled believing that the US did not have any responsibility to accept refugees, while 41% were adamant that the US should do so. At the time this poll was taken, the presidential election was nearly two weeks into the future, and President Obama's tenure was drawing to a close. The poll also covered how the fight against the Islamic State was transpiring: only 31% believed that it was progressing favorably and nearly two-thirds (64%) believed that it was not. These responses were of course split along partisan lines, but the percentages represented an average.[250] It seemed that domestic concerns trumped issues within Syria or Iraq. More importantly, it ignored the Constitutional issues, particularly that the federal government lacks the enumerated power to "help out" in certain circumstances.

To further complicate geo-political issues in Syria, November 2016 also witnessed Israel Defense Forces engaging with IS-affiliated groups in the Golan Heights after, evidently, the IDF established an ambush to catch the group unaware. Small-arms fire was exchanged, followed by IDF positions being targeted with mortar rounds. The Israeli air force then flew in, targeting a truck with a machine-gun mounted, thus ending the firefight. This was the first encounter with Israeli forces and the Islamic State. While the two had very few engagements, Israeli forces again fired on Islamic State fighters, this time in July 2018, after rockets landed in the Sea of Galilee. According to Russian media, the Islamic State was targeting Syrian positions and only inadvertently struck inside Israel. Some within Israel defense forces believe that the attack was deliberate in an effort to have Israeli forces strike Syrian positions.[251] Whatever the truth might have been, it pointed to the potential of Israel being dragged into the wider conflict.

CHAPTER 8

PEACE ATTEMPTS, CONTINUED

CEASEFIRE AND DEIR AL-ZOR (SEPTEMBER 2016)

After months of discussions between US Secretary-of-State John Kerry and his Russian counterpart Sergei Lavrov, a ceasefire was again agreed upon throughout Syria. It called for a halt to Syrian air force operations over opposition areas in order to allow for humanitarian aid to devastated areas. The US and Russia also agreed to the creation of a Joint Implementation Center that would facilitate information sharing in an effort to isolate al-Nusra Front and the Islamic State so that they could be identified and targeted. The US was reluctant to enter into such an agreement, given the tension and mistrust that had developed between the two nations throughout the years. Furthermore, any failures or incidents could be blamed on US forces, leaving Russia free of responsibility. One Obama White House official was quoted stating that the Joint Chiefs of Staff were against the idea and that the entire military command "got the Iraq part, but it was the Syria thing—even the counter-[Islamic State] part—that they didn't want. My theory is that everyone in DOD understands Iraq, and they don't understand Syria."[252] That is a fairly accurate summation of all of Washington, except for the understanding of Iraq; that still does not seem like the case 15 years later.

However, two days before execution of the Joint Implementation Center was to go into effect, the terms of the deal were undermined when US planes, operating over Deir al-Zor in eastern Syria, targeted Syrian military positions, killing at least 15, according to the US, and upwards of 62 according to Russia. Russian forces sent a warning to the US command that positions appeared to be Syrian, at which point the engagement was broke off; but the damage had been done. The ceasefire was cancelled and any cooperative US-Russian plans were permanently scrapped. It was the first time that the US had engaged Syrian forces, a mistake that the US admitted to, citing an "intelligence failure" in the belief that Islamic State fighters were actually being targeted. Russia called an emergency meeting of the UN Security Council to express its indignation and blamed the US for intentionally sabotaging the diplomatic efforts.

THIRD CEASEFIRE & ASTANA I (DECEMBER 2016–JANUARY 2017)

With Turkish allies having pulled out of Aleppo, and the pro-Assad forces' increased efforts, the Syrian opposition's strength faltered, allowing government-backed forces to begin fresh offensives to retake Aleppo. By December 2016, the majority of Aleppo was in government control, and the two sides agreed, with Russian and Turkish brokering, to a truce in which opposition fighters and tens-of-thousands of civilians would evacuate the city and redeploy elsewhere, with many going to Idlib, half-way between Aleppo and Latakia on the coast. Hampered by severe winter weather throughout, the evacuation was completed December 22.

Having captured Aleppo, Bashar al-Assad and his supporters were in a powerful position to force concessions on the opposition, as well as those world leaders calling for his removal. It seemed Turkey's withdrawal from Aleppo helped to pave the way for such a victory. Having been snubbed by the United States, which was siding with Turkey's Kurdish enemies, Turkey was turning more to Russia and less to the United States in partnership. Russia's pledge of March 2016 to soon draw-down its forces would put Iran in a position to wield hegemonic influence along Turkey's border, and a stable Syria would ensure a prosperous Turkey. If Turkey were to end up on the wrong side of that equation, there would be no end to Iran's ability to foment the Kurds against Turkey. Perhaps Ankara came to some sort of agreement with Damascus and Moscow? If so, it would seem to have been a carefully calculated move to undermine the US in an effort to secure its own security.

Meeting in Moscow on December 20, in what some would call the Moscow Declaration, the three nations (Russia, Turkey, and Iran) agreed to oversee an end to the fighting in Syria, the stabilization of the country, as well as the continued fight against terrorist groups. Fighting terrorists had been the Assad regime's narrative from the beginning, and with IS penetrating areas near the Turkish border, Turkey was more than willing to cooperate. However, unlike Russia that had invested heavily in backing Assad, Turkey realized that stabilization would not be likely, or come about easily, so long as Assad remained in power. Despite this realization, Turkey's most pressing concern was its own stabilization and security, therefore fighting IS and Kurdish separatist groups was more important than overthrowing the Syrian government. This cooperation came after the resultingly chilled relationship between Ankara and Moscow after Turkey shot down a Russian fighter in November 2015, in an apparent violation of Turkish sovereign airspace.

With Aleppo quieted, a truce was proposed by Ankara and Moscow, taking effect on December 30. This ceasefire was the third attempt at a truce between the warring parties just in 2016, and the third in which the United States was absent. The UN Security Council was not involved in these previous attempts, but quickly approved a Russian-drafted resolution. The opposition, however, was not completely on board with the agreement, stating that "a number of key and essential points that are non-negotiable" were missing, but leaving out further explanation.[253] While many looked hopefully to the future, the ceasefire did not end the fighting. As Turkey was a major actor in the ceasefire deal, and the YPG were viewed as a terrorist organization by Ankara, the YPG was not included in the ceasefire, and therefore, a valid target with which to engage in continued fighting.

Hoping to build off of this ceasefire, Turkey, Russia, and Iran met in the Kazahk capital of Astana in January 2017, along with elements of the opposition. Astana marked the first time that representatives from the Syrian government and actual fighters on the ground had met face-to-face. While these were distinct from past talks in Geneva, they were not viewed as a continuation of, but rather complementary to, those talks. Turkey, for its part, was definitively seen to back-pedal on its previous belief that Assad would not be capable of overseeing a stable Syria. The Turkish Deputy Prime Minister, Mehmet Şimşek, stated: "We have to be pragmatic, realistic. The facts on the ground have changed dramatically, so Turkey can no longer insist on a settlement without Assad. It is not realistic."[254] What had changed minds in Ankara in just a brief amount of time? It seems likely that Russia had some influence, a fact that certainly came about over Turkey's feeling of betrayal by the United States. It seemed likely that this was playing into Ankara's decision-making concerning its improving relationship with Russia, and its changing attitude towards Syria and Bashar al-Assad. Despite positive steps toward peace through Astana, neither party within Syria signed any agreements, leaving much work to be done.

ASTANA II (FEB 2017)

The second round of talks in Astana did not proceed far enough to guarantee an end to the fighting. It began even with the two backers, Russia and Turkey, failing to agree on the agenda: the former interested in moving forward on a constitution and the latter concerned over the precarious ceasefire. These two opposing viewpoints stemmed from the self-interest of the two parties: Russia wanted to ensure a stable Assad government so that it could draw-down troop levels; while Turkey, with a warring country so close, hoped for a ceasefire in order to stabilize its own border and strengthen its position in dealing with the refugees. Turkey had changed course concerning Assad since Astana I, now viewing Assad's tenure as president as an issue it could support.

The two belligerent sides refused to meet in-person, and the parties involved were unable to agree to a final statement. Bashar al-Jaafari, the Syrian government delegate, accused the opposition and Turkish delegates of arriving to the talks late, a point of contention. The opposition delegate, however, did reach consensus with Russia, which agreed to halt its shelling of rebel-held areas, as well as using its influence to obtain the release of political prisoners held by Syrian government forces. Al-Jaafari also accused Turkey of fomenting further violence within Syria and called for a withdrawal of all its forces from within Syria. Despite this, Russia, Turkey, and Iran formed an agreement that would realize continued monitoring of the ceasefire dating from December 2016. While the United States did not take part in the discussions, it was granted an observer role, along with representatives from Jordan.

With the United States still operating within Syria against IS, the Russians pushed for bilateral cooperation, particularly in matters involving their respective militaries and missions to wipeout terror groups. Iran balked at any involvement of the United States, due to its growing tension with the US, particularly after the election of President Donald Trump in January and the failing Iran Nuclear Deal. Despite these disagreements, the need was recognized for humanitarian assistance to be able to reach beleaguered areas throughout Syria, and all sides would assist in the free movement thereof. While these areas were in need of humanitarian supplies, discussions were also held for a system of prisoners and corpses to be exchanged across lines. This could help in seeing a return to normalcy for some communities and also undermine the spread of bacteria and viruses, allowing local communities to return to their day-to-day lives.

ASTANA III & GENEVA V (MARCH 2017)

March 2017 marked the sixth anniversary of the beginning of the Syrian Civil War and witnessed 400,000 people killed throughout that time. There was hope that the conflict might be in the process of ending, with four rounds of negotiations having already taken place in Geneva, and the third round of talks set to begin in Astana. No doubt aiming to undermine these talks, on March 11, 2017 militants detonated two explosives near a Shi'a pilgrimage site in Damascus, killing 40 and wounding 120 people, the majority of whom were visiting Iraqis. Although Tahrir al-Sham was believed to be responsible for this attack, the group denied it, claiming that they only target "security branches and military barracks of the criminal regime and its allies."[255] On March 15, a second set of explosives were detonated in Damascus, with suicide bombers targeting the Palace of Justice and a nearby restaurant, killing around 30 people and wounding another 100.[256]

Tahrir al-Sham was formed in January 2017, after several groups merged themselves into one organization: Jabhat Fath al-Sham (previously al-Nusra Front), Harakat Nur al-Din al-Zanki[ix], Liwa al-Haqq, Ansar al-Din, and Jaysh al-Sunnah. In English, the group's name means "Assembly for the Liberation of the Levant," and is led by Ahrar al-Sham's former head, Abu Jaber. Tahrir al-Sham was created to fight the Assad regime, and called for a ceasefire with other groups in the country as well as their joining under Abu Jaber's leadership. Apparently, these groups, and many others present in Syria, were disagreeing over the direction of the anti-regime fight, and many rivalries were developing. It seems that the creation of Tahrir al-Sham was an effort to alleviate some of those squabbles, as well as an attempt to distance themselves from any affiliation with al-Qaeda. Any relationship with al-Qaeda would undermine their efforts within Syria and bring increased international attention to their situation.[257]

Round three of Astana was held on March 14-15, with the opposition refusing to attend. Amid such a deadly environment in Syria, opposition officials placed blame on Russia for not taking appropriate steps necessary to safeguard the ceasefire. However, it was worked out between Turkey, Russia, and Iran, that the three countries would form a tripartite body in order to oversee responsibility for putting in place and monitoring progress ensuring violations of the ceasefire would be upheld. Despite this rhetoric, opposition elements launched two fresh offensives on March 21. The first was concentrated in the government-controlled city of Hama, and although militant groups took part in the operations, Free Syrian Army soldiers also took part.[258] On the same day, Damascus witnessed another operation launched against regime troops, the second in three days. Damascus had been relatively free of the violence, with these attacks being the first major operations carried out by the opposition against the capital in four years. The government was claiming these operations were initiated by Tahrir al-Sham, although groups falling under the FSA had spoken of the FSA's role in the attacks. Within just the first few days of fighting in and around Damascus, the government launched 143 air sorties, hoping to break the opposition's momentum.

In eastern Syria, regime forces had slowly been tightening its siege around Ghouta, which opposition attacks in Damascus had

---

ix   Al-Zanki had previously been vetted by the CIA, receiving anti-tank weapons in the process.

been aimed at relieving. With several past negotiations having taken place, and several more scheduled for the near future, these attacks were also designed to strengthen the opposition's ability at the negotiating table. Coupled with this, was the effort at driving a wedge between the government's reliance on Russia, and the latter's desire to withdrawal its forces from the country. It was the opposition's desire to demonstrate to Russia that the regime was still militarily weak, and completely dependent on Russian support.[259] The opposition believed that without this support, the government would not be able to maintain the fight, and most certainly would have little possibility of overseeing a political transition. Furthermore, without Russia and Iran, could the Syrian government maintain domestic security beyond a cessation of its civil war?

While Russia was taking the lead in the Astana negotiations, the UN was back at the fore in the fifth round of talks in Geneva, also held in March. UN mediator Staffan de Mistura drew up a proposal in order to restart talks concerning Syria's political future, but admitted that there seemed to be few items of common interest to the belligerent parties. Staffan de Mistura was somewhat successful in drawing out an agreement based on UN Security Council Resolution 2254, which called for a ceasefire and elections to be held within 18 months. The agreement called for an "overall political package for a negotiated transitional political process," including: an inclusive, non-sectarian government; a plan for the drafting of a constitution; the holding of elections within 18 months, supervised by UN mediators; and establishing "counterterrorism and security governance, and also confidence-building measures." While the first three were relatively clear cut and implementable within a relatively modest time-frame, the fourth caused some concerns. While objected by the opposition delegates, the Syrian government maintained it be added, with Russia's full support. It was not clearly understood what "counterterrorism and security governance, and also confidence-building measures" meant. According to the government, there was no civil war, but instead a fight against terrorists. Could this phrase be used to hamper or altogether scuttle progress towards a political solution?[260] As with the any government that claims to be fighting some vast enemy, the potential for a corrupted strategy was ever present. If the Syrian government needed to meet the opposition over these four points, then the government could claim no end to this counter-terrorist fight. Just as Hafez al-Assad kept the Emergency Laws in place for decades, so too did this measure have the potential to further undermine Syrian society. In any event, the delegates parted ways, with the understanding that another round in Astana would soon commence.

The ceasefire, for its part, was proving ever more fragile, with opposition representatives bellowing at government and Russian airstrikes targeting opposition holdouts, but the talks were almost completely aborted on February 25, 2017 after a suicide attack against government security offices in Homs killed dozens. Government forces responded with airstrikes against the western portion of the city still controlled by opposition groups. The government blamed the opposition for the attack and demanded their condemnation, while the opposition accused the government of complicity in an effort to undermine the talks. Tahrir al-Sham claimed credit for the attack.[261]

All-in-all, Astana III was a failure, although Turkey, Russia, and Iran did agree to meet for a fourth round in May. The Geneva process had failed at bringing about a resolution to the conflict as well, although the two sides agreed on reforms concerning governance, largely disagreeing, however, over how to reach that point.

KHAN SHEIKHOUN - MORE CHEMICAL WEAPONS

On April 4, 2017, reports circulated that 72 people, 11 of which were children, were killed, and 400 injured in an apparent chemical weapons attack in a rebel-controlled area of Syria. Newly-elected US President Donald Trump responded:

> Today's chemical attack in Syria against innocent people, including women and children, is reprehensible and cannot be ignored by the civilized world. These heinous actions by the [Bashar al-Assad] regime are a consequence of the past administration's weakness and irresolution. President Obama said in 2012 that he would establish a "red line" against the use of chemical weapons and then did nothing.[262]

President Trump also responded militarily by ordering 59 toma-hawk cruise missiles launched against the Shayrat Air Base in Syria during the early morning hours of April 7, 2017. It was believed this air base was the launching site of the aircraft that dropped the chemicals over Khan Sheikhoun. During this missile bombardment, there was a reported seven individuals killed, including a general and three soldiers, and possibly several children whose parents were stationed on the base. If the Syrian forces had in fact been warned hours before the attack, as has been alleged, they evidently did not take such news seriously.[263]

The tomahawk missiles launched by the US were primarily man-ufactured by Raytheon Missile Systems, and were capable of traveling 900 nautical miles to deliver a one-thousand-pound warhead. These missiles are equipped with two-way satellite communications (in order to change targets or abort a mission overall), Global Positioning Software (GPS) navigation, anti-jamming, and loitering capabilities. In 2015, each missile cost the U.S. taxpayer over $2 million, including procurement, research and development, and testing expenditures.[264] This particular US strike, therefore, cost the taxpayer $118 million, but at what benefit? In no way was the US made safer, nor were the American people benefited in any way. A message was undoubtedly sent, but what message was received and was $118 million necessary to do so? Given Russia's support of Syria, and Assad's continued tenure, it seems unlikely.

After the international efforts in 2013-2014 to remove the chemi-cal weapons after the attack in Ghouta, where did these "new" weapons originate? While the OPCW and the UN were rigorous in their efforts to destroy, not only Syria's stockpiled chemical weapons, but also its ability to further its manufacture of such weapons, there was a real possibility that the entire country could not be combed to locate such weapons or manufacturing sites. As was claimed from the previous removal of weapons, Assad simply moved some of Syria's chemical weapons out of the country, and when inspectors left, had them moved back. Therefore, it is possible that Assad utilized weapons that were not destroyed by the OPCW from 2013 to 2014. Despite Russian claims that rogue elements within the Assad regime were responsible for the attack, as well as blaming the Islamic State, it is also likely that Bashar al-Assad was convinced that he would face no direct opposition to such an attack, as his Russian overlords would be there to protect him and the US had already made empty threats. Instead of condemning Syrian forces for such an attack, would it not be appropriate to condemn Russia? After all, such an attack occurred under the watchful eyes of the Kremlin and its military on the ground within Syria. If Russia is working in tandem with Syria, how is it not at least complicit in the attack? Russia might not necessarily have provided such weapons to the Syrians, but surely the Russians were advising Syrian forces and were aware of their actions, which could explain why they would blame rogue elements.

Furthermore, as Russian and Syrian forces were co-located on Shayrat Air Base, this would further the idea that they were at least aware. In addition, according to a US official, a drone was flying over the hospital in Khan Sheikhoun that was admitting victims of the attack. Moments after the drone left station (how long was not mentioned) an aircraft appeared and bombed the hospital in an effort, some believed, to cover up evidence of the chemical attack. How it was known there was a drone flying over this particular hospital (assuming the drone was fairly advanced and not some cheap IS-controlled drone), the official did not say, but since the Syrians import their aircraft (from Russia, of course) they most certainly either do not have drones or are utilizing Russian drones.[265] If Russian forces took part in this, how would it have been known to target this hospital that just so happened to be receiving casualties from a chemical attack? This certainly shows Syrian forces at fault, with possible Russian collusion. This just goes to show, without multilateral cooperation, including from Russia and China, that the United States is not going to risk war with one or the other in order to remove Assad.

But, according to a defected Syrian general, Zaher al-Sakat, who was once Syrian Fifth Army's head of chemical warfare, Bashar al-Assad did not disclose all of the chemical stockpiles to inspectors in 2013. According to Sakat, before he defected from Syria, he was ordered on three separate occasions to launch chemical strikes, instead replacing the lethal substances with harmless ones. If this is accurate (and based on the attack at Khan Sheikhoun there does not seem to be a reason to believe it is not), Assad had plenty more, unaccountable chemical weapons. Furthermore, according to a French intelligence report: "France considers that Syria, despite the commitment to destroy all its stocks and capacities, has maintained a productive capacity."[266] The Organization for the Prohibition of Chemical Weapons has attempted to investigate this allegation; however, Russia has utilized its seat on the UN Security Council to block demands to cooperate with such measures.[267] This seems like further reason to believe Russia has aided Assad to this end.

In any event, the move did not improve relations on the ground between the various parties involved. Russia claimed it would cease cooperating with the United States concerning both side's air campaigns within Syria. As the Russian military dominated the area with a network of air-defense systems, any unknown or unidentified aircraft could become a target to such systems. Without clear lines-of-communication between Russia on the ground and in the air and the United States in the air, American pilots flying over the country in their missions against the Islamic State could be endangered. Furthermore, following the strike, Russia sent an advanced Black Sea frigate into the Eastern Mediterranean, where two U.S. destroyers remained on a "presence mission."[268] While there have been several occasions of Russian and American fighters having danger-close flybys over Syria, there is little doubt that these naval vessels will add to the tension. Just like US naval vessels have been forced to fire warning shots at fast-approaching Iranian vessels in the Persian Gulf, similar situations between Russian and American naval vessels could quickly escalate.

The Arab League, for its part, has called for a de-escalation of hostilities over Syria, deriding "regional and international powers' attempts to politick over the corpses of Syrians or at the cost of its sovereignty." The Arab League chief, Abu Gheit, had furthered stated that the "perpetrators [of the chemical attacks] must be held accountable one day."[269] There is no reason to believe that the Arab League is not fully capable of overseeing matters in Syria, not only in terms of its chemical weapons use, but also as pertains to refugees, peacekeeping operations, humanitarian assistance, and peace talks.

The fact that the US has more resources than others is plain to see; however, that does not mean they should be applied in every situation. The US has overstayed its welcome in the Middle East and, based on the shaky casus belli leading up to the 2003 invasion of Iraq, its credibility is not strong. The U.S. strike at the Shayrat Air Base was an act of war that lacked Congressional approval, had no national security implications, and cost the American taxpayers over a hundred million dollars. With all this stated, it seems that there are regional actors with more to gain by involving themselves in Syria's stability, and it seems likely that the Arab League could lead such an effort. It is poised to deliver a far better response to issues forming or stagnating throughout the Middle East.

ASTANA IV, GENEVA VI, AND "DE-ESCALATION ZONES" (MAY 2017)

The fourth round of Astana hoped to make significant contributions to ending hostilities. On May 4, Russian officials released their proposal for four safe zones to be established throughout Syria to this this end, which would allow for the safe return of refugees and provide medical and humanitarian relief to besieged areas.[270] While some supported what might be viewed as an important step in ending the years-long conflict, others viewed it as undermining the national integrity of the country, and with no mention of how such a plan would be enforced, many believed it would be another opportunity for more violence.[271] The opposition representatives walked out the first day in protest to the agreement. They cited continued government bombardment of opposition-held areas, the questionable intentions emanating from Moscow, and the hostility and bitterness of having a continued Iranian presence into the unforeseeable future.[272] The Kurdish forces were displeased with such a proposal as well, believing it was an attempt to divide Syria demographically.

With such bitter opposition to the proposal, and no plan to implement and enforce one, the safe zones precariously took hold. Russia would have liked the formality of a UN Security Council backing, although Bashar al-Assad refused any deals that might involve the intervention of UN forces or any UN oversight. Syrian government forces also expected opposition forces to pull their weight in expelling Tahrir al-Sham and the Islamic State forces from Syria, while the opposition was hesitant to trust the Assad government, Russia, or Iran. The United States was concerned with Iran's role in the negotiations, believing, per the US State Department, that

Iran's activities in Syria have only contributed to the violence, not stopped it, and Iran's unquestioning support for the Assad regime has perpetuated the misery of ordinary Syrians. In light of the failures of past agreements, we have reason to be cautious. We expect the regime to stop all attacks on civilians and opposition forces, something they have never done. We expect Russia to ensure regime compliance.[273]

While the entirety of Syria would still be at war, especially against terror groups, these safe zones would be the exception. They would allow humanitarian groups to establish operations conducive to stable and long-term support, with the intention of decreasing the fatality rates, and possibly reducing the refugee crisis being imposed on the surrounding countries and the global community. One question raised, however, was what would happen to these safe zones if the Islamic State, Tahrir al-Sham, or other such groups began operating inside of them? As the Syrian government had already remarked that all its enemies were terrorists, it seemed unlikely that any safe zones would persist, as terror groups would likely exploit such soft targets, thereby incurring responses from the Assad regime or its allies. In addition to this, there was a belief that the safe zones might have been proposed in an effort to safeguard Syria's continued chemical weapons production.

In any event, with such prevalent mistrust between the parties involved in the establishment and safeguarding of these zones, a reliable, objective party would be needed to oversee such an operation; otherwise, tensions would remain and potentially increase. These de-escalation zones included: Idlib Province in the north; Homs Province, near the border with northern Lebanon; the eastern portion of Ghouta, the area held by opposition forces; and the Syrian-Jordanian border.

That same month, despite the rhetoric supporting such zones, Syrian forces began building what appeared to be fighting positions about 35 miles away from a de-escalation zone along the Jordanian border, occupied by US forces and its coalition partners. They also began advancing towards US forces. Coalition forces, coupled with Russia, attempted to contact this approaching Syrian unit. When this failed, US aircraft flew a show-of-force and fired warning shots, before firing directly on the Syrian column. Then-Secretary of Defense James

Mattis stated that the US was "not increasing our role" in the conflict, but would "defend our troops, and that is a coalition element made up of more than just US troops, and so we'll defend ourselves. If people take aggressive steps against us," it has been a long-term policy of the US to respond.[274] While the missile attacks against Shayrat Air Base were a response after a chemical weapons incident, this was the first of such incidents involving a direct, intentional attack on Syrian forces perceived to be poised to do harm. It also demonstrated the danger of having US forces in a foreign country and then permitting those forces self-defense. As the US's previous engagement of Syrian forces was unintentional, caused by confusion, certainly Syrian forces could be expected to operate similarly, particularly within their own borders. This is precisely how situations can escalate.

And again, on June 18, 2017, US forces engaged Syrian forces, shooting down a Syrian aircraft approximately 30 miles west of Raqqa after it dropped munitions close to coalition positions. The US military asserted, in a statement following the incident, that the "coalition's mission is to defeat [the Islamic State] in Iraq and Syria. The coalition does not seek to fight Syrian regime, Russian, or pro-regime forces partnered with them, but will not hesitate to defend coalition partner forces from any threat."[275] This is the role everyone has come to expect the United States to play; however, it is a role that has unnecessarily dragged it into conflicts in the past; take Vietnam for example. The US Congress passed the Gulf of Tonkin Resolutions in 1964 after a US vessel, patrolling the waters off the North Vietnamese coast, came into contact with North Vietnamese vessels. This resolution intensified America's role in Vietnam, a role that had come about in order to contain Communism and prevent its spread from North Vietnam into the South. In no way, did this assist or benefit the Vietnamese people. Russia described the downing in Syria as "a cynical violation of Syria's sovereignty" and threatened to "track any air targets, including the international coalition's planes and drones, found to the west of the Euphrates [R]iver." In response, a US coalition spokesman stated that "we have taken prudent measures to reposition aircraft over Syria" but added "we will retain the right of self-defense of coalition forces aligned against" the Islamic State.[276] The US and Russia have been in communication since Russia's entry into Syria in October 2015, establishing a de-confliction line-of-communication in order to avoid unnecessarily escalating the conflict. While it has been used in the past, it evidently failed in this situation.

This incident came days before a fresh round of negotiations took place in Geneva. Deliberations were set to discuss the political transition, the process for writing a new constitution, and the status of prisoners. The High Negotiation Committee again insisted that for any political transition to be successful, Bashar al-Assad must be removed from his office. This, of course, was not an option for the government negotiators. De Mistura, sensing that talks would again fail, tried to maintain momentum by focusing on developing a new constitution; however, his suggestion that an outside group assist, was not a welcome idea by either party. Despite the awful idea and lack of progress, de Mistura labeled the talks as an "incremental progress."[277]

While such mediations are undoubtedly frustrating and taxing, suggesting that a new Syrian constitution be written with help, even from "experts" undermines the efforts of all the parties in Syria. This is the very reason why intervening in such a situation can be disastrous: the internal actors do not want their processes tainted by international interference, and the international actors should not want their presence to be construed as interfering. This is the stigma that attached itself to the British and French during their respective mandates throughout the region after World War I, and unfortunately, this same mentality is following the United States after 9/11. Its occupations of Iraq and Afghanistan (as well as operations and presence in many other Middle Eastern countries) have lent credibility to this argument for many throughout the world, in addition to its support of Israel throughout the years, oftentimes at the expense of the Arab countries. The Syrian people alone should be responsible for their form of government, not any third party or other country.

OPERATION INHERENT RESOLVE: PHASE III - DEFEAT

In June 2017, YPG forces began the battle to retake Raqqa from IS after months of battles leading to and encircling the city. The US, for its part and against the wishes of Turkey, began supplying small-arms and light machine guns to the YPG for this fight. Naturally, Ankara believed that any proliferation of small-arms would circulate back to

PKK fighters, but Washington assured Ankara that every weapon distributed would be accounted for and tracked.[278] This, no doubt, boosted little confidence within the Turkish government; after all, the US government lost track of weapons during Operation Fast and Furious, and failed to account for weapons that headed into Afghanistan in the 1980s.

On June 29, 2017, Iraqi Prime Minister Haider al-Abadi declared an end to the caliphate of IS, at least as within Iraq. This end came as fighting continued in Mosul, Iraq, which was liberated the following month. While al-Abadi's pronouncement was certainly political, it is also likely, given the advances made by Iraqi and other coalition forces, that the Islamic State's caliphate had been unraveling. However, it was estimated that 2,500 IS fighters remained in Raqqa, with another 100,000 civilians trapped between the fighting.[279] To add to these complications, IS fighters had dug tunnels, undermining civilian safety by eliminating front lines and further endangering YPG fighters. If the Islamic State had intent on holding Raqqa, the fight would no doubt prove strenuous, and in the end, hard won. The destruction of IS will be difficult to measure, but their expulsion from Iraq and Syria will not necessarily be the end of IS.

FIFTH CEASEFIRE, ASTANA V, AND GENEVA VII (JULY 2017)

The fifth round of Astana talks began in July 2017, although they had previously been scheduled for June, with the safe zones in Syria being a major sticking point. It was also a sticking point during the talks as well, resulting in no consensus being reached. The issue was that both Syrian opposition and the regime did not agree to safe zones, now being referred to as de-escalation zones. The opposition again balked at the idea of an Iranian presence overseeing such zones, while Russia's relationship with the regime raised questions of bias along with Turkey's view of the Kurds, all the while undermining their ability to effectively safeguard these zones. Aleksandr Lavrentyev, the Russian chief negotiator, stated that there was an "essentially agreed" framework that was in "need [of] finalizing."[280] How could this be if the two parties directly affected, the Syrian government and the opposition, were nowhere near agreement?

Lavrentyev stated that Russia had asked some member states belonging to the Commonwealth of Independent States (CIS) if they would assist in securing these de-escalation zones. The CIS was formed after the fall of the Soviet Union, bringing together many former Soviet states[x], whereby they would cooperate on various transnational issues. It remains to be seen whether or not any of the CIS members would go along with Russian adventures, particularly when Russia's past actions have not always been favorable for said states (Russo-Georgian War of 2008 and Russia's annexation of Crimea, formerly a part of the Ukraine). Also, in light of their past relationships during the Cold War, it seems likely that they would want to distance themselves from a Russia calling the shots in anything resembling a new Cold War.

In June 2018, Russian Defense Minister Sergei Shoigu, made it be known that Russia was again seeking assistance from the CIS member states. While they were not materially wealthy, perhaps in lieu of monetary assistance, they could provide vehicles and troops for mine clearances, joint patrols, and humanitarian assistance, humanitarian issues created by Russian military forces. CIS member states balked at this as well; they had been subjected to threats from the Islamic State (by way of Afghanistan) and were therefore not supporters of Assad or the Islamic State. However, with such threats emanating so near the borders of the CIS states, it made more sense for their efforts to be concentrated on a stable Afghanistan before they began considering efforts at cleaning up Russia's messes (although that argument could be made with Afghanistan as well).[281]

On July 9, 2017, a fresh ceasefire went into effect in southern Syria, centered around three provinces, a deal reached by the United States, Russia, and Jordan while Presidents Trump and Putin were attending the G20 Summit held in Hamburg, Germany. Ultimately, the ceasefire went into effect for the provinces of Dera'a, Suwayda, and Quneitra, areas bordering Jordan and the Golan Heights. While at Astana that same month, the opposition voiced concerns over this

---

x   The CIS is composed of a dozen countries: Russia, Ukraine, Belarus, Moldavia, Armenia, Azerbaijan, Kazakhstan, Turkmenistan, Uzbekistan, Tajikistan, Kyrgyzstan, and Georgia.

tripartite agreement, expressing "great concern over the secret meetings between Russia and Jordan and America" which they believed "divides Syria and the opposition."[282] Despite the regime gaining ground with Russian and Iranian assistance, and talks leading to naught, US Secretary of Defense Rex Tillerson did not appear to be optimistic about the ceasefire. He did not foresee a "long-term role for the Assad family or the Assad regime. And we have made this clear to everyone. We certainly made it clear in our discussions with Russia."[283]

This ceasefire was a surefire sign of potential progress for the next round of talks in Geneva, where Stefan de Mistura was hoping to guide the two sides into exploring key issues vital to a political transition: writing a constitution, establishing a strong government, holding elections, and combating terrorism. This again was shot down by government representatives who had stated that no talks could take place without the acknowledgement of Assad's continued tenure as president. Ever frustrated, the opposition described the failed talks as a failure of the international community. Nasser al-Hariri, the lead opposition negotiator, stated that

> [t]he political process is in danger because, after all these rounds, the international community doesn't put enough pressure on the regime and its allies to engage in this negotiation. Now we are coming for rounds of negotiations without a framework, without direct negotiations, without sharing or exchanging papers and now returning back without specific results.[284]

In fairness, the international community had not been putting pressure on the Assad regime, but neither had it put pressure on the opposition. The opposition had slowly been losing physical ground throughout Syria, and the regime was likely aware that the opposition was only attempting to hold on to what it had, while waiting out and hoping for a political resolution to be reached. In the meantime, the country was being destroyed and the people were forced to suffer through it. The opposition did not want US assistance before the conflict erupted, so why would they want US involvement after, or any other country for that matter?

Along with Astana and Geneva, another meeting was held in July, this one in Cairo, Egypt, with Russian military and Syrian opposition representatives present. They agreed to a ceasefire in eastern Ghouta, one of the last major urban areas held by the opposition as well as the site of the chemical attack in 2013. The Egyptians held talks in Cairo in 2015 as well in an effort to air grievances. Egyptian political officials were present, but did not head the talks; a freedom of dialogue was granted to the opposition in an effort to reach consensus for more formal talks in the future. This previous talk did lead to the approval of ten points, notably the removal of foreign forces from Syria and a political solution that would lead to a stable, democratic government.[285] It did not come to fruition, but it was hoped, at least by the Egyptian government, that a formal relationship between Egypt and Syria might undermine Turkey's efforts in pushing for solutions and instead grant Syria an Arab alternative to its current relationship with Iran or any potential relationship with Turkey.[286] Perhaps not in the same vein as the United Arab Republic of old, but it could lead to the similar cultures working together for an amicable solution, as opposed to Turkish or Persian interference that could lead to the creation of an unstable, hegemonic, sectarian struggle.

ASTANA VI & VII (SEPTEMBER & OCTOBER 2017)

Meeting again for the sixth time in Kazakhstan, Russia, Turkey, and Iran hammered out details for the implementation of de-escalation zones throughout Syria. While the idea was worked out in previous Astana talks, the three countries agreed on the precise locations of the zones and agreed to act as underwriters throughout the process. For six months, with the possibility of an extension, four de-escalation zones would be guaranteed in: eastern Ghouta, and in or around the provinces of Aleppo, Hama, Homs, Idlib, and Latakia. These were predominantly opposition-controlled areas, with the exception of Idlib, which was controlled by Tahrir al-Sham.[287] Tahrir al-Sham would still be engaged by Syrian and Russian forces, but the de-escalation zones would not contain any hostilities, including air sorties. The opposition continued to disagree over Iranian forces overseeing any of these areas, let alone remaining in Syria. It seemed Iran's presence securing these de-escalation zones has showed their continued commitment to a long-term presence throughout Syria and the region.

The following month, a seventh round was convened in Astana, Kazakhstan in order to continue toward the path of establishing these de-escalation zones. The hope for these de-escalation zones was that ceasefires could be initiated in these areas, facilitating humanitarian aid, the return of hostages and prisoners, and the recovery and identification of those killed-in-action and missing-in-action.

ASTANA VIII AND GENEVA VIII (DECEMBER 2017)

The eighth round of Geneva talks were held in December of 2017, and, as should be expected, were a complete failure. Again, mediating for the United Nations, Staffan de Mistura held the Syrian government responsible, citing its refusal to entertain new elections or even discuss a new constitution. As Bashar al-Assad and the Syrian government had stated all along, the fight has been against terrorism, and that is what the discussion in Geneva needed to be focused on. Staffan de Mistura had hoped to burden the Russian government into pressuring Bashar al-Assad, but the Geneva processes had appeared to be losing quite a bit of steam, having reached little consensus over the years. He as much as admitted that the Syrian government had no need to negotiate without the opposition gaining concessions on the battlefield, while also recognizing that their strongest unification was in his, Assad's, opposition, and little else. So long as the Syrian government was in a position of strength militarily, the opposition could not hope to garner any concessions for itself.

On the heels of this failure, Astana VIII was held the following week. The discussions at Astana were aimed at more tangible issues, such as the de-escalation zones, detainees, the bodies of those killed-in-action, those missing-in-action, and the rising violence then taking part in eastern Ghouta. Following Astana VIII, the head of the Syrian government delegation, Bashar al-Jaafari, released a statement calling for the immediate removal of Turkish and US forces, which were illegally positioned throughout sovereign Syrian territory without the approval of the Syrian government. He also stated that US and EU economic sanctions levied against Syria were illegal as they were not sanctioned by the UN Security Council.

SOCHI PEACE TALKS (JANUARY 2018)

Russian President Vladimir Putin called for a peace conference to be held in Sochi, Russia on January 30, 2018. Fifteen-hundred delegates arrived, although opposition delegates refused to attend. One member of the opposition stated that "it's obvious they're not intending to have serious discussions. The Russians are trying to control us, if not directly, they will try to find a way." The opposition was still voicing concern over Russia's lack of conviction in seeing the fighting end, with it still conducting airstrikes throughout the country. Perhaps another reason the opposition did not attend the talks was that all the delegates were vetted by Syrian security. Although some dissidents were allowed to do so, all the delegates for the government received training on how to conduct themselves before leaving Syria. Also, they were forbidden from: discussing the formation of a new constitution, discussing Syria's armed forces, discussing the removal of Bashar al-Assad as president, and shaking hands with any members of the opposition.[288] With such restrictions, it is no wonder that such fruitless talks were seen in any other light. Suffice it say, the talks in Sochi accomplished nothing, except perhaps a public relations boon for President Putin and a further marginalized role for the United States.

ASTANA IX (MAY 2018)

Astana IX, in May 2018, was the continued discussion from previous Astana talks. No political solutions were reached or even discussed, but the military realities on the ground were highlighted. Bashar al-Jaafari, the Syrian delegate, expressed the Syrian government's resolve in its continued efforts in "the fight against terrorism and colonial regimes that wanted to divide Syria." He also praised its army for creating a "safe place for the southern part of Syria and also southern part of Aleppo" by clearing eastern Ghouta and Damascus of "terrorists."[289]

CHAPTER 9

BEGINNING OF THE END
FOR THE ISLAMIC STATE

ROAD TO RAQQA—OPERATION
WRATH OF THE EUPHRATES

While Phase II of Operation Inherent Resolve was aimed at destroying the Islamic State's two major cities of Mosul and Raqqa, Operation Wrath of the Euphrates was the campaign within Phase III to retake Raqqa itself.

In March 2013, the Free Syrian Army, looking to gain possession of a major city, along with some Islamist forces, took control of Raqqa and tore down the statue of Hafez al-Assad. The opposition had taken control of a city of roughly 240,000 residents; however, after two years of fighting throughout Syria, many had been forced to flee their homes, pushing 800,000 to seek refuge in Raqqa. Islamic State fighters began creeping into the city, and by May 2013, began fighting with those FSA soldiers. Assisted by Islamic State's brutal tactics, fear swept through the FSA ranks, causing many to defect to the IS ranks. Through this attrition, the Islamic State was able to defeat or absorb all resistance in Raqqa, and by January 2014, the city was under the complete control of the Islamic State, at which point, it was declared the capital of their self-proclaimed Islamic caliphate.

In November 2016, from an area north of Raqqa, Syrian Democratic Forces announced that the offensive to retake the city had begun, which they broke down into five phases, aimed at completely surrounding and isolating Raqqa, and ultimately culminating in the assault of the city. Phase I was retaking areas north of the city and was completed by the end of the month. At that time, the first US servicemember was killed in Syria in the town of Tal Saman. Phase I was successful (from a military standpoint), seeing dozens of towns liberated from IS. Phase II began in December 2016, aimed at isolating Raqqa from the west. Phase III was initiated in February 2017, aimed at severing the eastern lands from Raqqa. One area of importance was severing Islamic State's lines-of-communication between Raqqa and Deir al-Zor, a city about 85 miles south-east of Raqqa. Islamic State fighters were attempting to take the city from Syrian government forces and it was also the site of the US's attack on Syrian forces the previous September.

Twenty-five miles west of Raqqa lies the Tabqa Dam, the piece of infrastructure responsible for the creation of Lake Assad, which is a major source of water for the city of Aleppo as well as agriculture in the region. The Islamic State was defending the dam in an effort to divert pressure away from Raqqa, threatening to severely damage the dam by strategically placing explosives around it. It was the last major town before reaching Raqqa along the Euphrates River, and SDF units launched their assault on IS positions around the dam in March, wanting to capture the dam in order to secure their own lines-of-communication, while also securing an important piece of infrastructure. With US assistance, Tabqa Dam was captured in May 2017; the Islamic State was allowed to surrender and withdrawal from the area in exchange for surrendering their heavy weapons and dismantling the bombs placed around the dam. Syrian Democratic Forces sustained around 450 casualties, with IS sustaining an equal number throughout the fighting. Phase IV began in April 2017, with the aim of capturing the environs immediately north of Raqqa, furthering the noose around the city. Preparations and staging were readied soon thereafter, and Phase V, the plan to retake Raqqa itself began.

On June 6, SDF elements began their assault on Raqqa, with the Islamic State defending the city with approximately 2,500 fighters. Within weeks, SDF fighters had completely isolated Raqqa, while Mosul was falling to Iraqi forces. With the noose tightening around Raqqa, the Islamic State slowly began shifting personnel and material to its new de-facto headquarters along the Euphrates River Valley between al-Mayadin, Syria and al-qa'm, Iraq. It was believed that the Islamic State was also utilizing the area to establish a sort of research and development site for chemical weapons.[290] While it is no doubt logical to assume that forces opposing the Islamic State pushing into this area might well have had to face threats from these weapons, much more sinister than this is the possibility of Islamic State utilizing such weapons against soft targets. The operations inside Iraq and Syria to push back Islamic State has not stopped them from continuing its operations around the world, which would become much more devastating if they were able to smuggle such weapons outside of Iraq and Syria. The question remains: was the Islamic State able to obtain such weapons and/or technologies due to the failed state that Syria had become?

Capturing Raqqa was not a simple or quick fight. Coalition forces were supporting fighters on the ground with heavy airstrikes against Islamic State positions, and may have destroyed half of the city, conducting 4,000 airstrikes. This all played havoc with the local civilian population as well, with 270,000 displaced, and at least 1,200 killed.[291] Raqqa was completely retaken in October 2017 through US and SDF efforts; however, the Syrian government was not satisfied, as it was not controlled by an Arab army. The fall of Raqqa corresponded with the last of the Islamic State's major strongholds, Hawja, falling in Iraq at the beginning of the same month.

In November 2017, the Syrian government claimed victory over the Islamic State, attacking and capturing its last urban center in Syria, Abu Kamal. This operation was launched concurrently with fighting in western Iraq, itself successful, leading to the Iraqi prime minister, Haider al-Abadi, to declare victory over IS as well. With this came the US drawdown from Iraq, which stood at nearly 8,900 troops. Per an agreement initially reached between the US and Iraq, 4,000 personnel would remain in order to conduct training and support to Iraqi forces.

On the heels of the Syrian proclamation of victory over IS, the US and Russia issued a joint statement to show their solidarity in combatting IS. With IS largely defeated in Syria and Iraq (at least conventionally and in major urban areas), and the US supposedly drawing down its own personnel, this statement seemed largely unnecessary. It did, however, show consensus as to the outlook of the overall conflict in Syria, confirming "that the ultimate political solution to the conflict must be forged through the Geneva process pursuant to UNSCR 2254."[292]

After Raqqa and Abu Kamal, the last official pocket of the Islamic State in Syria needed to be taken. Beginning in September 2018, Syrian Democratic Forces began battling in the Deir al-Zor Governate of eastern Syria to root out the last major pocket of the Islamic State in Syria. By February 2019, they had them nearly surrounded in the Syrian village of Baghouz. Iraqi forces, in conjunction with French units, had closed the border to any fleeing fighters. As of mid-February 2019, the fighting had killed 400 civilians, nearly 700 SDF personnel, and nearly 1,300 IS fighters.[293] In March 2018, SDF elements assaulted the Syrian town of Baghouz, driving Islamic State fighters out in a hard-fought victory, and claiming the last piece of IS territory in Syria.

With the fighting winding down in Iraq, then-Secretary of State Rex Tillerson made it clear that the US would not be drawing down forces from Syria, stating in January 2018 that US personnel in Syria would help ensure "[the Islamic State] cannot re-emerge... We cannot make the same mistakes that were made in 2011 when a premature departure from Iraq allowed al-Qaeda in Iraq to survive and eventually morph into [the Islamic State]." This fed into the Trump Administration's counterterrorism policy, which was "to protect Americans at home and abroad from attacks by terrorists. Central to this policy is to deny terrorist and terrorist organizations the opportunity to organize, raise money, recruit fighters, train, plan, and execute attacks." This of course misses the strategic picture, which is not just denying terrorists the opportunities that they seek, but forging a policy that denies the creation of terrorists in the first place.

Although the Islamic State had been losing territory throughout Iraq and Syria into 2018, it did not lose the will to attempt or inspire continued attacks. In the US and Western Europe, arrests were on the rise, with law enforcement becoming more diligent and experienced in their investigations. Leading up to 2018, Islamic State attacks had been steadily increasing in Europe and North America, from 14 in 2015, to 22 in 2016, and 27 in 2017. In the first eight months of 2018, there had been only four attacks. The severity of the attacks had also declined with 130 in 2015, 86 in 2016, and 22 in 2017. It would seem likely that a correlation could be drawn between combat losses and the evident reduction in global attacks and the lethality of such attacks. According to the Center for the Analysis in Terrorism, located in Paris, this is not necessarily the case. According to the director, Jean-Charles Brisard, the center was "able to conclude that there is no correlation between their military set-backs and the loss of territory and the intensity of the threat. Even if the Islamic State is losing both militarily and in terms of terrain, the ideology of [IS] remains present in the hearts of individuals who want to harm us."[294] This points to the idea that the Islamic State specifically, and terrorism in general, cannot be defeated on the bat-tlefield alone. While law enforcement was becoming progressively more diligent and experienced in their investigations, this alone would not be enough either; political and diplomatic efforts would need to be efficiently exercised.

On a more strategic level, Secretary Tillerson mentioned the positioning of Iran, both as it related to its own interests through-out the region, and also as a threat to the United States. There is no doubt that Iran has hegemonic aspirations, and it is supporting Syria, while undermining Iraq, but it does not pose an existential threat to the United States. The US has been at odds with Iran at least since 1979, and there has been no cogent reason to permanently station US troops in the region in an effort to check Iranian foreign policy. Secretary Tillerson further outlined five reasons to keep US forces in Syria:

1. to ensure the ultimate defeat of [the Islamic State] and al-Qaeda and a guaranteed assurance that they cannot regroup elsewhere,

2. to ensure an end to the conflict in Syria, resulting in a stable and united country free of a Bashar [al-Assad] presidency,

3. to ensure an Iran incapable of spreading its influence,

4. to ensure an environment necessary for resettlement of refugees, and

5. to ensure Syria is free of, and incapable of securing, weap-ons of mass destruction.

He further stated that the defeat of terrorist groups within the country would allow for local governments to reclaim control, and in turn, allow for the peaceful and stabilizing transition in a post-Assad country. A Bashar government was not conducive to a stable and free Syria. Tillerson believed that American disengagement would encourage Iran to continue to seek "dominance in the Middle East and the destruction of our ally, Israel. As a destabilized nation and one bordering Israel, Syria presents an opportunity that Iran is all too eager to exploit." "We must be clear: 'Stabilization' is not a synonym for open-ended nation-building or a synonym for reconstruction. But it is essential." This is anything but clear. The military will remain in Syria to stabilize but will not remain for nation-building or recon- struction? Specifically, as it relates to reconstruction, the US would "not provide international reconstruction assistance to any area under control of the Assad regime." Based on the five points, outlined by Secretary Tillerson above, it did seem like a great deal of US resources and time would need to be involved.

Since Russia is protecting Assad, there is no real way to remove him short of war, so the US will execute the next best thing: economic pressure. The US would encourage international economic investment in areas recovered from IS and only when Assad is no longer in power will the US encourage and seek to normalize economic ties with Syria. This sounds terribly close to nation-building; the US owned the responsibility of ridding Syria of IS and afterwards would assume responsibility of investing in those same areas. If you're a Syrian who just happens to live in an area controlled by Syrian government forces or one of its allies, then you are on your own. The US will help you, just as soon as you get rid of your president. Tillerson did state that the US military's presence in Syria was "conditions-based."

According to Tillerson, "The safe and voluntary return of Syrian refugees serves the security interests of the United States, our allies, and our partners." He added that it would "be impossible to ensure stability on one end of the Mediterranean, in Europe, if chaos and injustice prevail on the other end, in Syria." And where is the United States in relation to the Mediterranean?

TURKEY VS. YPG—OPERATION OLIVE BRANCH (JANUARY 2018)

The Kurdish autonomous area that was springing up in northern Syria was allegedly utilizing heavy-handed tactics in an effort to undermine terrorism and any support for the Islamic State. Amnesty International released several reports blaming the PYD of unlawful detentions while denying trials, habeus corpus, or use of counsel. One report in particular accused YPG forces of demolishing homes and forcing displacement of local residents, the majority of which were Arab and Turkmen, but also some Kurdish residents. The PYD claimed any such incidents were isolated and necessary for safety and security.[295] The report did not explicitly state that this was an attempt to redefine the demographics of the region, although the accusation has certainly been levelled by Turkish President Erdogan. This belief alone could be enough to force Turkey's hand in intervening in the region, particularly when it comes to protecting the Turkomen ethnic groups and also further securing its shared border with norther Syria.

Perhaps Turkey was looking for an excuse to move against northern Syria, because YPG activities were not comforting in Ankara. When Turkey first conducted operations within Syria in October 2012, it was to undermine the Islamic State's ability to conduct indirect-fire into Turkey. At the beginning of 2018, Turkey's concern over the Kurdish People's Protection Units goaded it into a renewal of offensive operations, beginning on January 20.

Ankara informed Damascus of its impending offensive aimed at Afrin; in response, Russian units were pulled from the area in an effort to avoid collateral damage and escalation. The Turkish military offensive would be aimed at establishing "security and stability on our borders and region, to eliminate terrorists of PKK/KCK/PYD-YPG" and the Islamic State. Damascus, of course, was not pleased and condemned the Turkish assault on its territory. "The Syrian Arab Republic decisively condemns Turkish aggression against the town of Afrin, which is an inseparable part of Syria." Also, "Syria completely denies claims by the Turkish regime that it was informed of this military operation."[296]

Within two months of its offensive in northern Syria, Turkey had cleared pockets of resistance up to the town of Afrin in conjunction with Free Syrian Army units, reaching the city on March 12 and gaining complete control on March 18. As the United States was allied with the Syrian Democratic Forces, under which the YPG falls, Turkey's operations directly impacted Operation Inherent Resolve, causing units to conduct an "operational pause."[297] As the US was operating in northern Syria with SDF units, there was a great deal of concern over collateral damage with the Turkish military advancing. With the US already having developed a tense relationship with Syrian and Russian troops on the ground and in the skies, Turkish troops were only adding to the mix. The US had deployed troops in early 2017 in an effort to appeal to its Kurdish allies by deterring Turkey from any aggression, but it could also be viewed as a reassurance to Ankara that the Kurds would not become a threat to Turkish security.

With Afrin secured, Turkey was threatening to push further along Syrian territory and conduct an assault on Manbij. Manbij was the site of the YPG's fight against the Islamic State which ended in the latter's expulsion from the city in August 2016. In an effort towards goodwill and security assurances, US Secretary of State Mike Pompeo and his Turkish counterpart, Mevlüt Çavuşoğlu, met in Washington, DC in June 2018. The two sides called for a roadmap for mutual cooperation in Syria and a way forward in securing Manbij. According to Çavuşoğlu, "[t]he aim of this roadmap is the clearing of Manbij of all terror organizations and the permanent instatement of safety and stability." Furthermore, the parties involved would need to make a "determination of parameters for common plans for the removal of YPG-PYD from Manbij—you can also call it PKK—will be determined."[298]

In June 2018, the US came to an agreement with Ankara whereby YPG fighters would be forced out of Manbij, Syria, near the Turkish border. As of December 2018, the US and Turkey had not finalized any roadmaps for Manbij and the YPG; YPG fighters were fortifying their positions in the city, while Free Syrian Army units, with Turkish support, were moving to positions for a possible assault. Turkish president Erdogan stated earlier in December that Turkish military units would conduct operations to drive out the YPG, thus securing Turkey's border from what it perceives as a terrorist organization.[299] However, in January 2019, Turkey and Russia reached an agreement whereby Turkish-backed groups would withdrawal from Manbij concurrently with the withdrawal of Kurdish groups, at which point the Syrian government would assume control.[300] Despite this, US National Security Advisor John Bolton stated in January 2019 that US forces would remain in the area until the defeat of IS and assurances could be reached detailing the protection of Kurdish fighters.

As of January, US forces were maintaining a presence in Manbij. On January 16, while conducting a dismounted patrol, a suicide bomber detonated his explosives in front of a restaurant frequented by US troops. The blast killed four US personnel (two of which were servicemembers), wounded three others, and caused multiple deaths and injuries among the locals that were nearby. The Islamic State claimed credit for the attack, despite having little presence in the area. As of January 2019, and since the US began its intervention in Syria in 2014, six US servicemembers have been killed in total.[301] This attack is a reminder of the volatility on the ground and the ever-present dangers to US forces deployed to such austere environments.

THE BEGINNING OF THE END OF US INVOLVEMENT?

On February 7, 2018, a group of Wagner mercenaries, augmented by Syrian regime forces, attacked an SDF position, a location that also housed US soldiers. The soldiers at the base began noticing elements maneuvering into place for an assault, followed by artillery fire (this indirect fire could have been an indication of a pending ground assault). During the assault, US airstrikes were called, resulting in 200 to 300 killed, according to the commander's estimate (no US servicemembers were killed). The US commander attempted to contact his Russian counterparts throughout this engagement utilizing a deconfliction line-of-communication; the Russians assured him no Russians troops were taking part in the assault. In the face of such firepower, the attacking force retreated, but only to a point three miles away.[302] In any military operation, three miles is not a great distance and was undoubtedly enough to keep the SDF and US forces on edge.

Wagner was part of Russia's overall efforts to support the Syria regime; however, Wagner concluded a deal with the Syrian government by which the company could seize oil and gas fields held in opposition territory. The head of Wagner, Yevgeniy Prigozhin, would no doubt reap huge profits from such a deal. With that knowledge, it was believed that the mercenaries' main objective in attacking the SDF position was to gain possession of a nearby oilfield.[303] The whole situation begs the question of whether or not Moscow had direct knowledge of the attack. If Prigozhin's company had such deals with Damascus, and given Prigozhin's close, personal relationship with President Putin, it is not unreasonable to assume that Prigozhin ordered such an attack on his own volition, knowing that he would not receive much blowback from Moscow, but it is just equally likely that he had direct blessings from Moscow. There are certainly enough rogue elements on the battlefield without adding Russian defense contractors (if they were in fact that) to the mix; such an action has the catastrophic potential of drastically escalating the situation in Syria into far more than a civil war.

In addition, Prigozhin was pointed out in the Mueller Report as one of the elements directly involved in funding the company that was setup to conduct social media operations within the United States. While it initially may have seemed that such operations came about after the US and Russia became involved in Syria, the Mueller Report stated that such operations possibly began sometime in 2014. This seems to correspond with Russia's annexation of Crimea, and the United States' outrage. This action came about, as some believe, due to the North Atlantic Treaty Organization's (NATO) expansion along Russia's borders, necessitating Russia's annexation of Crimea in order to prevent further encirclement of NATO.

In order to hit back at the Russians, the US government leveled sanctions against Russia. On December 29, 2016, the Obama White House, weeks before newly elected Donald Trump was sworn in as US President, announced reprisals for Russia's interference in the 2016 US presidential election that supposedly included hacking into Democratic hopeful Hilary Clinton's campaign website, as well as hacks against the Democratic National Committee (DNC). Economic sanctions were levied against individual Russians (including Wagner head Prigozhin), as well as several entities within the country, including the GRU and the FSB. The GRU is the Main Intelligence Agency of the General Staff of the Russian Armed Forces, Russia's foreign military intelligence agency; while the FSB is the Federal Security Service, responsible for counterintelligence, counterterrorism, and general domestic security. The US seized two properties utilized by Russian diplomats, while also reducing the number of Russian diplomatic personnel, expelling 35, which the Russian government willingly reciprocated. President Obama claimed that some further actions would be initiated, but not publicized. Global US-Russian relations showed no signs of cooling moving into 2017 and a new American administration, a point that President Trump was willing to confront.

In May 2017, the US Attorney General's Office appointed a special prosecutor, Robert Mueller, to investigate whether or not Russia played a role in any election interference and did then-candidate Trump's team play a role. While Russian President Putin denies any Russian interference, Mueller's investigation concluded that they did, including a disinformation campaign aimed at undermining the US democratic process, while attempting to influence the vote for then-candidate Trump (no evidence has come to light, however, indicating that Donald Trump collaborated with any Russians). In addition, it was believed that the Russians had conducted various other cyber-attacks, including one aimed at the US energy infrastructure.

In March 2018, President Trump made the decision to impose further sanctions, zeroing in on five Russian organizations and 19 individuals that Mueller's investigation had pointed out. Two of these organizations, however, were the previously sanctioned FSB and GSU. These sanctions were somewhat moderate, blocking certain persons from entering the US, freezing any assets that might be tied up in the US, and preventing US companies from doing businesses with them. While certain Russian government organizations had been named, President Putin himself was not found to have been personally involved, although it had not been completely ruled out either. In response to US sanctions, President Putin and Moscow imposed sanctions against the United States, forbidding some Americans to travel or do business in Russia.

The point of all this being that this back-and-forth between the US and Russia created an incredibly dangerous situation on the ground in Syria, not only for US troops, but Syrian civilians.

With Wagner's group's attack on this US position so near a Syrian oilfield, the role of the region's oil reserves, and the superpowers aim at them, comes into question. It has long been part of the US foreign policy, particularly in the Middle East: safeguarding the world's oil infrastructure and logistics routes to feed its own, and the globe's, insatiable demand for oil. As a major producer and exporter of crude oil, Russia might view this same situation from a different lens. In a Washington Times article from 1986, located in the CIA library, then-CIA Director William Casey had been accusing the Soviets of attempting to control oilfields and logistics routes in Libya and Syria. He stated that the Soviet's "creeping imperialism" was a threat to the oilfields throughout the Middle East, and,

> [t]he greatest hedge against Soviet influence in the Middle East is the peace process aimed at resolving Arab-Israeli differences. The invigoration of the peace process is, in my view, of overriding geopolitical importance in order to deny the Soviets a lever of entry into the Middle East.[304]

This would have been a great idea to keep both superpowers out of the Middle East; factors, however, have changed since then.

In July 2017, the US stated that it would end the CIA program that was putting arms in the hands of the Syrian opposition. According to a military spokesman, it was not carried out as a concession to Russia, simply to ease tension with the country and lead toward better relations. While Russia certainly reacted positively to such news, Jordan itself was not disappointed either. As Jordan shares a border with Syria, some opposition fighters had conducted training inside the Hashemite Kingdom. That shared border also puts Jordan in the path of possible small-arms proliferation routes. As Jordan has been on the receiving end of terrorist attacks in its own country, it does not want the same terrorist groups seizing these same arms in Syria and moving them across the border into Jordan where they could be utilized for operations inside Jordan, or for cross-border operations launched from Jordan.

Arming the opposition, supporting allied fighters, and air operations were part of a three-prong strategy to remove terrorist group and help stabilize Syria. With an end to such a program, resources could be diverted to the other two elements of the strategy, or it could be the first step in a drawdown of US forces. President Trump has been adamant about "America First" and holding partner countries accountable for security, particularly when it comes to funding. As far as transition and stabilization efforts in Syria following the ouster of the Islamic State, President Trump asked the king of Saudi Arabia, Salman bin Abdulaziz al-Saud, if The Kingdom could contribute $4 billion for Syrian stabilization. While Saudi Arabia would likely question such a sum, their interests align very much with a peaceful and stable Syria. Furthermore, if past actions are any indication of Saudi Arabia's willingness to pay such a sum, one would need to look no further than the Soviet invasion of Afghanistan, and the subsequent funding of the mujahideen. Saudi Arabia vowed to spend $1 for every $1 spent by the United States, amounting to tens of billions of dollars flowing through Pakistan into Afghanistan.

According to the United States Agency for International Development (USAID), in a fact sheet released in January 2018, the US spent nearly $8 billion since the start of the civil war in Syria; in 2017, the US spent $200 million on non-humanitarian assistance alone. USAID believes this level of spending contributes to a more stable Syria and broader Middle East, a national security imperative for the United States. It quoted former-Secretary of State Rex Tillerson as stating, "[a] stable, unified, independent Syria will serve the national security interests of the United States, its allies, and our partners. If that reality can come to pass, it will be a victory for all, and it will support the ability of the Syrian people to pursue their own God-given rights of life, liberty and the pursuit of happiness."[305] Of course, this is not the responsibility of the US government. According to the Declaration of Independence, "governments are instituted amongst men" in order to secure one's freedoms and rights. The government of the United States was instituted amongst the several states for the several states and its people, not for the people of Syria. The Syrian people are best positioned to support themselves with a viable constitution that will work for Syria; one that will protect their lives, liberties, and the pursuit of their own form of happiness, without overbearing foreign oversight.

THE SEVEN YEAR ITCH

On February 24, 2018, United Nations Resolution 2401 was adopted, calling for an immediate ceasefire throughout Syria to allow for humanitarian services and evacuations of the sick and injured. This coming after nearly seven years of fighting, over 400,000 people having been killed, and half of Syria's pre-war population having been displaced from their homes.[306] Two weeks after the UN resolution, the US circulated a draft resolution calling for an immediate ceasefire, one in which contained "no counterterrorism loopholes for Assad, Iran and the Russians to hide behind," according to Nikki Haley, the then-US Ambassador to the UN. She continued,

> When the international community consistently fails to act, there are times when states are compelled to take their own action. We warn any nation determined to impose its will through chemical attacks and inhuman suffering, but most especially the outlaw Syrian regime, *the United States remains prepared to act if we must* [author's italics]. It is not a path we prefer. But it is a path we have demonstrated we will take and we are prepared to take again.[307]

Such a statement seems to suggest that the US is willing to impose its will over Syria. To state that the US "must act" is utter nonsense; it has no constitutional enumerated power to act, unless the Congress declares such. But the US does not, and should not, need to act unless directly attacked, something for which Syria is completely incapable of doing.

The fighting showed perhaps a few signs, if any, of slowing down, as the seventh anniversary of the conflict appeared; the multiple countries involved in the conflict were not helping matters. Iran had been involved in Syria at least since 2012, when, over the summer, Free Syrian Army units captured Iranian soldiers, although Tehran denied they were part of any large-scale, sanctioned operation, instead, referring to them as "pilgrims." This contradicted a May 2012 statement from the then-Quds Force deputy commander, Brigadier General Esmail Qaani, in which he detailed an Iranian military presence to "prevent great massacres." Furthermore, in September 2012, the IRGC commander, Mohammad-Ali Aziz Jafari, went so far as to admit to the presence of Quds Force units within Syria, but denied an Iranian military presence, limiting Iran's role to one of "consultancy and economic assistance."[308]

The conflict has allowed Iran to shield its weapons transfers to Hezbollah via Syria, while also being shielded by Russian troops and aircraft that have been moving into Syria since 2015. While the Israelis have conducted several strikes inside Syria in an effort to curb the lethality of Hezbollah, the Israeli military estimated that Hezbollah's rocket cache had grown to 150,000 since the beginning of the civil war.[309] A year before the war began, Hezbollah claimed to have just 40,000 in its possession.[310] This places Israel in a precarious position as any future conflict will force it to fight on Hezbollah's terms; potentially goading it into another invasion of Lebanon that has accomplished little in the past. The real tragedy in such a situation would be the Lebanese people being subjected to yet another round of war due to Hezbollah's (and by extension Syria's and Iran's) desire to undermine Israel.

The presence of Iranian troops has raised alarm both in Israel and Jordan, where shared borders are always porous enough to allow spillage from the conflict. Jordan has been a partner of the US in the fight against terrorism; Jordan has also assisted in stabilization efforts in Afghanistan. Jordan had been pursuing efforts towards a solution in Syria early in the conflict, troubled over the presence of IS and concerns over Iran's efforts at regional destabilization. Jordan has been hosting Syrian refugees despite their past experiences with Palestinian refugees, and despite the crippling costs, which has threatened the fabric of its economy. Jordan began flying sorties over Syria in September 2014 in an effort to destroy IS targets from the air. Their efforts had been aimed at disabling IS military capabilities while attempting to contain the Syrian civil war in the hopes that a peaceful resolution could be reached without a considerable amount of spillover. These efforts soon came to the forefront in December 2014 when a Jordanian pilot, Muadh al-Kasasbeh, crashed the F-16 he was flying near the IS capital of Raqqah. Jordanian officials were quick to offer a swap for al-Kasasbeh, but hesitated when no proof of his safety was forthcoming. Jordanian authorities had arrested Sajida al-Rishawi in 2005 after her suicide-vest failed to detonate inside a posh hotel in

Amman, Jordan. Her partner in the attack (who was also her husband) succeeded in detonating his own vest, killing dozens of wedding attendees in the process (this was part of a larger series of attacks throughout Jordan's capital). Al-Qaeda in Iraq, the predecessor to IS, took responsibility for the attack. Jordanian officials were hoping that an exchange could be brokered, al-Kasasbeh for al-Rishawi. Instead, IS marched al-Kasasbeh into a locked cage, doused him in gasoline, and burned him alive. When Jordanian officials learned of al-Kasasbeh's execution, al-Rishawi was executed in turn.

However, a ground war is inconceivable for Jordan, at least into the near future. A Jordanian military presence inside Syria could be destabilizing for Jordan, undermining its own domestic security. The notion of being bogged down in Syria on behalf of Russo-American foreign policies is not popular with the Jordanian people either.[311] King Hussein tried to keep Jordan out of past conflicts with Israel in previous Arab-Israeli conflicts, and the present monarch, King Abdullah, surely wishes to do the same. With this stated, however, Iran's militarized hegemony could become a threat to Jordan's stability. In any event, what is best for Jordan is doing what is best for Jordan, not for Western governments or Israel, necessarily.

Within Syria, Iranian proxies had greatly assisted in building up a force around Bashar al-Assad so that he could turn his full attention to combating opposition forces. This Iranian-backed ground force has alarmed Syrian government officials, as it has largely assisted Assad regain control of his position of power.[312] This cannot be good news for Syria, as these forces will either prove to be the muscle for Iran playing puppet master with Assad, or Assad will have a foreign militia to do his bidding, granting him even greater power in a country reeling from civil war, and before that, angered over a repressive government. In any event, it seems unlikely that Iran would sacrifice so many resources in Syria just to pull those forces out of the country after it has stabilized. Just like with Hezbollah in Lebanon, Iran's intentions in Syria are evidently long-term.

Iran's presence in Syria has created increased tensions with Israel. There has been tension between Israel and Iran throughout the years, particularly after Israel's invasion of Lebanon and Iran's subsequent creation of Hezbollah. With fighting in Syria and Hezbollah and Iranian forces very much taking part, tensions were bound to erupt.

One serious confrontation involving Israeli forces in Syria came about on February 10, 2018, when Israel shot down a drone it claimed was operating within its airspace. It then sent a pair of F-16s over Syria in order to strike what Israel believed was the command-and-control center for the drone at a Syrian air base near Palmyra. Returning from their mission, one F-16 was hit by Syrian anti-aircraft fire, subsequently crash landing in northern Israel. In response, Israel then sent a dozen aircraft back in order to strike Syrian and Iranian military targets, including those air defense systems. The episode marked the first time the Israeli air force had lost a fighter to hostile fire in over three decades; no doubt a shocking and embarrassing blow to the Israelis, and a pleasant surprise to the Syrians and Iranians. It also witnessed an escalation of hostilities, the degree to which had mostly been avoided between Israel and Syria since the latter's internal troubles began.

In April, Israel targeted a military base near Palmyra, Syria, supposedly utilized to coordinate Iran's militias; the same base attacked in February. Four Iranian advisors were killed, including a senior Iranian officer working in its drone program. While Israel, throughout the remainder of 2018, launched many additional strikes within Syria against Iranian and Hezbollah positions, Israel has officially remained mum. However, Israeli Air Force Major General, Amir Eshel, stated that as of August 2017, Israel had launched 100 strikes on military convoys in Syria since 2012.[313] This trend was undermined in January 2019, when Israel launched attacks against Quds Force positions, an Iranian intelligence site and military training camp, as well as a weapons depot. According to Israeli Prime Minister Benjamin Netanyahu, the Israeli "air force strongly attacked Iranian targets in Syria after Iran launched a missile from there at our territory. We will not ignore such acts of aggression as Iran attempts to entrench itself militarily in Syria. He further added that Israel was maintaining a "permanent policy, to strike at the Iranian entrenchment in Syria and hurt whoever tries to hurt us." Israel's consistent aggression within Syria brings to light Iran's continued presence in Syria, and its relationship with Syria and Hezbollah that is no doubt possible due to Syria's willingness to undermine Israel for not returning the Golan Heights. Iran remains in Syria, so it would seem, in its efforts to undermine Israel as well, which it does, chiefly, through Hezbollah. If a relationship could be formed between Israel and Syria, a situation that could be initiated through Israel's relinquishing of the Golan Heights, Iran's hegemony would be drastically undermined, as Syria would no longer need to maintain a relationship with Iran.

In March 2018, the Syrian regime, with Russian support, made significant gains in the eastern suburbs of Damascus and the opposition-controlled area of Ghouta. By mid-March, the opposition had been pushed from 80% of the city, signaling the main opposition group's willingness to enter into negotiations with Russia to bring about a ceasefire. It should come as no surprise that the opposition would desire ceasefire negotiations in the midst of such drastic losses. The heavy fighting in eastern Ghouta has caused thousands to flee their homes and the chaos, and despite this, opposition forces were blocking some from leaving.[314]

On March 22, 2018, fighters under the opposition group Ahrar al-Sham, began leaving the city after an agreement reached with regime and Russian troops. Ahrar al-Sham is not to be mistaken for Tahrir al-Sham, although the two groups were once considered allies. Ahrar al-Sham was also allied with the Islamic State until January 2014, when bad blood formed, and attacks were stepped-up against one another.[315] As many as 1,500 Ahrar al-Sham fighters and their accompanying families left the city of Ghouta under assurances that they would not be molested in the process, while also retaining their weapons. Ghouta remained one of few significant pockets of opposition forces remaining. Ahrar al-Sham's departure from Ghouta provided a morale boost to regime forces while placing increased pressure on the remaining opposition forces.

Faylaq al-Rahman was the next opposition group to negotiate a deal, evacuating Ghouta on March 24. Russian military police (MPs) deployed to those evacuated areas to maintain order and attempt to facilitate a restoration of normalcy to the area. There was one opposition group that remained in Ghouta, Jaysh al-Islam. By early April 2018, they too had struck a deal with the government to evacuate, providing a huge victory for Bashar al-Assad and his allies. In total, some 40,000 opposition fighters and their families had relocated to northern Syria. In addition, the months-long campaign had killed 1,000 people, including several hundred women and children.[316]

STILL MORE CHEMICAL ATTACKS

Before Jaysh al-Islam could be convinced to leave Ghouta, however, civilians in Douma (about six miles northeast of Damascus) were taken to a local hospital on April 7, 2018, suffering from respiratory issues, leading many to believe chemical weapons had again been utilized. The Organization for the Prohibition of Chemical Weapons conducted tests from samples taken from two separate sites throughout the city, finding explosive residue and "various chlorinated organic chemicals." The Syrian government denied its use while Russia blamed Great Britain for the incident. Various sources quoted different levels of fatalities, but it seemed approximately 40 deaths were caused by respiratory issues in this attack conducive to chlorine.[317]

Russia threatened retaliation if the US conducted any strikes inside Syria as a result of this incident. President Trump responded in a tweet for Russia to be ready "because they will be coming, nice and new and 'smart!' You shouldn't be partners with a Gas Killing Animal who kills his people and enjoys it!" The Trump Administration ignored such rhetoric from Moscow, launching several strikes inside Syria on April 14, 2018, in conjunction with British and French actions, although the attacks were launched Friday night / Saturday morning in the US. This seems coincidentally timed, taking place at the end of the work week when US citizens would be winding down and then ramping up their weekend plans. It seems likely the intent was to strike inside Syria while Americans would not be in front of their televisions, while hoping for the story to die out by Monday morning.

Clearly these actions were aimed at deterrence and little else. If the US knew the locations of Syria's chemical weapons, would it not have said or done something before such weapons were utilized? The strikes targeted a science research facility in Damascus along with two production and storage facilities in Homs. In total, the United States launched 105 missiles against Syria, of which the Russians claimed to have intercepted 83 of them. They further claimed to have sent two of them back to Russia in order to reverse-engineer the technology. While it is unlikely that Russia was successful in any of its claims, reverse engineering is always a real threat, made successful by China and various other countries without the budget of the US military. Based on the previous calculations conducted for the previous US missile strike, these 105 missiles cost the US taxpayer another $210,000,000, a cost incurred without much benefit attached.

IDLIB PROVINCE—REMAINING STRONGHOLD

In September 2018, Turkey and Russia agreed to create a demilitarized zone in Idlib Province aimed at avoiding an all-out assault and bombardment on the city. Turkey has been housing three million Syria refugees and is concerned that a major offensive would result in more refugees streaming to its border, as well as the potential for collateral damage along its border with Syria. In addition, as a result of its role in policing the de-escalation zones in Syria, Turkey constructed observation posts throughout Idlib Province, manned by Turkish troops, a scenario that places Turkish military units in the way of any offensives in the area. Turkish military units and Russian military police were to oversee the area, with moderate opposition groups remaining, but heavy weapons and some groups (like Tahrir al-Sham) would have to be moved by October. There were approximately three million civilians residing in Idlib, which was being controlled primarily by Tahrir al-Sham. Purportedly maintaining 10,000 fighters, Tahrir al-Sham was controlling a border crossing with Turkey and the provincial capital. Many groups had been spread throughout the city, with the potential for a combined force of 70,000 fighters opposing any assault. In January 2019, Tahrir al-Sham signed ceasefire agreements with rival groups throughout Idlib, consolidating control and potentially prepping for upcoming offensives.[318]

Tahrir al-Sham and its affiliates began striking at military facilities throughout the region, prompting the start of a Syrian government offensive in April 2019. Some had claimed it was not a full-blown offensive to recapture the entire territory, but more so an operation to retake key terrain: a major highway running north to Turkey and other supply routes, and to claim a larger buffer between government-controlled territory and the fighters within Idlib.

As of the writing of this book, the situation in and around Idlib is ever-changing. It will most likely end with the Syrian government reclaiming this territory, assuming that its allies do not abandon it. While some things seem like foregone conclusions, like Bashar's willingness and ability to reclaim Syria as it was pre-2011, including the north-east territory currently controlled by the Kurds. With Russia's assistance there is little to indicate that Bashar will not push to reclaim this area, which could put Syrian forces in opposition to US forces, the de facto protectors of these Kurdish fighters.

CHAPTER 10

SYRIA'S FUTURE

"The sinews of war are infinite money" was as true in Cicero's time as it is today. Funding any conflict places great strain upon a country, which is already exacerbated by the other issues caused by the conflict. In interviews given to Russian media outlets in 2016, Bashar al-Assad claimed that the war to that point had cost $200 billion.[319] This might be true (although it seems conservative, given the level of destruction and displacement), but it no doubt lacks the clarity of the full economic picture. A government has three ways to raise revenue: impose or increase taxes, borrow money, or create money. Increasing taxes on a population suffering from the impact of war (displacement, unemployment, scarcity of goods, health, and uncertainty) is most likely not going to increase revenue by any significant level. As of 2016, taxes accounted for 2% of Syria's gross domestic product (GDP), the lowest in the world. And with its unemployment at 50% in 2016, and over 82% of its population under the poverty line in 2014, this would create a further strain on the country and its economy.[320]

In order for the Syrian government to borrow money, the lender would have to feel that they were acquiring a return for the risk that they would be assuming for such lending. The government could also issue bonds, but the same principle applies; in this case, the buyer of the bond must be confident that the government will follow through with payments, but also offer competitive rates to entice buyers. As the conflict has increasingly ruined Syria's economy, its credit rating has suffered in tandem; this, coupled with the fact that Syria has not serviced its debt since 2012,[321] makes it unlikely that many countries would be willing to lend Syria money, at least not until stability is returned.

While Russia is assisting Syria militarily, costing Russia over $4 million per day, its economy has its own woes, with a devaluing of the ruble, decreased foreign direct investment (FDI), decreased oil prices, and assets frozen after its foray into Ukraine;[322] Russian assistance beyond military spending seems unlikely and unsustainable into the future.

Lastly, the Syrian government could easily print money, which it is likely doing. However, from 2015 to 2016, inflation in Syria increased 25% to nearly 48%.[323] This is likely a result of an increased amount of currency circulating throughout the country; coupled with the fact that domestic production has decreased, infrastructure is not being serviced, and the devaluation of the Syrian currency, there is likely a surplus of money chasing after a limited amount of goods, leading to such high rates of inflation. As more money goes after fewer goods, prices rise, and consumers' purchasing power diminishes as well. If the country desires to undermine this effect, it must either create an economic environment conducive to producers increasing their goods and services, or it will need to decrease the money supply, something unlikely to happen.

Overall, Syria's economy has shrunk 62% between the years 2010 to 2014. The conflict has extensively destroyed the country's infrastructure with most fighting taking place in major cities. With inflation so high, personal savings has no doubt suffered, diminishing the banks' ability to lend. These economic woes have undoubtedly affected businesses' confidence in their own investment, and thereby their inability to produce, or to move goods via the country's infrastructure. This further erodes the efforts of businesses to provide basic goods to consumers. In order to fix the problem, many years of peace and stability will be required to rebuild the country, allowing FDI to return to the country. While security forces will need to be maintained, reducing government's footprint will allow for the balancing of budgets and trade and restart the economy. While Bashar al-Assad initially began economic reforms upon his election, the Syrian economy is highly regulated; reducing this will go a long way into rebuilding the country, and potentially solve the issues of high unemployment and high inflation, which could help bring in much needed stimulus for the economy. However, as the Ba'ath Party is inherently socialist, it is unlikely the Syrian economy will witness a large growth trend into the long-term.

But very little is possible without the manpower to sustain it, which means resettling the refugees who fled the country during the fighting. Since the outbreak of fighting, there has been an estimated 11 million refugees. The vast majority are displaced within Syria (just over 6.5 million), with another approximately 5 million being cared for in countries near Syria: Turkey, Lebanon, Jordan, Egypt, and Iraq. Countries from around the world have accepted Syrian refugees as well, with Europe receiving 1 million asylum requests (although they are unlikely to return).[324] In addition, one million Syrian have been born outside Syria; the Syrian government has agreed to recognize their citizenship,[325] but it seems unlikely that they will return to a country torn by war.

The problem with countries outside Syria accepting refugees, is that it does not solve any long-term problems for Syria, without which, will just create more refugees. There is the added complication of culture that has to be addressed; that is not to state that Muslims are incapable of reaching the point of shared values, but it is certainly fair to state that the values between western states and that of Muslim states do not always align. When cultures and values do not align, it creates a problem for the rule-of-law for the host countries. An even more nefarious, but plausible possibility, is the potential for these refugees to be infiltrated by terrorist groups, thereby providing such groups the opportunity to place their people throughout the society of a country it is hostile to.

Once these refugees return to Syria, many problems remain, the largest of which is economic. Aside from providing security and stability throughout the country, the government will need to provide an environment where private enterprise can quickly thrive. The vast majority of refugees were living below the poverty line, so economic stability will prove to be important in regaining their normalcy. With this, will come the issues of proving ownership of homes and properties, amnesty for deserting soldiers, mines and unexploded ordinance (UXO), as well as day-to-day necessities: healthcare, water, food, education, and coping with their past traumas. The UN estimated that 250,000 Syrians might be able and willing to return to their homes throughout 2019.[326] This is a healthy start, but much work would need to be done in order to get the millions returned.

If the situation in Syria were not bad enough, a long-term issue for many countries in the region is the growing pressure on sustainable water sources. Increasing pressure from hydro-electricity, agriculture, growing populations and industries, have all led to growing concerns over sources of water, leading many to believe the next major crisis facing the region will not have to do with oil and natural gas, but water. This is not only an economic issue, but one that will affect the standard of living of all Syrians, and one that will require a working relationship with its neighbors in order to amicably resolve.

While economic stability will ensure a return to normalcy for many Syrians, it is territorial integrity that will ensure lasting peace within Syria, and without amongst its several neighbors. This will further the prospect of stability. With this, comes the prevention of terrorism, to a degree, but, more importantly, creates a vacuum with which terrorism cannot thrive. The first part of acquiring this territorial integrity comes from an evacuation of US forces; the US was not invited into Syria, and therefore must leave. Furthermore, it is not for the US to decide the fate of the Syrian territory occupied by the Kurds, and therefore not a reason for its military to remain. Turkey does not want an autonomous Kurdish area within Syria from which the PKK can launch attacks into Turkey. While this is not for Turkey to decide, it will inevitably lead to many issues between Ankara and Damascus. Establishing a semi-autonomous Kurdish state within Syria ultimately rests between Damascus and the Kurdish authorities, but this seems unlikely to play out.

In February 2019, Bouthaina Shaaban, a senior advisor to Bashar al-Assad stated that dividing Syrian territory was not an option. She called autonomy for the Kurds a partition of Syria, which feels that the Kurds are "a precious and very important part of the Syrian people." She further stated that Syria "is a country that is a melting pot for all people and all people are equal in front of Syria law and in front of the Syrian constitution."[327] The following month Syrian authorities agreed to merge their forces with Syrian government forces if, in exchange, Damascus conceded to an autonomous Kurdish region.[328] Whatever the outcome with the Kurds might be, a Syrian assault into this area could draw US forces into a fight, but not doing so, could lead to long-term hostilities with the Kurds of the region and the Turks as well.

At the top of its list in securing its territorial integrity, will no doubt be the return of the Golan Heights from Israel. A return of the Golan would go a long way in ensuring a lasting peace in Syria, as well as the Middle East as a whole, undermining the necessity of further US efforts in the region. But this matter is much more complicated...

MIDDLE EAST PEACE

The return of the Golan Heights is not a situation that the Syrian people, or the Arabs in general, see as an event likely to happen, given the relationship between the US and Israel. This is further exacerbated by the status of Jerusalem, Israeli settlement building, and the status of the Golan itself.

Jerusalem has been a contentious issue between the Israelis and the Arabs since the state of Israel came into being. Jerusalem has maintained a sacred status among the world's three major religions. In Christianity, Jerusalem was the site of the crucifixion of Jesus; Jews hold that the first temple built by Solomon was erected in Jerusalem; and to Muslims, Jerusalem was the city to which the Prophet Muhammed journeyed and subsequently ascended to heaven. Known in Islam as Isra and Mi'raj, respectively, the Quran describes a journey of one night taken by the Prophet Muhammed in which he saw Heaven and Hell, and met the Prophets of the Old and New Testaments. The Israelis have not been content in allowing a separation of Jerusalem for which they claim both a political and spiritual connection, despite the city being nearly completely razed by the Romans in 135 AD.

According to the US Jerusalem Embassy Act of 1995, "[i]n 1990, the Congress unanimously adopted Senate Concurrent Resolution 106, which declares that the Congress 'strongly believes that Jerusalem must remain an undivided city...'"[329] Who is the US Congress to make such a declaration? How does such a declaration strengthen US national security or improve the lives of its citizens? Should not such a statement be debated by those affected? It was such questions that kept US administrations since from acting on the legislation; however, this changed on December 6, 2017, when US President Donald Trump, in a speech from the White House, acknowledged Israeli sovereignty over the city, and promised to move the US embassy to the city. This went a terribly long way in undermining the Palestinians' hopes to locate their own capital to eastern Jerusalem.[xi] President Trump stated that "Israel is a sovereign nation with the right, like every other sovereign nation, to determine its own capital. Acknowledging this fact is a necessary condition for achieving peace."[330] This view completely undermines the sovereignty of the Palestinian State. Currently, 420,000 Palestinians are residing in East Jerusalem, and the Arabs residing in the city are not considered residents of Israel, Jordan, or the State of Palestine.[331] They are allowed Jordanian passports in order to travel, but they are temporary in nature and do not extend any further rights upon those Palestinians.

Following the announcement, the United States spent nearly $400,000 to upgrade its consulate in Jerusalem to a full embassy, adding an additional $21 million to upgrade the security systems and an extension to the already existing structure. It seems that the Trump Administration is putting top dollars at work on security; no doubt many security concerns are being anticipated, and no doubt the US embassy is there to stay, and a likely target it will become for some future terrorist.

The US announcement has also undermined the UN Partition Plan, established as UN Resolution 181 in 1947. In it, the UN acknowledged the situation in Palestine was "likely to impair the general welfare and friendly relations among nations," and an attempt to facilitate peace, called for a separate Jewish and Palestinian state, with an international governance over Jerusalem, administered by the United Nations. On December 21, 2017, the United Nations General Assembly held its own vote to consider Jerusalem. Despite the US's attempts at persuading nations to take its side, the UN countered Israel's claim of Jerusalem as its capital with a vote of 128 for and 9 against, with 35 abstaining.[xii] While many countries are opposed to the whole of Jerusalem belonging to Israel, many believe that Jerusalem should be shared between Israel and a Palestinian State, including:

---

xi   While Palestine is recognized as an independent country by a great many UN countries, the US, Israel, and many western European countries recognize the area as the Palestinian Territories, per the Oslo Accords.

xii   The nine countries that voted "no" were: Guatemala, Honduras, Israel, the Marshall Islands, Micronesia, Nauru, Palau, Togo, and of course, the United States.

Russia, the United Nations, Great Britain, China, France, and the European Union.

In August 2018, the Trump Administration cancelled $200 million in aid for projects aimed at residents of the West Bank and Gaza Strip. It also cut $25 million in aid that would have gone to hospitals throughout East Jerusalem; since the US government now officially recognizes Jerusalem as the capital of Israel, it makes sense that any projects that go towards helping those Arabs would be defunded.

On September 10, 2018 the Trump Administration ordered the closing of the PLO office in Washington, DC, citing the PLO's inability to engage in "direct and meaningful negotiations with Israel." A US State Department spokesperson stated that the PLO office was closed due to congressional concerns, further adding that "PLO leadership has condemned a US peace plan they have not yet seen and refused to engage with the US government with respect to peace efforts and otherwise."[332] The "otherwise" sounds dubious, but most seriously, why is the PLO handcuffed to engage with the US government and how would shutting its office in DC compel it do so? Can the PLO not engage with other actors in the peace process? Considering the US's recent moves, it should come as no surprise. It seems like further cause as to why the US has been unsuccessful in its efforts.

Following on the heels of the US' recognition of Jerusalem, the Israeli Knesset voted in March 2018 to enact a "breach of loyalty" or "breach of allegiance" bill. Per this legislation, the Israeli Ministry of the Interior can revoke the residency documents of Palestinians deemed a threat to Israel or Israelis or who have falsely claimed residence. The law was first proposed in 2017 after the Israeli Supreme Court shot down the Interior Ministry's attempt to strip the residency of four individuals living in Jerusalem. An amendment to this bill was first raised in September 2017, which would have prohibited the Supreme Court from challenging the Ministry's decisions. Through 2017, 14,000 people living within Jerusalem have had their residency revoked.[333] Is this an Israeli attempt to deny Arabs citizenship?

To add to this, in July 2018 the Israeli Knesset passed the Jewish Nation State Law. It further affirmed, despite the disagreement throughout the world, that Jerusalem is, and will remain, the capital. It did not, however, stop there. The law went on to define what is meant by the State of Israel, which "is the historical homeland of the Jewish people" and "the nation-state of the Jewish people" in which the "actualization of the right of national self-determination... is unique to the Jewish people." It defines the symbols (such as the flag and the national anthem) of the country, and specifies Hebrew as the official language, granting Arabic a "special status." Incidentally, the law also applies to the land outside of Israel: "Jewish settlement as a national value and will labor to encourage and promote its establishment and development."

With the passage of this law it seemed very clear that Israel was attempting to undermine the Arab minority within the country, which makes up around 20% of the population, and solidify the status of the country should Arabs one day make up a larger percentage of the population. While Israel has no constitution, it has passed several Basic Laws (such as the Jewish Nation State Law) which are constitutional-like and require a majority within the legislature to amend. So, if and when Jews become the minority, it will require a great deal of votes within the Knesset to overturn the Jewish Nation Law. It further undermines the Palestinian State with its insistence of settlement building.

Settlement building is conducted by the Israeli government, taking place outside the defined borders of the country; the government even offers incentives to Jews to live in the West Bank. In 1993, the government of Israel and the PLO signed the Oslo Accords, calling for the withdrawal of the IDF from the West Bank and Gaza Strip. In exchange, the Palestinian Authority (PA) would be created in order to oversee these areas. Israel would recognize the PA as a representative body for all Palestinians, while the PLO would recognize Israel's right to exist and renounce terrorism. While not all Palestinian factions have done so, the PLO, under the leadership of Yasser Arafat, did just that. Oslo was no doubt possible due to Arafat's conciliatory diplomacy by the late 1980s, but he furthered this rhetoric in 1993 by sending a letter to the then-Israeli Prime Minister Yitzhak Rabin, recognizing the PLO commitment to do its part in curbing violence.[334]

At the time, there were approximately 100,000 Israeli settlers in the West Bank, but by 2016, that number had grown to 400,000 spread throughout 130 settlements. In 2016, East Jerusalem had an additional 200,000 Israeli citizens. Since 1995, the population growth of Israeli settlements was four times faster than the population within Israel's borders. To make matters worse, these settlements must be connected with roads and require further buffer zones for security purposes in some areas. These areas dissect Palestinian lands and restrict their freedom-of-movement throughout their own lands. These areas are also scenes of attacks, targeting both Palestinians and Israelis; however, they are prosecuted unequally. When Palestinians are accused in such attacks, they are faced with Israeli military law, while Israeli accused go before an Israeli civil court.[335]

Less than two weeks after President Trump announced the American Embassy move to Jerusalem, the defense minister of Israel, Avigdor Lieberman, announced the approval of 3,900 new homes to be constructed in pre-existing settlements throughout the West Bank. He was quoted as saying: "In the coming months we will bring thousands of more units for approval. We will continue to settle and develop Judea and Samaria [the West Bank] through actions."[336] While this does not necessarily add settlements to the map, it certainly solidifies Israel's claims to its preexisting settlements. This should show that Israel is not (and perhaps never was) content to live peaceably within the confines of UN Resolution 242, never mind the borders outlined by UN Resolution 181.

The Trump Administration has not taken much action on such obviously illegal actions on the part of Israel. The US Ambassador to Israel, David Friedman, declared that these settlements are a part of Israel, although a US State Department spokesperson did not seem entirely convinced that he was the best official to make such remarks.[337] Who better than the ambassador? There is little doubt this causes a great deal of confusion for Palestinian grievances. To add to this, is the belief by some Palestinians that as the US was so adamant in recognizing Jerusalem as Israel's capital, so too will the US be adamant in recognizing such settlements as inherently part of Israel.[338] How long before the US recognizes Israel's "right" to keep the Golan Heights as well? What will that do to an already unstable Syria? What will that do to encourage terrorist recruitment and continued operations? In November 2018, the US and Israel, voted against a UN resolution condemning Israel's occupation of the Golan Heights, the only two countries to do so. This was a first for the US; in previous votes, the US had abstained.[339]

So, as the US is adamant in support of Israel by declaring Jerusalem its capital, thus depriving the Palestinians' claim to such, while simultaneously failing to hold Israel accountable of its settlement building, the Syrian people have little hope that the Golan Heights will be returned peaceably.

US WITHDRAWAL

The United States, Iran, and Russia were purportedly building bases in Syria during their "occupations". Russia singed a deal with Syria in which Russia was granted a 49-year concession to a naval base in Tartus and indefinite use of Hmeimim Air Base.[340] Russian Defense Minister Nikolay Pankov even stated that Soviet-era facilities were under consideration for revitalization throughout Africa, Southeast Asia, and Latin America.[341] This would have indicated that there was a long-term intention for remaining in Syria, even though the US did not have agreements from Damascus to remain (the Iraqis certainly want the US gone as well based on their previously stated attitudes). While this seemed to indicate the worst-case scenario for all involved, in December 2018, President Trump announced that US forces would be withdrawing from Syria. This was not an indication of an impending departure from Iraq, however. With 5,000 US troops still in Iraq, President Trump had "no plans at all" to withdrawal them. He further stated that, "[i]n fact, we could use this as a base if we wanted to do something in Syria. I will say this, if you take [the Islamic State] and if we see something happening with [the Islamic State] that we don't like, we can hit them so fast and so hard, they won't—they really won't know what the hell happened."[342] President Trump quickly backpedaled on this assurance however, citing a US need to protect the Kurds from Turkey (and perhaps Syria as well), while also guarding against any resurgence of the Islamic State, he called for a presence of 400 US personnel to remain inside Syria.

Despite the fight against the Islamic State, the presence of US forces in Syria had done nothing to end the Syrian Civil War; if anything, it made it easier for Bashar al-Assad and his allies to retake the country from the opposition (who were also tied down themselves in some cases) by essentially tying down the Islamic State and allowing government forces to be engaged elsewhere. There is a moral issue here in that the US government was not created to impose its will on the international community, but there is also an economic interest in that it is not for the US government to allocate US resources to the international community. As has previously been stated, the Islamic State did not pose a serious threat to the United States, but despite this, the attitude existed that they had to be targeted, most especially with tax dollars, like much of the US government's problem-solving.

According to the Department of Defense, operations against the Islamic State in Syria and Iraq (between August 2014 and June 2017) was costing $13.6 million per day. If these funds were theoretically split 50/50 between operations in Iraq and Syria, the four years of a US presence in Syria could potentially have cost the US taxpayer nearly $10 billion in total (half of $13.6M = $6.8M x 1,460 days = $9.928B). That is an awful lot of borrowed money (it could not possibly all have been from taxed revenue); at the end of 2018, the United States was nearly $22 trillion in debt.

Gross funds have been thrown at the Islamic State, but the fact remains that war has not been declared and no invitation extended to US forces, and therefore a US presence in Syria has been unconstitutional. Before the invasion of Iraq, the case had been made that Iraq had been producing WMD and had even been in contact with al-Qaeda operatives. While this was the selling point needed for the American public's approval, it was also needed as Congress had granted President George W Bush the authority to attack those, and their supporters, that had attacked the United States on 9/11. By making the case that the Saddam regime had been in contact with al-Qaeda, the US was thereby justified (Constitutionally at least) in attacking Iraq.

And it is from 9/11 that the United States government continues to conduct military operations in the Middle East. One week after the Twin Towers came down, the 107th Congress passed the "Authorization for Use of Military Force," granting the President use of,

all necessary and appropriate force against those nations, organizations, or persons he determines planned, authorized, committed, or aided the terrorist attacks that occurred on September 11, 2001, or harbored such organizations or persons, in order to prevent any future acts of international terrorism against the United States by such nations, organizations or persons.

This, evidently, continues to provide relatively broad powers to the president, particularly when the legislation is left up to the president's determination.

In September 2017, the Kurds of Iraq held a referendum in which they sought the answer to: "Do you want the Kurdistan Region and the Kurdistani areas outside the Region to become an independent state?" 3.3 million Iraqi Kurds cast their vote, and nearly 93% answered yes, they would desire to be independent.

With the SDF butting heads with Turkey in northern Syria, and the Kurds seeking independence from Iraq, there was a perception that the US withdrawal from Syria was a betrayal to the Syrian Kurds. The United States never supported Kurdish independence. The US has supported a strong, Iraqi government post-2003, which would undermine US efforts at supporting Kurdish independence in Iraq, but also elsewhere. The Kurdish areas of northern Iraq are awash in oil; losing these resources would be a major blow to any Iraqi government; this is the reason that the area was incorporated into the British mandate of Iraq after World War I. If anything, it was the Kurds using the US to build momentum of their own that would lead to the independence of the area. The Kurds, however, failed to leverage their military accomplishments into the required political capital necessary to successfully pursue independence. This is not support for or opposition to any one side, simply an opinion based on pragmatism.

As regards the Kurds in northern Syria, it does beg the question what line the US is walking in regards to its NATO ally Turkey and also its anti-IS ally, the Kurdish People's Protection Units. President Trump proposed a 20-mile "safe zone" to protect the Kurds, but also warned Turkey against attacks, threatening economic sanctions against the country. Turkey, of course, responded defiantly, vowing to continuing their fight against IS and the YPG.

While Bashar al-Assad gave the Kurds of Syria relative autonomy early in the Syrian conflict, it was likely more of an effort to quell any Kurdish dissent so he could concentrate on the real opposition. While the Kurds are willing to negotiate with Damascus, Bashar al-Assad has claimed his intention of reclaiming "every inch" of territory.[343]

This seems more likely, particularly if Iranian militias and Russian forces are assisting as well. Likely Assad is making an effort to buy time as it remains to be seen how efforts will unravel in Idlib and no campaign there would turn out well for the YPG, as it would likely prevent Assad from antagonizing the Kurds so long as an opposition-held Idlib remained to threaten his position.

Twenty thousand fighters made their way to Syria and Iraq to take part in the fighting with the Islamic State, 4,000 of which were nationals of western European countries; that exceeded the number of jihadis fighting the Soviets in Afghanistan.[344] While its infrastructure is almost non-existent, along with its recruitment efforts, the Islamic State still maintains forces. While many of its leadership ranks have been assassinated in drone strikes and targeted killings, its upper echelons remain, including its leader, Abu Bakr al-Baghdadi. Killing him would not end the Islamic State, proof enough exists in the fact that al-Qaeda remains a viable force after the death of Osama bin Laden. While they are on the run, they are not defeated, nor is their ideology been checked. One measure of success against the Islamic State, aside from depriving them of territory, was to measure their presence on social media and other internet sites. After the fall of Raqqa, Islamic State's media outlets dropped from 30 to 10 items posted per day. This might simply mean they had concentrated their media operations around Raqqa or Mosul, and not necessarily a true measure of their constitution in maintaining the fight.[345] This, of course, is dramatically less than it was pushing out before the offensive or after its take-over of the city, and seeing as the world is connected, this would likely only be a minor setback. In an audio recording from September 2017, IS leader Abu Bakr al-Baghdadi called on fighters to target "media centers of the infidels."[346] Perhaps media is just that important to IS. With the Islamic State's "caliphate" drastically undermined, and no "brick-and-mortar" location with which to beckon followers, the group would likely be dependent on such propaganda, as a "headquarters" is not required for it to launch operations. This is another reason why merely fighting Islamic State (or any terrorist group for that matter) is not enough. Their message must be attacked and degraded before any hope of killing such an organization can play out. Hence, US military operations in Syria, and throughout the region for that matter, are short-term, political solutions to a broader issue, one that cannot be won with military might alone. Peace in the region must be obtained, and this starts with the US withdrawing from Syria, allowing for Syrian autonomy and integrity, and holding Israel accountable for its illegal actions.

A viable Syrian will ensure a defeat of terrorists, and the return of the Golan, will likely lead to improved relations between Syria and Israel, and undermine Syria's relationship with Iran.

CONCLUSION

Who would have guessed that nearly 30 years after the end of the Cold War, peace in the Middle East is as yet, still unattainable? The US has continually failed, despite its best intentions at resolving these issues. Intentions are of course irrelevant, what is most important are the outcomes. The US relationship with Israel has soured its ability to effectively broker any peace in the region, which undermines its own national security. Its military presence in the Middle East has only grown since September 11th, with no signs of significant withdrawals. This too, has undermined its credibility throughout the region and made its efforts at a resolution nearly impossible.

In a March 2016 report released by the State Department Inspector General, it was found that one-third of the Iraqis interviewed believed that the US was in some way supporting terrorism and the Islamic State, while 40% felt that the US was pursuing efforts at destabilizing Iraq and pushing for control of its resources. In addition, half of Iraq's Muslim population (both Sunni and Shi'a), were opposed to the US-led coalition to fight the Islamic State.[347] While this is not an overwhelming majority, it points to the idea that the United States has overstayed its welcome in Iraq and no doubt throughout the Middle East. Furthermore, Iraqi parliamentary elections held in May 2018 saw a political movement opposed to a US presence win 100 out of 329 seats[348]. This was clearly not a majority, but nevertheless an indication of growing anti-US discontent.

The United States is right to withdrawal from Syria, not because the Islamic State has been pushed from huge chunks of territory, but because a continued US presence perpetuates such groups. Even if the Islamic State were wiped out of existence, another would rise from those ashes; the ideology persists and cannot be defeated entirely with force. It can be defeated, however, through understanding; but it takes an understanding of how actions can affect issues in the region, and how history has come to define those issues.

These historical issues can be seen in Syria into the present; a country now wracked by instability and uncertainty. There have been many external forces that have contributed to this: the French mandate, the creation of Israel, interference by the US government and the CIA, and Israel's occupation of the Golan Heights.

Great Britain, France, and the League of Nations perhaps had good intentions for the Middle East following the collapse of the Ottoman Empire, particularly in assisting in the establishment of well-governed, viable countries. These good intentions led to the British and French forcing their ideas of governance on a populace that had been governing themselves even during Ottoman times, and were certainly ready to do so after its defeat. In Palestine, the British forced the Arabs into an untenable position whereby hundreds of thousands of Zionists were permitted by British officials to locate to Palestine. The Arabs' sense of betrayal led them to side with the Nazis during WWII, furthering the cause of the Zionists, which further undermined the Arabs' position.

In Syria, the French forced the population to submit to their Mandate by force. The fact remains that following the chaos of World War I, the Syrians were poised to form their own self-governed land, a move undermined by French intransigence; the French did not believe the Syrians capable of standing on their own despite having security forces and a governing body. The present will be no different; just as the US was hailed by many Iraqis for the overthrow of Saddam in 2003, the continued presence of US forces has come to be resented. The US intervened in Libya following the Arab Spring in 2011, and despite such "goodwill," two civil wars have wracked the country, with disparate factions vying for control. Intervention is not always appreciated, nor does it necessarily lead to improvement.

Following the Soviet expansion into the Middle East during the early years of the Cold War, the United States followed suit, assuming the responsibility of supporter of Israel. What flowed from this was the US involvement in Lebanon in the 1980s, US involvement in the Israeli-Arab peace process in which the US has spent perhaps billions of dollars, and a military presence throughout the Middle East and Persian Gulf to ostensibly protect oil logistics, including its defense of Saudi Arabia and offensives against Iraq. A Soviet expansion and, some would claim, an American expansion necessitated by the flow of oil.

The discovery of oil in the Middle East led to the continuation of Western policies in the area. After US companies built the Trans-Arabian pipeline through Syria, many Syrians perceived such a move as imperialistic and a way for the US government to interfere in domestic Syrian politics, thus promoting American interests. It is not imperialistic for a developed nation to step-in and assist a country such as Syria in developing its natural resources, particularly when that country does not possess the know-how or infrastructure to do so efficiently. It is, however, wrong for that country to attempt to control the host country. This Tapline gave the US government the excuse to interfere in domestic Syrian politics, reasoning that such interference was necessary to protect the flow of oil and US business interests. With British, followed by American interference, coupled with the tension with Israel, it is no wonder that Syrian nationalism came to the fore.

In addition to these external factors, and maybe as a result of this increasing nationalism, there have been a number of Syrian policies that have contributed to the country's instability as well. Some of these were implemented, however, in an effort to counter the above external: an authoritarian government (and the crony economics and restriction of civil liberties that was brought with it), siding with the Soviet Union, Syria's invasion of Lebanon, its support of terrorism, and the loss of the Golan Heights (Syria can be blamed for losing the territory, but Israel is responsible for its continued illegal possession).

It is no wonder, particularly after the Golan Heights were seized, that the Ba'ath Party and then Hafez al-Assad were able to seize power and maintain control. Authoritarian measures became necessary in order to maintain control, preserve a war footing to counter Israel, and take back the Golan Heights. The animosity between Syria and Israel, particularly after the loss of the Golan, in addition to Cold War tensions, led to heightened defense spending, a level with which Syria could not maintain after the collapse of the Soviet Union. Opportunity costs, and Syria's crony economy, led Syria further into financial ruin, exasperated by its dwindling oil reserves and mounting water pressures. Although failing in Lebanon and realizing that it could not standup in a conventional fight with Israel, the Syria-Iran duo was born, breathing life into Hezbollah and Syria's support of terrorism.

The authoritarian regime of the Ba'ath Party and the Assads resulted in a closed state, one in which the people lacked opportunities, and one where the tightening of civil liberties led people to desperations, forcing the government to crack down. As soon as the Bashar al-Assad government lost control of the population in 2011, it became a failed state. This decline was furthered through the assistance of foreign powers. Small arms proliferation is not the means by which to win these conflicts; the US role in Afghanistan during the 1980s should be proof enough of this. Certainly, the role played by the US had some effect on the Soviets' withdrawal from Afghanistan; however, the very effort led to the rise of the Taliban and the exporting of military-style skills to the host countries of these fighters. In the first case, there were a great many weapons and equipment left over that led to in-fighting amongst the various groups. Small arms proliferation serves to exacerbate the situation; it would be a shame to think foreign governments might use that tool for just such a purpose. This policy failed in Afghanistan, and did little to end the fighting in Syria; only time will tell what impact this will have on the country and the region into the future.

This failed state in Syria ultimately led to the creation of the Islamic State; security forces were tied up combatting opposition elements to notice the rise of this group. Many in the United States are quick to claim that a premature withdrawal of US forces from Iraq led to the creation of the Islamic State; however, if the wrong of Iraq created IS, why would the US continue on a path of flawed Middle East policies? That is not to state that the US should not step in and offer assistance to countries, but it should most certainly be invited by the host country and such a move should be agreed upon by the vast majority in the Congress. Partisan politics is no doubt to blame, with the left and right blaming one another for problems created by both parties throughout the years.

Robert Gates wrote a great passage in his 2014 book, *Duty: Memoirs of a Secretary at War* that sums up the challenges of US foreign policy in a post-Cold War world. A world in which the United States succeeded as the sole superpower, a feat only made possible by its productive economy and its relative isolation prior to the world wars, yet has witnessed threats arising all over the world:

> On the left, we hear about the "responsibility to protect" as a justification for military intervention in Libya, Syria, the Sudan, and elsewhere. On the right, the failure to use military force in Libya, Syria, or Iran is deemed an abdication of American leadership and a symptom of a "soft" foreign policy. Obama's "pivot" to Asia was framed almost entirely in military terms as opposed to economic and political priorities. And so the rest of the world sees America, above all else, as a militaristic country too quick to launch planes, cruise missiles, and armed drones deep into sovereign countries or ungoverned spaces.[349]

It is this perception that the United States must guard against, particularly if it desires an end to the quagmire of Middle East relations. Those on the left of the aisle desire to export and prop-up democratic principles, while the opposing party seems to be concerned with projecting a powerful image to the world in order to maintain its status as "leader". The former is not truly democratic if it is coming from outside the country, and the latter can tend towards aggressive actions and fiscal irresponsibility; in either case, money is required, and a whole lot of it. Since the federal government does not actually produce goods and services, the money is ultimately coming from the taxpayer. Furthermore, neither option is supported by the U.S. Constitution and neither is directly safeguarding the United States or its people, and therefore not worth the enormous price.

This is precisely what is happening in Syria; no thought is given to the long-term effects of such overwhelming actions. The complicated interrelationships that have been playing out within Syria and the Middle East, on a most basic of levels, is as good as any reason for the United States to remain aloof throughout the conflict and in what outcome may transpire. The political players within the US do not fully understand this complexity: Sunni versus Shia, Kurds versus Turkey and Kurds versus Syria, Arabs versus Turks and Arabs versus Persians and Arabs versus Kurds, Hezbollah versus Israel, Iran versus

Israel, and the role the US has played throughout the Middle East in the last several decades. The complications can destabilize negotiations quickly, and outcomes reached could fall apart just as quickly if all sides are not properly analyzed; the US has shown that long-term results in the region are not as desirable as quick, short-term solutions. Again, partisan politics at work.

After the chemical attack in April 2017, President Trump stated that "the United States stands with our allies across the globe to condemn this intolerable attack."[350] The fact of the matter is that the Syrian Civil War has killed tens of thousands of individuals, women and children among them, without the use of chemical weapons. Why do chemical weapons change the response of the United States? Only politics forces the United States government to respond, which is why it was acceptable for the US to make threats and then fail to follow through with them under the Obama Administration; it gave the appearance of concern. No punishments have been meted out to the parties responsible for utilizing chemical weapons, to include Saddam Hussein's use during the Iran-Iraq War and again in Halabja against the Kurds; and recently Bashar al-Assad's use during the Syrian Civil War. Intervention is one thing, but prevention is quite another. It is not in the national security interest of the US (until a point is determined that such weapons will be used against American citizens or sovereign US territory), and therefore should not be the armed forces' role to intervene to disarm Assad. This most important take-away in this, however, should be the question of why Syria acquired chemical weapons in the first place. The answer clearly seems that it was looking for a force-multiplier against Israel (perhaps to be used, but much more likely as a deterrent). As a short-term solution, absolutely Syria should need to rid itself of such weapons; however, for the sake of a viable peace, it needs to rid itself of the reason of having them at all, and that means negotiations with Israel. In order for this to work, however, Israel must be willing to give up its own chemical, biological, and nuclear weapons.

The struggle in Syria has been framed in the context of morality and security; it would be immoral for the United States to do nothing in Syria's opposition to tyranny, and the American people are safer in combatting IS abroad, or so the argument goes. However, it is unjust for the Syrian opposition to demand international assistance;

it is for them to shape their own government how they see fit. They attempted to shuck the authority of Assad's regime and it is not for the United States to play sides in such a contest. Furthermore, it is unjust to demand that US taxpayers and soldiers expend their resources in order to aid the Syrian opposition; it is unfair and unequitable for politicians to take from Americans by force and then give to the Syrians. It remains that the people of Syria have the right to resist their government if they see fit, and the United States should stay out of it. Governments are a necessary evil, installed to ensure life's pursuit of happiness is not infringed. People have the right to install whichever form of government they see fit, but in order to be successful, the support of the people is necessary; it should not be for other governments to step in and choose sides. The Syrian people chose to resist their government, but there are no guaranteed outcomes.

If, however, a situation was to become so great as to directly threaten US national security, then certainly it would be great enough to cause action. In the event of a direct threat, the Congress would certainly vote for military actions; unilateral if need be. However, if a direct threat were not forthcoming, the Congress must still take action, but US unilateral involvement would be inappropriate. In this case, the US should vie for multilateral involvement and collective security, particularly among the nations affected. In the Middle East, there is no reason that the Arab League, or individual Arab States could not involve themselves, as has been done throughout the Syrian Civil War. But, oftentimes, there is an overreliance on the United States to fix problems. As long as the United States exhibits a willingness to intercede in global conflicts, others will exhibit an unwillingness to fix their own regional and national issues. Just as the King-Crane Commission stated in 1919 that "[t]he wishes of these communities must be a principal consideration in the selection of the Mandatory," so too must America ask itself whether or not a US presence will benefit or harm the native people. Even with the best of intentions, a clear lack of understanding can harm the process and endanger American lives and the country's security. To truly solve the ongoing problems within the Middle East, the international community must understand them on a fundamental level, and that means recognizing the role that history has played. For the United States and other Western governments, throwing money at the problems is a near-sighted, short-term solution, one that merely recognizes that there is a problem, not necessarily the issues at hand. The United States and other Western governments have done much to undermine peace and stability in the region, and if they want to play active roles in resolving the problems, they must bring all parties into agreement as to what is best to move forward. If foreign intervention were necessary, it should be an issue large enough to engage a multilateral effort, multilateral in both physical and economic forces, preceded by a debate in the Congress. Rarely is this the case, as the US covers the vast majority of the costs as well as the military forces employed, and is committing forces around the world without a declaration of war from the Congress.

The most important consideration, however, should be the impact on the US Constitution, the American people, and US national security. If such an intervention undermines the Constitution, does not bring greater freedom or prosperity to its citizens, and adversely impacts security, then there is no doubt that it should not be undertaken. The economic and human costs are too great. There is also the issue of checks-and-balances within the United States government. While the President is the Commander-in-Chief, overseeing the nation's armed forces and warfighting capabilities, only the Congress has the Constitutional authority, under Article 1, Section 8, "to declare war." Launching 59 cruise missiles at a Syrian military installation should surely require Congressional consent; if that is not an act of war, what is it and what would constitute an act of war? While many have reasoned that the War Powers Resolutions grants the commander-in-chief the right to make such decisions, it seems to be an unchecked power in regards to executing military operations. Placing the country's resources in harm's way should not be relegated to the limits of one man's reasoning.

While many things have come together to undermine the stability of Syria, there are some things that cannot be undone; history cannot be altered. However, for Syria, the linchpin remains: Israel and the Golan Heights. In addition to what Syrians feel has been Western and American interference in Syria's past, is the US policy towards Israel. Syrians are still bitter over Israel's continued occupation of the Golan Heights, a territory that was captured from Syria during a war initiated by Israel. The issues of Jerusalem and settlement building are contentious for all Arabs, and give the Syrians little hope for the future of their country. To this end, combatting terrorism can only work for the US if it holds Israel accountable for its actions. If the US were to bring its full weight to bear on Israel to make concessions and end the issues that have been plaguing the region, stability in the region could soon be achieved, including an end to weapons proliferation and the desire of acquiring nuclear weapons. Would Syria have felt the need to obtain chemical weapons had the Golan Heights remained in its possession? In addition, the real enemies of the Middle East, groups like al-Qaeda and the Islamic State could be effectively combatted, while undermining their messages. If enough pressure was applied to Israel, and the Golan Heights were returned to a stable, unified Syria, the two countries could begin to enjoy a vibrant, productive stability and economic growth.

After the discovery of gas in the eastern Mediterranean, Egypt hosted a gas forum in an effort to coordinate efforts, with many regional countries represented, including Israel. Israeli Energy Minister Yuval Steinitz called it "the most significant economic cooperation between Egypt and Israel since the singing of the peace treaty 40 years ago."[351] The two countries agreed on a $15 billion deal for Israel to begin exporting gas to Egypt by the spring of 2019. The European Union is encouraging such cooperation in the hopes of importing its own stores and thus reducing its reliance on Russian supplies. Such a relationship could not have been possible if Israel was still occupying the Sinai Peninsula. Such a relationship could exist between Syria and Israel, as well.

Furthermore, if the Golan were returned, the Iranian position would be undermined, diminishing its hegemonic ambitions as well as delivering a blow to Hezbollah. This could further increase security and cooperation between Israel, Syria, and Lebanon. In addition, the Israelis should be forced to remove all settlers from the lands of a Palestinian state; if they refuse, those settlers should then assume the role of subjects of a Palestinian state. In 2005, Israel removed all 8,000 settlers from the Gaza Strip, far less than the 600,000 that would be required to remove from East Jerusalem and the West Bank, but it does demonstrate an ability to get it done. With that as well, East Jerusalem should be recognized as belonging to a Palestinian State; the vast majority of the international community recognizes it as such. If the United States was interested in mediating peace between Israel and its Arab neighbors, it would relegate itself to a truly unbiased position; this is the only way to successfully combat IS, al-Qaeda, and terrorism more broadly, and it is the only way to assist Syria in obtaining a stable and prosperous country.

The current "War on Terror" has blurred the lines of acceptable conduct; conducting military operations within the borders of a sovereign country is an act of war, no matter the intent. The past has shown that good intentions can lead to serious consequences, therefore serious debate should occur before such actions are executed. The continued prosperity of the United States depends on this. Following the French and Indian Wars, which Great Britain spent handsomely to undertake, it began levying taxes on the American Colonies to refill its coffers. This was the duty of the American Colonies, Great Britain reasoned, as it had been waging this war in protection of the Colonies. During the American Revolution, the French crown largely supported the American cause, leading to many financial woes that unfortunately resulted in the French Revolution. These two events serve to illustrate that it is such expensive government spending that leads to such wasteful and unnecessary taxation. But when it comes to conflicts, the government takes up the mantle of protecting the people (rightly or wrongly), and for this, the people must assume their patriotic duty of supporting such an endeavor through taxation. However, how often is such protection necessary? After all, Great Britain and France were merely fighting a proxy war on the North American continent; is today's Middle East any different? With the United States $22 trillion in debt, is it not time that we start pondering the long-term consequences of such debt? Is it not time that the role of the United States in global affairs be reevaluated? It seems so; the future of America's children and grand-children require it. When the US begins to drawdown its Middle Eastern presence, peace and stability will truly triumph throughout the region and fiscal responsibility will become the norm throughout the US government. When Israel becomes convinced of returning the Golan Heights to a stabilized Syria, long-term economic prosperity and peace will follow suit, undermining terrorism and hegemony in the region, and finally bring an end to the US's destructive and consuming presence in the region. Ending such a presence will go a long way in assuring these countries that their domestic affairs are their own, and not for the US, or any other country, to alter. Without such burdensome military deployments, the United States can fix its debt crisis and return the country to an era of low taxes and increased personal freedoms. Without such burdensome interventions, the US can return, not necessarily to an era of isolationism, but perhaps an era of sustained peace.

ACTION GROUP FOR SYRIA

Final Communiqué - 30.06.2012

1. On 30 June 2012, the Secretaries-General of the United
    Nations and the League of Arab States, the Foreign
    Ministers of China, France, Russia, United Kingdom,
    United States, Turkey, Iraq (Chair of the Summit of the
    League of Arab States), Kuwait (Chair of the Council of
    Foreign Ministers of the League of Arab States) and Qatar
    (Chair of the Arab Follow-up Committee on Syria of the
    League of Arab States), and the European Union High
    Representative for Foreign and Security Policy met at the
    United Nations Office at Geneva as the Action Group for
    Syria, chaired by the Joint Special Envoy of the United
    Nations and the League of Arab States for Syria.

2. Action Group members came together out of grave alarm
    at the situation in Syria. They strongly condemn the con-
    tinued and escalating killing, destruction and human rights
    abuses. They are deeply concerned at the failure to protect
    civilians, the intensification of the violence, the potential
    for even deeper conflict in the country, and the regional
    dimensions of the problem. The unacceptable nature and
    magnitude of the crisis demands a common position and
    joint international action.

3. Action Group members are committed to the sover-
    eignty, independence, national unity and territorial
    integrity of Syria. They are determined to work urgently

and intensively to bring about an end to the violence and human rights abuses and the launch of a Syrian-led political process leading to a transition that meets the legitimate aspirations of the Syrian people and enables them independently and democratically to determine their own future.

4. To secure these common objectives, the Action Group members:

(i) identified steps and measures by the parties to secure full implementation of the six-point plan and Security Council resolutions 2042 and 2043, including an immediate cessation of violence in all its forms;

(ii) agreed on guidelines and principles for a political transition that meets the legitimate aspirations of the Syrian people; and

(iii) agreed on actions they would take to implement the above in support of the Joint Special Envoy's efforts to facilitate a Syrian-led political process. They are convinced that this can encourage and support progress on the ground and will help to facilitate and support a Syrian-led transition.

IDENTIFIED STEPS AND MEASURES BY THE PARTIES TO SECURE FULL IMPLEMENTATION OF THE SIX-POINT PLAN AND SECURITY COUNCIL RESOLUTIONS 2042 AND 2043, INCLUDING AN IMMEDIATE CESSATION OF VIOLENCE IN ALL ITS FORMS

5. The parties must fully implement the six-point plan and Security Council resolutions 2042 and 2043. To this end:

- All parties must re-commit to a sustained cessation of armed violence in all its forms and implementation of the six-point plan immediately and without waiting for the actions of others. The government and armed opposition groups must cooperate with UNSMIS with a view to furthering the implementation of the above in accordance with its mandate.

- A cessation of armed violence must be sustained with immediate, credible and visible actions by the Government of Syria to implement the other items of the six-point plan including: o Intensification of the pace and scale of release of arbitrarily detained persons, including especially vulnerable categories of persons, and persons involved in peaceful political activities; provision without delay through appropriate channels of a list of all places in which such persons are being detained; the immediate organization of access to such locations; and the provision through appropriate channels of prompt responses to all written requests for information, access or release regarding such persons;

- Ensuring freedom of movement throughout the country for journalists and a non-discriminatory visa policy for them;

- Respecting freedom of association and the right to demonstrate peacefully as legally guaranteed.

- In all circumstances, all parties must show full respect for UNSMIS' safety and security and fully cooperate with and facilitate the Mission in all respects.

- In all circumstances, the Government must allow immediate and full humanitarian access to humanitarian organizations to all areas affected by the fighting. The Government and all parties must enable the evacuation of the wounded, and all civilians who wish to leave to do so. All parties must fully adhere to their obligations under international law, including in relation to the protection of civilians.

AGREED PRINCIPLES AND GUIDE-LINES FOR A SYRIAN-LED TRANSITION

6. Action Group members agreed on the following 'Principles and Guide-lines on a Syrian-led transition':

Any political settlement must deliver to the people of Syria a transition that:

- Offers a perspective for the future that can be shared by all in Syria;

- Establishes clear steps according to a firm time-table towards the realization of that perspective;

- Can be implemented in a climate of safety for all, stability and calm;

- Is reached rapidly without further bloodshed and violence and is credible.

PERSPECTIVE FOR THE FUTURE

The aspirations of the people of Syria have been clearly expressed by the wide range of Syrians consulted. There is an overwhelming wish for a state that:

- Is genuinely democratic and pluralistic, giving space to established and newly emerging political actors to compete fairly and equally in elections. This also means that the commitment to multi-party democracy must be a lasting one, going beyond an initial round of elections.

- Complies with international standards on human rights, the independence of the judiciary, accountability of those in government and the rule of law. It is not enough just to enunciate such a commitment. There must be mechanisms available to the people to ensure that these commitments are kept by those in authority.

- Offers equal opportunities and chances for all. There is no room for sectarianism or discrimination on ethnic, religious, linguistic or any other grounds. Numerically smaller communities must be assured that their rights will be respected.

CLEAR STEPS IN THE TRANSITION

The conflict in Syria will only end when all sides are assured that there is a peaceful way towards a common future for all in Syria. It is therefore essential that any settlement provides for clear and irreversible steps in the transition according to a fixed time frame. The key steps in any transition include:

- The establishment of a transitional governing body which can establish a neutral environment in which the transition can take place. That means that the transitional governing body would exercise full executive powers. It could include members of the present government and the opposition and other groups and shall be formed on the basis of mutual consent.

- It is for the Syrian people to determine the future of the country. All groups and segments of society in Syria must be enabled to participate in a National Dialogue process. That process must not only be inclusive, it must also be meaningful—that is to say, its key outcomes must be implemented.

- On this basis, there can be a review of the constitutional order and the legal system. The result of constitutional drafting would be subject to popular approval.

- Once the new constitutional order is established, it is necessary to prepare for and conduct free and fair multi-party elections for the new institutions and offices that have been established.

- Women must be fully represented in all aspects of the transition.

SAFETY, STABILITY AND CALM

Any transition involves change. However, it is essential to ensure that the transition can be implemented in a way that assures the safety of all in an atmosphere of stability and calm. This requires:

- Consolidation of full calm and stability. All parties must cooperate with the transitional governing body in ensuring the permanent cessation of violence. This includes completion of withdrawals and addressing the issue of the disarming, demobilization and reintegration of armed groups.

- Effective steps to ensure that vulnerable groups are protected and immediate action is taken to address humanitarian issues in areas of need. It is also necessary to ensure that the release of the detained is completed rapidly.

- Continuity of governmental institutions and qualified staff. The public services must be preserved or restored. This includes the military forces and security services. However, all governmental institutions, including the intelligence services, have to perform according to human rights and professional standards and operate under a top leadership that inspires public confidence, under the control of the transitional governing body.

- Commitment to Accountability and National Reconciliation. Accountability for acts committed during the present conflict must be addressed. There also needs to be a comprehensive package for transitional justice, including compensation or rehabilitation for victims of the present conflict, steps towards national reconciliation and forgiveness.

RAPID STEPS TO COME TO A CREDIBLE POLITICAL AGREEMENT

It is for the people of Syria to come to a political agreement, but time is running out. It is clear that:

- The sovereignty, independence, unity and territorial integrity of Syria must be respected.

- The conflict must be resolved through peaceful dialogue and negotiation alone. Conditions conducive to a political settlement must now be put in place.

- There must be an end to bloodshed. All parties must re-commit themselves credibly to the six-point plan. This must include a cessation of armed violence in all its forms and immediate, credible and visible actions to implement items 2-6 of the six-point plan.

- All parties must now engage genuinely with the Joint Special Envoy. The parties must be prepared to put forward effective interlocutors to work expeditiously towards a Syrian-led settlement that meets the legitimate aspirations of the people. The process must be fully inclusive to ensure that the views of all segments of Syrian society are heard in shaping the political settlement for the transition. The organized international community, including the members of the Action Group stands ready to offer significant support for the implementation of an agreement reached by the parties. This may include an international assistance presence under a United Nations Mandate if requested. Significant funds will be available to support reconstruction and rehabilitation.

AGREED ACTIONS GROUP MEMBERS WILL TAKE TO IMPLEMENT THE ABOVE IN SUPPORT OF THE JOINT SPECIAL ENVOY'S EFFORTS TO FACILITATE A SYRIAN-LED POLITICAL PROCESS

7. Action Group members will engage as appropriate, and apply joint and sustained pressure on, the parties in Syria to take the steps and measures outlined in paragraph 5.

8. Action Group members are opposed to any further militarization of the conflict.

9. Action Group members underscore to the Government of Syria the importance of the appointment of an effective

empowered interlocutor, when requested by the Joint Special Envoy to do so, to work on the basis of the six-point plan and this communiqué.

10. Action Group members urge the opposition to increase cohesion and be in a position to ensure effective representative interlocutors to work on the basis of the six-point plan and this communiqué.

11. Action Group members will give full support to the Joint Special Envoy and his team as they immediately engage the Government and opposition, and consult widely with Syrian society, as well as other international actors, to further develop the way forward.

12. Action Group members would welcome the Joint Special Envoy's further convening of a meeting of the Action Group should he deem it necessary to review the concrete progress taken on all points agreed in this communiqué, and to determine what further and additional steps and actions are needed from the Action Group to address the crisis. The Joint Special Envoy will also keep the United Nations and the League of Arab States informed.

UN SPECIAL ENVOY'S PAPER ON POINTS OF COMMONALITIES

March 2016

1. Respect for the sovereignty, independence, unity and territorial integrity of Syria. No part of the national territory shall be ceded. As an integral part of the Arab nation, Syria is committed to a peaceful and active role in the international community. As a founding member, Syria is dedicated to the UN Charter and its purposes and principles. The people of Syria remain committed to the restoration of the occupied Golan Heights by peaceful means.

2. The principles of sovereign equality and non-intervention shall apply, in conformity with the UN Charter. The Syrian people alone shall determine the future of their country by democratic means, through the ballot box, and have the exclusive right to choose their own political, economic and social system without external pressure or interference.

3. Syria shall be a democratic, non-sectarian state based on citizenship and political pluralism, the representation of all components of Syrian society, the rule of law, the independence of the judiciary, equal rights, non-discrimination, human rights and fundamental freedoms, transparency, accountability and the principles of national reconciliation and social peace.

4. Syria cherishes its history of diversity and the contributions and values of all religions, traditions and national identities to Syrian society. Acts of revenge against individuals or groups shall not be tolerated. There shall be no discrimination against, and full protection of, all national, ethnic, religious, linguistic and cultural identities. Members of all communities, men and women, shall enjoy equal opportunities in social, economic, cultural and public life.

5. Women shall enjoy equality of rights and representation in all institutions and decision-making structures at a level of at least 30 per cent during the transition and thereafter.

6. As per Security Council resolution 2254 (2015), the political transition in Syria shall include mechanisms for credible, inclusive and non-sectarian governance, a schedule and process for drafting a new constitution and free and fair elections pursuant to the new constitution, administered under supervision by the United Nations, to the satisfaction of the governance and to the highest international standards of transparency and accountability, with all Syrians, including members of the diaspora, eligible to participate.

7. Such governance shall ensure an environment of stability and calm during the transition, offering safety and equal chances to political actors to establish themselves and campaign in the forthcoming elections and participate in public life.

8. Continuity and reform of state institutions and public services, along with measures to protect the public infrastructure and private property, shall ensure stability in accordance with international standards, principles of good governance and human rights. The governance will take effective measures to combat corruption. Citizens will benefit from effective mechanisms of protection in the relations with all public authorities, ensuring full compliance with human rights.

9. Syria categorically rejects terrorism and strongly opposes terrorist organizations and individuals identified by the UN Security Council and will engage in a national endeavor, in international partnership, to defeat terrorism and to address the causes of terrorism. Syria calls on all states in accordance with the relevant UNSC resolutions, to prevent terrorist groups from being supplied with weapons, money, training, shelter, intelligence or safe havens and to refrain from inciting acts of terrorism.

10. Syrians are committed to rebuilding a strong and unified national army, also through the disarmament and integration of members of armed groups supporting the transition and the new constitution. That professional army shall protect the borders and population of the State from external threats in accordance with the principle of the rule of law. The state and its reformed institutions will exercise the exclusive right of controlling weapons of war. There shall be no intervention by foreign fighters on Syrian soil.

11. All refugees and internally displaced people wishing it shall be enabled to return safely to their homes with national and international support and in line with international protections standards. Those arbitrarily detained shall be released and the fate of the disappeared, kidnapped or missing shall be resolved.

12. There shall be reparations, redress, care, and restitution of rights and property lost for those who have suffered loss or injury in consequence of the conflict. As peace and stability are being restored, Syria shall call for the holding of a major donor conference to gain funds for compensation, reconstruction and development of the country, and the lifting of all coercive economic measures and other unilateral actions affecting the people of Syria. Syria looks forward to international guarantees and support for the implementation of the political process in a way that does not infringe upon the sovereignty of Syria.

BIBLIOGRAPHY

Aleppo Project, The. Timeline. Accessed from
    http://www.thealeppoproject.com/conflict-timeline/.

Anderson, Scott. *Lawrence in Arabia: War, Deceit, Imperial
    Folly and the Making of the Modern Middle East.* New York:
    Doubleday, 2013.

Barr, James. *A Line in the Sand: The Anglo-French Struggle for the
    Middle East, 1914-1948.*

New York: W. W. Norton & Company, 2012.

Barr, James. Setting the Desert on Fire: *T.E. Lawrence and Britain's
    Secret War in Arabia, 1916-1918.* New York: W.W. Norton &
    Company, 2008.

Boot, Max. Invisible Armies: *An Epic History of Guerrilla Warfare
    from Ancient Times to the Present.* New York: Liverlight
    Publishing Corporation, 2013.

Bregman, Ahron. *A History of Israel.* New York: Palgrave
    Macmillan, 2003.

Bruno, Greg. "Inside the Kurdistan Workers Party (PKK)." Council
    on Foreign Relations, October 19, 2007. Accessed from
    http://www.cfr.org/turkey/inside-kurdistan-workers-par-
    ty-pkk/p14576.

Bush, George W. *Decision Points.* New York: Crown
    Publishers, 2010.

Byman, Daniel. *Al Qaeda, The Islamic State, and the Global Jihadist Movement: What Everyone Needs to Know*. New York: Oxford University Press, 2015.

Cambanis, Thanassis. *A Privilege to Die: Inside Hezbollah's Legions and Their Endless War Against Israel*. New York: Free Press, 2010.

"Chapter VII." *United Nations*. Accessed from http://www.un.org/en/sections/un-charter/chapter-vii/.

Clinton, Bill. *My Life*. New York: Alfred A. Knopf, 2004.

Cohen, Martin and Andrew McKillop. *The Doomsday Machine: The High Price of Nuclear Energy, the World's Most Dangerous Fuel*. New York: Palgrave Macmillan, 2012.

Collelo, Thomas. *Syria: A Country Study*. Washington: GPO for the Library of Congress, 1987.

Dayan, Moshe. *Moshe Dayan: Story of My Life: An Autobiography*. New York: William Morrow and Company, Inc., 1976.

Dowty, Alan. *Israel/Palestine*. Cambridge: Polity Press, 2008.

Eisenhower Diaries, The, Edited by Robert H. Ferrell. New York: W.W. Norton & Company, 1981.

Erlich, Reese. *Inside Syria: The Backstory of Their Civil War and What the World Can Expect*. New York: Prometheus Books, 2014.

Gates, Robert M. *Duty: Memoirs of a Secretary at War*. New York: Alfred A. Knopf, 2014.

Gates, Robert M. From the Shadows: *The Ultimate Insider's Story of Five Presidents and How They Won the Cold War*. New York: Simon & Schuster, 1996.

General Atomics Aeronautical. Predator C Avenger RPA. Products and Services, Aircraft Platforms. http://www.ga-asi.com/predator-c-avenger.

Gilbert, Martin. *Israel: A History*. New York: Harper Perennial, 1998.

Gordis, Daniel. *Israel: A Concise History of a Nation Reborn*. New York: HarperCollins, 2016.

Haddad, Bassam. "Enduring Legacies: The Politics of Private Sector Development in Syria." In Demystifying Syria, edited by Fred Lawson, 29-55. London: The Middle East Institute, 2009.

Hitchcock, William I. *The Age of Eisenhower: American and the World in the 1950s*. New York: Simon & Schuster, 2018.

Hook, Steven W and John Spanier. *American Foreign Policy Since World War II, Eighteenth Edition*. CQ Press. Washington, DC, 2010.

Hussein I. *Uneasy Lies the Head: The Autobiography of His Majesty King Hussein I of the Hashemite Kingdom of Jordan*. New York: Bernard Geis Associates, 1962.

Hussein, King. *My "War" With Israel*. New York: Morrow, 1968.

Lacey, Robert. *Inside the Kingdom: Kings, Clerics, Modernists, Terrorists, and the Struggle for Saudi Arabia*. New York: Viking, 2009.

Ladis, Joshua and Joe Pace. "The Syrian Opposition: The Struggle for Unity and Relevance, 2003-2008." In Demystifying Syria, edited by Fred Lawson, 120-143. London: The Middle East Institute, 2009.

Lawrence, T.E. *Seven Pillars of Wisdom: A Triumph*. New York: Dell Publishing Co., Inc., 1962.

Lesch, David W. *Syria: The Fall of the House of Assad*. New Haven: Yale University Press, 2012.

Lewis, Bernard. *The Crisis of Islam: Holy War and Unholy Terror*. New York: Random House, 2004.

Lewis, Bernard. *The Middle East: A Brief History of the Last 2,000 Years*. New York: Scribner, 1995.

McHugo, John. *Syria: A History of the Last Hundred Years*. New York: The New Press, 2014.

Michaels, Walter B. and June P. Wilson, trans. *Hussein of Jordan: My "War" With Israel*, as Told to and With Additional Material by Vick Vance and Pierre Lauer.

New York: William Morrow and Company, Inc., 1969.

Morgan, Patrick M. *International Security: Problems and Solutions.* Washington, D.C.: CQ Press, 2006.

Morris, Benny. Righteous *Victims: A History of the Zionist-Arab Conflict*, 1881-1999. New York: Alfred A. Knopf, 1999.

Mueller Report, The. The Final Report of the Special Counsel into Donald Trump, Russia, and Collusion, as Issued by the Department of Justice. New York: Skyhorse Publishing, 2019.

Oren, Michael B. *Six Days of War: June 1967 & the Making of the Modern Middle East.* New York: Presidio Press, 2002.

Owen, Roger. *The Rise and Fall of Arab Presidents for Life.* New York: Harvard University Press, 2012.

Panetta, Leon with Jim Newton. *Worthy Fights.* New York: Penguin Press, 2014.

Peres, Shimon. *No Room for Small Dreams: Courage, Imagination, and the Making of Modern Israel.* New York: HarperCollins, 2017.

"President Nixon and the Role of Intelligence in the 1973 Arab-Israeli War." Yorba Linda, CA: Richard Nixon Presidential Library and Museum, 2013.

"Pre-State Israel: The Hussein-McMahon Correspondence." Jewish Virtual Library. Accessed from http://www.jewishvirtuallibrary.org/ the-hussein-mcmahon-correspondence-july-1915-august-1916.

Program Acquisition Cost by Weapon System, United States Department of Defense Fiscal Year 2016 Budget Request. Undersecretary of Defense (Comptroller). Accessed from http://comptroller.defense.gov/Budget-Materials/Budget2016/.

Reich, Bernard. *A Brief History of Israel*. Washington, DC: George Washington University, 2008.

Rogan Eugene. *The Arabs: A History*. New York: Basic Books, 2009.

Rogan, Eugene. *The Fall of the Ottomans: The Great War in the Middle East*. New York: Basic Books, 2015.

Sahner, Christian C. *Among the Ruins: Syria Past and Present*. New York: Oxford University Press, 2014.

"Security Council Requires Scheduled Destruction of Syria's Chemical Weapons, Unanimously Adopting Resolution 2118 (2013). *United Nations*. September 27, 2013. http://www.un.org/press/en/2013/sc11135.doc.htm.

Sekulow, Jay with Jordan Sekulow, Robert W. Ash, and David French. Rise of ISIS: A Threat We Can't Ignore (New York: Howard Books, 2014).

Sykes-Picot Agreement, The: 1916. Yale Law School, The Avalon Project. Accessed from http://avalon.law.yale.edu/20th_century/sykes.asp.

Syria: Dozens of Government Attacks in Aleppo. Human Rights Watch. December 21, 2013. Accessed from https://www.hrw.org/news/2013/12/21/syria-dozens-govern-ment-attacks-aleppo.

Syrian Refugees, Home. Accessed from http://syrianrefugees.eu/.

Tabler, Andrew. *In the Lion's Den: An Eyewitness Account of Washington's Battle with Syria*. Chicago: Lawrence Hill Books, 2011.

Tessler, Mark, ed. *A History of the Israeli-Palestinian Conflict, 2nd ed.* Indianapolis: Indiana University Press, 2009.

Thucydides. *History of the Peloponnesian War*. Translated by Rex Warner. New York: Penguin Books, 1972.

Truman, Harry S. *Memoirs, Volume 2: Years of Trial and Hope*. Garden City: Doubleday & Company, Inc., 1956.

Ulrichsen, Kristian Coates. *The First World War in the Middle East.* London: Hurst & Company, 2014.

Warrick, Joby. *Black Flags: The Rise of ISIS.* New York: Doubleday, 2015.

West, Nigel. *The Friends: Britain's Post-War Secret Intelligence Operations.* London:

Weidenfeld and Nicolson, 1988.

Wieland, Carsten. *Syria, A Decade of Lost Chances: Repression and Revolution from Damascus Spring to Arab Spring.* Seattle: Cune Press, 2012.

World War I Document Archive, The. Conventions and Treaties, Peace Treaty of Sevres Section 1, Articles 1-260. Accessed from https://wwi.lib.byu.edu/index.php/Section_I,_Articles_1_-_260.

Zorob, Anja. "Partnership with the European Union: Hopes, Risks and Challenges for the Syrian Economy." In Demystifying Syria, edited by Fred Lawson, 144-158. London: The Middle East Institute, 2009.

Zuckoff, Mitchell with the Annex Security Team. *13 Hours: The Inside Account of What Really Happened in Benghazi.* New York: Twelve, 2014.

INDEX

NOTES

1   Hussein I, Uneasy Lies the Head: The Autobiography of His Majesty King Hussein I of the Hashemite Kingdom of Jordan (New York: Bernard Geis Associates, 1962), 84.

2   "Operation Inherent Resolve: Report to the United States Congress, January 1, 2017—March 31, 2017," Lead Inspector General for Overseas Contingency Operations, page 4, accessed March 25, 2017 from https://oig.state.gov/system/files/lig_oco_oir_mar2017_0.pdf.

3   "Syria: 560,000 Killed in Seven Years of War, SOHR," Syrian Observatory for Human Rights, December 12, 2018, accessed January 14, 2019 from http://www.syriahr.com/en/?p=108829.

4   "Syria Emergency," UNHCR, accessed January 14, 2019 from https://www.unhcr.org/syria-emergency.html.

5   "In the 50th Month of its Operations in Syria, International Coalition Killed About 200 Civilians, the Highest Death Toll in 17 Months," Syrian Observatory for Human Rights, November 23, 2018, accessed January 15, 2019 from http://www.syriahr.com/en/?p=107264.

6   "Pre-State Israel: The Hussein-McMahon Correspondence," Jewish Virtual Library, accessed May 20, 2017 from http://www.jewishvirtualli-brary.org/the-hussein-mcmahon-correspondence-july-1915-august-1916.

7   Anderson, Lawrence in Arabia, 142.

8   Bernard Lewis, The Middle East: A Brief History of the Last 2,000 Years (New York: Scribner, 1995), 23.

9   "Pre-State Israel," Jewish Virtual Library.

10   Lawrence, *Seven Pillars, 93.*

11   Lawrence, *Seven Pillars, 104*

12   Lawrence, *Seven Pillars, 656.*

13   "The Sykes-Picot Agreement: 1916," Yale Law School, The Avalon Project, accessed April 2, 2017 from http://avalon.law.yale.edu/20th_century/sykes.asp.

14   Lawrence, *Seven Pillars, 58.*

15   Lawrence, *Seven Pillars, 555.*

16   Lawrence, *Seven Pillars, 276.*

17   Lawrence, *Seven Pillars, 555.*

18   Lawrence, *Seven Pillars, 276.*

19   Lawrence, *Seven Pillars, 275-76.*

20   Lawrence, *Seven Pillars, 132.*

21   "Anglo French Declaration," Balfour Project, July 1, 2013, accessed July 31, 2018 from http://www.balfourproject.org/anglo-french-declaration/.

22   Kristian Coates Ulrichsen, *The First World War in the Middle East (London, Hurst & Company, 2014), 117.*

23   "President Woodrow Wilson's Fourteen Points," Yale Law School, The Avalon Project, accessed April 8, 2017 from http://avalon.law.yale.edu/20th_century/wilson14.asp.

24   "The King-Crane Report," World War I Document Archive, accessed April 2, 2017 from https://wwi.lib.byu.edu/index.php/The_King-Crane_Report.

25   "San Remo Resolution-Palestine Mandate 1920," MidEast Web, accessed May 1, 2017 from http://www.mideastweb.org/san_remo_palestine_1920.htm.

26   James Barr, *A Line in the Sand: The Anglo-French Struggle for the Middle East, 1914-1948 (New York: W.W. Norton & Company, 2012), 92.*

27 The World War I Document Archive, https://wwi.lib.byu.edu/index.php/ Section_I,_Articles_1_-_260.

28 Thomas Collelo, *Syria: A Country Study (Washington, GPO for the Library of Congress, 1987),* 24.

29 CIA World Factbook

30 David W. Lesch, *Syria: The Fall of the House of Assad (New Haven: Yale University Press, 2012),* 125.

31 Lewis, *The Middle East, 371-72.*

32 "Pact of the League of Arab States, March 22, 1945," Yale Law School, the Avalon Project, accessed April 9, 2017 from http://avalon.law.yale. edu/20th_century/arableag.asp.

33 "Pact of the League of Arab States, March 22, 1945," Yale Law School, The Avalon Project, accessed July 16, 2018 from http://avalon.law.yale. edu/20th_century/arableag.asp.

34 Theodor Herzl, The Jewish State (New York: Dover Publications, Inc.), 95, accessed June 27, 2018 from https://www.gutenberg.org/ files/25282/25282-h/25282-h.htm.

35 Alan Dowty, *Israel/Palestine (Cambridge, Polity Press, 2008),* 13.

36 Bernard Reich, *A Brief History of Israel, 2nd Ed., (Washington, DC: George Washington University, 2008),* 19.

37 "The Palestine Mandate, The Avalon Project, Yale Law School Library, accessed June 27, 2018 from http://avalon.law.yale.edu/20th_century/pal-manda.asp.

38 Mark Tessler, ed., *A History of the Israeli-Palestinian Conflict, 2nd ed. (Indianapolis: Indiana University Press, 2009),* 118.

39 Benny Morris, *Righteous Victims: A History of the Zionist-Arab Conflict, 1881-1999 (New York: Alfred A. Knopf, 1999),* 121.

40 Morris, *Righteous Victims, 147.*

41 Peel Commission Report, Jewish Virtual Library, accessed November 24, 2018 from https://www.jewishvirtuallibrary.org/ text-of-the-peel-commission-report.

42   Peel Commission Report, Jewish Virtual Library, accessed
      November 24, 2018 from https://www.jewishvirtuallibrary.org/
      text-of-the-peel-commission-report.

43   Peel Commission Report, Jewish Virtual Library, accessed
      November 24, 2018 from https://www.jewishvirtuallibrary.org/
      text-of-the-peel-commission-report.

44   Palestine Partition Commission Report (London: October
      1938, 18), accessed July 4, 2018 from https://archive.org/details/
      WoodheadCommission.

45   Palestine Partition Commission Report, 18.

46   Palestine Partition Commission Report, 19.

47   Palestine Partition Commission Report, 23.

48   Alan Macfarlane, "Some Reasons Why an Industrial Revolution Did Not
      Occur in the Ottoman Empire," University of Cambridge, Video File,
      August 6, 2004, accessed December 30, 2018 from https://www.repository.
      cam.ac.uk/handle/1810/598.

49   British White Papers: White Paper of 1939, Jewish Virtual Library,
      accessed July 11, 2018 from https://www.jewishvirtuallibrary.org/
      british-white-paper-of-1939.

50   "Zionist Congresses: The Biltmore Conference (May 6-11, 1942), Jewish
      Virtual Library, accessed October 7, 2018 from https://www.jewishvirtu-
      allibrary.org/the-biltmore-conference-1942.

51   "Zionist Congresses: The Biltmore Conference (May 6-11, 1942), Jewish
      Virtual Library, accessed October 7, 2018 from https://www.jewishvirtu-
      allibrary.org/the-biltmore-conference-1942.

52   Nigel West, The Friends: Britain's Post-War Secret Intelligence
      Operations (London, Weidenfeld and Nicolson, 1988), 37-8, accessed
      from CIA Library on August 30, 2018 from https://www.cia.gov/library/
      readingroom/docs/CIA-RDP96B01172R000100060001-5.pdf.

53   Harry S. Truman, *Memoirs, Vol. 2: Years of Trial and Hope (Garden City:
      Doubleday & Company, Inc., 1956), 153.*

54   Truman, *Memoirs, 160.*

55 Truman, *Memoirs, 162.*

56 Truman, *Memoirs, 164.*

57 Truman, *Memoirs, 133.*

58 "The Consequences of the Partition of Palestine," CIA Library, November 28, 1947, accessed June 27, 2018 from https://www.cia.gov/library/readingroom/docs/CIA-RDP78-01617A003000180001-8.pdf, page 8.

59 "The Consequences of the Partition of Palestine," CIA Library, November 28, 1947, accessed June 27, 2018 from https://www.cia.gov/library/readingroom/docs/CIA-RDP78-01617A003000180001-8.pdf, page 9.

60 "Cabinet Meeting 61," September 1948, accessed July 15, 2018 from http://filestore.nationalarchives.gov.uk/pdfs/small/cab-128-13-cm-48-61-21.pdf.

61 Truman, *Memoirs, 169.*

62 Martin Gilbert, *Israel: A History (New York: Harper Perennial, 1998), 231.*

63 Gilbert, *Israel, 231.*

64 Ahron Bregman, *A History of Israel (New York: Palgrave Macmillan, 2003), 60.*

65 "The Arab-Israeli Wars: Five Major Wars Define the Ongoing Arab-Israeli Conflict," Al Jazeera, December 9, 2003, accessed March 4, 2019 from https://www.aljazeera.com/archive/2003/12/2008410115114656999.html#1948.

66 "Near East/Africa Branch Intelligence Summary, for Week Ending 18 August 1948," CIA Library, accessed November 25, 2017 from https://www.cia.gov/library/readingroom/docs/CIA-RDP78-01617A004700010016-2.pdf.

67 "Near East/Africa Branch Intelligence Summary, for Week Ending 1 September 1948," CIA Library, accessed November 25, 2017 from https://www.cia.gov/library/readingroom/docs/CIA-RDP78-01617A004700010018-0.pdf.

68 Lewis, *The Middle East, 372.*

69   "Syria Without Assad: Succession Politics," CIA Library, November 7, 1978, accessed December 10, 2017 from https://www.cia.gov/library/readingroom/docs/CIA-RDP80T00634A000400010052-5.pdf.

70   "General CIA Record," CIA Library, March 29, 1949, accessed January 6, 2018 from https://www.cia.gov/library/readingroom/docs/CIA-RDP78-01617A006000020077-6.pdf.

71   "Intelligence Summary, Vol. 4, No. 15," CIA Library, April, 20 1949, accessed January 6, 2019 from https://www.cia.gov/library/readingroom/docs/CIA-RDP78-01617A004700010049-6.pdf.

72   "Miles Copeland on the Failed CIA Instituted Syrian Coup D'état 1969," YouTube, October 5, 2014, accessed September 2, 2018 from https://www.youtube.com/watch?v=JRa11vtonWw.

73   Yost, Charles. "Interview with Charles Yost." Interview by Dr. Thomas Soapes. Dwight D. Eisenhower Library, September 13, 1978.

74   "Syria's Rulers and Their Political Environment," CIA Library, December 7, 1973, accessed January 2, 2019 from https://www.cia.gov/library/readingroom/docs/CIA-RDP80T01002A000200040027-2.pdf.

75   "Communist Economic and Military Aid to Syria," CIA Library, July 1972, accessed January 6, 2019 from https://www.cia.gov/library/readingroom/docs/CIA-RDP85T00875R001700030111-4.pdf.

76   "Arab Threats Against US Interests: More Bark Thank Bite," CIA Library, October 18, 1972, accessed January 6, 2019 from https://www.cia.gov/library/readingroom/docs/CIA-RDP85T00875R001100130104-7.pdf.

77   Robert H. S. Eakens, "Oral History Interview with Robert H. S. Eakens, " Interview by Richard D. McKinzie, Truman Library, June 13, 1974, accessed January 3, 2018 from https://www.trumanlibrary.org/oralhist/eakens.htm.

78   "Communist Propaganda About Tapline," CIA Library, January 8, 1948, accessed from January 6, 2019 from https://www.cia.gov/library/readingroom/docs/CIA-RDP82-00457R001200400005-3.pdf.

79   NSC Briefing, "Tapline," CIA Library, July 31, 1960, accessed January 5, 2018 from https://www.cia.gov/library/readingroom/docs/CIA-RDP79R00890A001200080002-4.pdf.

80   NSC Briefing, "Tapline," CIA Library, 19 October 1959, accessed January 5, 2019 from https://www.cia.gov/library/readingroom/docs/CIA-RDP79R00890A001100100007-7.pdf.

81   "Mossadeq Plans to Announce End of Oil Negotiations," CIA Library, February 17, 1953, accessed March 4, 2019 from https://www.cia.gov/library/readingroom/docs/CIA-RDP91T01172R000200290007-3.pdf.

82   "Current Intelligence Bulletin," CIA Library, November 15, 1956, accessed January 21, 2019 from https://www.cia.gov/library/readingroom/docs/CIA-RDP79T00975A002800230001-5.pdf.

83   "Central Intelligence Bulletin," CIA Library, May 15, 1971, accessed January 5, 2019 from https://www.cia.gov/library/readingroom/docs/CIA-RDP79T00975A019000080003-0.pdf.

84   Moshe Dayan, *Moshe Dayan: Story of My Life: An Autobiography (New York: William Morrow and Company, Inc., 1976),* 402.

85   Walter B. Michaels and June P. Wilson, trans., *Hussein of Jordan: My "War" With Israel, as Told to and With Additional Material by Vick Vance and Pierre Lauer (New York: William Morrow and Company, Inc., 1969),* 32.

86   Bregman, *History of Israel,* 106.

87   *The Eisenhower Diaries, ed. Robert H. Ferrell (New York: W.W. Norton & Company, 1981),* 319.

88   William I. Hitchcock, *The Age of Eisenhower: American and the World in the 1950s (New York: Simon & Schuster, 2018),* 326.

89   "The Eisenhower Doctrine, 1957," US State Department, Office of the Historian, accessed August 28, 2018 from https://history.state.gov/milestones/1953-1960/eisenhower-doctrine.

90   Dayan, *Moshe Dayan,* 289.

91   Adi Cohen, "Netanyahu Says Plan for New Golan Community Named After Trump Under Way," Haaretz, May 13, 2019, accessed May 13, 2019 from https://www.haaretz.com/israel-news/.premium-netanyahu-says-plan-for-new-golan-community-named-after-trump-under-way-1.7225713.

92   Clinton, *My Life,* 575.

93   Lewis, *Crisis, 95-6.*

94   "Resolution 242 (1967)," UN Docs, accessed August 28, 2018, from https://undocs.org/S/RES/242(1967).

95   Michael B Oren, Six Days of War: June 1967 & the Making of the Modern Middle East (New York: Presidio Press, 2002), 325.

96   National Intelligence Estimate, No. 35-68, CIA Library, April 11, 1968, Page 7, accessed June 26, 2018 from https://www.cia.gov/library/reading-room/docs/DOC_0001518686.pdf.

97   Lewis, *The Middle East, 348-49.*

98   Christian C. Sahner, *Among the Ruins: Syria Past and Present (New York: Oxford University Press, 2014), 61.*

99   John McHugo, *Syria: A History of the Last Hundred Years (New York: The New Press, 2014), 188-89.*

100   Reese Erlich, *Inside Syria: The Backstory of Their Civil War and What the World Can Expect (New York: Prometheus Books, 2014), 69.*

101   Hussein of Jordan, My "War" With Israel (New York: Morrow, 1968), 22.

102   McHugo, *Syria, 181.*

103   "Michel Kilo: Freed Dissident Analyzes US-Syrian Future," Wikileaks, accessed March 22, 2018 from https://wikileaks.org/plusd/cables/09DA-MASCUS747_a.html.

104   "President Nixon and the Role of Intelligence in the 1973 Arab-Israeli War," (Yorba Linda, CA: Richard Nixon Presidential Library and Museum, 2013), 43.

105   "Military Expenditure (% of GDP)," The World Bank, accessed September 3, 2018 from https://data.worldbank.org/indicator/MS.MIL.XPND.GD.ZS?end=2007&locations=SY&name_desc=true&start=1960&view=chart.

106   Owen, *Arab Presidents, 80.*

107   Erlich, *Inside Syria, 73.*

108   Zorob, *Demystifying Syria, 145.*

109   Zorob, *Demystifying Syria, 146.*

110   Joshua Hammer, "Is a Lack of Water to Blame for the Conflict
       in Syria?" Smithsonian Magazine, June 2013, accessed June
       3, 2017 from http://www.smithsonianmag.com/innovation/
       is-a-lack-of-water-to-blame-for-the-conflict-in-syria-72513729/.

111   "Background Note: Syria," U.S. Department of State, accessed June 3,
       2017 from https://web.archive.org/web/20110817013711/http://www.
       state.gov/r/pa/ei/bgn/3580.htm.

112   "Public Information Notice: IMF Executive Board Concludes 2006
       Article IV Consultation With the Syrian Arab Republic," International
       Monetary Fund, News, August 7, 2006, accessed June 4, 2017 from http://
       www.imf.org/en/news/articles/2015/09/28/04/53/pn0689.

113   "Syrian Arab Republic - - 2008 Article IV Consultation, Concluding
       Statement, International Monetary Fund, News, November 26,
       2008, accessed June 4, 2017 from http://www.imf.org/en/news/
       articles/2015/09/28/04/52/mcs102908.

114   "Public Information Notice: IMF Executive Board Concludes 2005
       Article IV Consultation with the Syrian Arab Republic, International
       Monetary Fund, News, October 3, 2005, accessed June 4, 2017 from
       http://www.imf.org/en/news/articles/2015/09/28/04/53/pn05138.

115   "Public Information Notice: IMF Executive Board Concludes 2008
       Article IV Consultation with the Syrian Arab Republic, International
       Monetary Fund, News, January 26, 2009, accessed June 4, 2017 from
       http://www.imf.org/en/news/articles/2015/09/28/04/53/pn0907.

116   "President Nixon and the Role of Intelligence in the 1973 Arab-Israeli
       War," 17.

117   "President Nixon and the Role of Intelligence in the 1973 Arab-Israeli
       War," 17.

118   Dayan, *Moshe Dayan, 481.*

119   Dayan, *Moshe Dayan, 485.*

120   "Telecon, Lord Cromer and Kissinger, 4:25 p.m. October 6, 1973, Richard
       Nixon Presidential Library and Museum, Virtual Library, accessed on

November 12, 2017 from https://www.nixonlibrary.gov/virtuallibrary/releases/jan17/telcon-4-25pm.pdf.

121 "Telecon, Ambassador Cromer and Kissinger, 9:38 p.m. October 6, 1973, Richard Nixon Presidential Library and Museum, Virtual Library, accessed on November 12, 2017 from https://www.nixonlibrary.gov/virtuallibrary/releases/jan17/telcon-9-38pm.pdf.

122 "Telecon, Lord Cromer and Kissinger, 4:25 p.m. October 6, 1973, Richard Nixon Presidential Library and Museum, Virtual Library, accessed on November 12, 2017 from https://www.nixonlibrary.gov/virtuallibrary/releases/jan17/telcon-4-25pm.pdf.

123 Dayan, *Moshe Dayan, 501.*

124 Dayan, *Moshe Dayan, 517.*

125 Dayan, *Moshe Dayan, 510.*

126 Dayan, *Moshe Dayan, 506.*

127 Dayan, *Moshe Dayan, 513.*

128 Dayan, *Moshe Dayan, 511.*

129 Dayan, *Moshe Dayan, 578.*

130 "Security Council Declares Support for Free, Fair Presidential Election in Lebanon; Calls for Withdrawal of Foreign Forces There," UN, Meetings Coverage and Press Releases, September 2, 2004, accessed July 5, 2017 from https://www.un.org/press/en/2004/sc8181.doc.htm.

131 "Profile: Iran's Revolutionary Guards," BBC, October 19, 2009, accessed May 14, 2017 from http://news.bbc.co.uk/2/hi/middle_east/7064353.stm.

132 Lesch, *Syria, 4.*

133 Bush, *Decision Points, 414.*

134 Derk Roelofsma, "Syria's Assad Uses Terror Groups to Stay as Mideast Power Broker," Washington Times, September 25, 1985, accessed May 13, 2019 from https://www.cia.gov/library/readingroom/docs/CIA-RDP90-00965R000605300045-2.pdf.

135 "Assad: Ready to Dialogue with Obama, but 'Without Conditions,'" Asia News, January 27, 2009, accessed June 11, 2017 from http://www.asianews.it/news-en/Assad:-ready-to-dialogue-with-Obama,-but-without-conditions-14326.html.

136 Carsten Wieland, *Syria, A Decade of Lost Chances: Repression and Revolution from Damascus Spring to Arab Spring (Seattle: Cune Press, 2012), 47.*

137 "Profile: Bashar al-Assad," Al Jazeera, April 17, 2018, accessed May 15, 2019 from https://www.aljazeera.com/news/middleeast/2007/07/200852518514154964.html.

138 "Syria in Crisis: The Damascus Spring," Carnegie Middle East Center, accessed May 31, 2017 from http://carnegie-mec.org/diwan/48516?lang=en.

139 Ladis and Pace, *Syrian Opposition, 121.*

140 The Damascus Declaration, Carnegie Middle East Center, March 1, 2012, accessed June 3, 2017 from http://carnegie-mec.org/diwan/48514?lang=en.

141 "Michel Kilo: Freed Dissident Analyzes US-Syrian Future," Wikileaks, accessed March 22, 2018 from https://wikileaks.org/plusd/cables/09DAMASCUS747_a.html.

142 Andrew Tabler, *In the Lion's Den: An Eyewitness Account of Washington's Battle with Syria (Chicago: Lawrence Hill Books, 2011), 145.*

143 Ladis and Pace, *Syrian Opposition, 127.*

144 "The 'Spark' That Started It All," Cornell University Library, accessed February 20, 2017 from http://guides.library.cornell.edu/c.php?g=31688&p=200750.

145 "'Day of Rage' Protest Urged in Syria," NBC News, February 3, 2011, accessed February 17, 2017 from http://www.nbcnews.com/id/41400687/ns/world_news-mideastn_africa/#.WPVrRXQ2ypp.

146 Joe Sterling, "Daraa: The Spark That Lit the Syrian Flame," CNN, March 1, 2012, accessed March 11, 2017 from http://www.cnn.com/2012/03/01/world/meast/syria-crisis-beginnings/.

147 "Death Toll Rises as Syria Crackdown Continues," Al-Jazeera, April 30, 2011, accessed March 11, 2017 from http://www.aljazeera.com/news/middleeast/2011/04/2011430174959835564.html.

148 "Scores Killed on Syria's 'Day of Rage,'" Al-Jazeera, April 29, 2011, accessed March 11, 2017 from http://www.aljazeera.com/news/middleeast/2011/04/201142993412242172.html.

149 Daniel Byman, *Al Qaeda, The Islamic State, and the Global Jihadist Movement: What Everyone Needs to Know (New York: Oxford University Press, 2015), 179.*

150 Gates, *Duty, 523.*

151 Jeffrey White, "Asad's Armed Opposition: The Free Syrian Army, The Washington Institute, November 30, 2011, accessed March 11, 2017 from http://www.washingtoninstitute.org/policy-analysis/view/asads-armed-opposition-the-free-syrian-army.

152 Erlich, *Inside Syria, 94.*

153 Erlich, *Inside Syria, 220.*

154 Ruth Sherlock, "'15,000 Strong' Army Gathers to Take on Syria," The Telegraph, November 3, 2011, accessed December 2, 2018, from https://www.telegraph.co.uk/news/worldnews/middleeast/syria/8868027/15000-strong-army-gathers-to-take-on-Syria.html.

155 "Syrian Opposition Groups Reach Unity Deal," USA Today, November 11, 2012, accessed April 17, 2017 from https://www.usatoday.com/story/news/world/2012/11/11/syrian-opposition-deal/1697693/.

156 "Riad Seif Elected Head of Leading Opposition Syrian Group," al-Arabiya English, May 6, 2017, accessed May 31, 2017 from https://english.alarabiya.net/en/News/middle-east/2017/05/06/Riad-Seif-elected-head-of-the-opposition-Syrian-National-Coalition-.html.

157 Richard Spencer, "Syria: Thousands Demand Arab League Take Action Against Bashar al-Assad,"Telegraph, December 27, 2011, accessed on December 23, 2018 from https://www.telegraph.co.uk/news/worldnews/middleeast/syria/8979580/Syria-thousands-demand-Arab-League-take-action-agasint-Bashar-al-Assad.html.

158 Nick Meo, "Geneva Meeting Agrees 'Transition Plan' to Syria Unity Government," The Telegraph, June 30, 2012, accessed on November 26, 2018 from https://www.telegraph.co.uk/news/worldnews/middleeast/syria/9367330/Geneva-meeting-agrees-transition-plan-to-Syria-unity-government.html.

159 "Security Council Unanimously Adopts Resolution 2042 (2012), Authorizing Advance Team to Monitor Ceasefire in Syria," United Nations, April 14, 2012, accessed June 4, 2017 from http://www.un.org/press/en/2012/sc10609.doc.htm.

160 "Syrian Government and Opposition Forces Responsible for War Crimes," UN News, August 15, 2012, accessed May 15, 2019 from https://news.un.org/en/story/2012/08/417632-syrian-government-and-opposition-forces-responsible-war-crimes-un-panel.

161 Luke Harding and Martin Chulov, "Syrian Rebels Fight Assad Troops in Aleppo," The Guardian, July 22, 2012, accessed April 17, 2017 from https://www.theguardian.com/world/2012/jul/22/syrian-rebels-fight-aleppo.

162 The Aleppo Project, Timeline—2012, accessed June 26, 2017 from http://www.thealeppoproject.com/aleppo-conflict-timeline-2012/.

163 The Aleppo Project, Timeline—2013, accessed June 26, 2017 from http://www.thealeppoproject.com/aleppo-conflict-timeline-2013/#_edn69.

164 "Syria: Parties Discuss Forming Kurdish Regional Government," Asharq al-Awsat, August 13, 2013, accessed June 26, 2017 from https://english.aawsat.com/theaawsat/news-middle-east/syria-parties-discuss-forming-kurdish-regional-government.

165 "Syria: Dozens of Government Attacks in Aleppo," Human Rights Watch, December 21, 2013, accessed June 26, 2017 from https://www.hrw.org/news/2013/12/21/syria-dozens-government-attacks-aleppo.

166 Joby Warrick, Black Flags: The Rise of ISIS (New York: Doubleday, 2015): 251-52.

167 Mona Mahmood and Ian Black, "Free Syrian Army Rebels Defect to Islamist Group Jabhat al-Nusra," The Guardian, May 8, 2013, accessed

April 22, 2017 from https://www.theguardian.com/world/2013/may/08/
free-syrian-army-rebels-defect-islamist-group.

168   "Syrian Nusra Front Announces Split from al-Qaeda," BBC News, July
       29, 2016, accessed April 22, 2017 from http://www.bbc.com/news/
       world-middle-east-36916606.

169   Byman, *Al Qaeda, 179.*

170   David Usborne, "Syria Crisis: America Tells the World 'We Have the
       Evidence—Now We HAVE to Punish Assad, Independent, August 30,
       2013, accessed March 12, 2017 from http://www.independent.co.uk/
       news/world/americas/syria-crisis-america-tells-the-world-we-have-the-
       evidence-now-we-have-to-punish-assad-8792337.html.

171   Leon Panetta, *Worthy Fights, 448.*

172   Mithcell Zuckoff with the Annex Security Team, *13 Hours: The Inside
       Account of What Really Happened in Benghazi (New York: Twelve, 2014), 62.*

173   Zuckoff, *13 Hours, 65.*

174   Zuckoff, *13 Hours, 36.*

175   Michael Kelly, "How US Ambassador Chris Stevens May Have Been
       Linked to Jihadist Rebels in Syria," Business Insider, October 19,
       2012, Accessed May 13, 2017 from http://www.businessinsider.com/
       us-syria-heavy-weapons-jihadists-2012-10.

176   Simon Chase and Ralph Pezzullo, Zero Footprint: The True Story of a
       Private Military Contractor's Covert Assignments in Syria, Libya, and
       the World's Most Dangerous Places (New York: Mulholland Books,
       2016), 211.

177   Chase and Pezzullo, Zero Footprint, 209.

178   "10 Days in Iraq: Aid Drops, Air Strikes and 200,000 New Refugees,"
       BBC News, August 19, 2014, accessed September 4, 2017 from http://
       www.bbc.com/news/world-middle-east-28761383.

179   "U.S. Aircraft Conducted Targeted Airstrike in Northern Iraq," DoD
       News, Defense Media Activity, August 8, 2014, accessed September
       4, 2017 from https://www.defense.gov/News/Article/Article/603032/
       us-aircraft-conduct-targeted-airstrike-in-northern-iraq/.

180 Sellström, Åke, Head of Mission, United Nations Mission to Investigate Allegations of the Use of Chemical Weapons in the Syrian Arab Republic.

181 Usborne, "Syria Crisis," August 30, 2013.

182 Usborne, "Syria Crisis," August 30, 2013.

183 CNN Wire Staff, "Obama Warns Syria Not to Cross 'Red Line,'" CNN, August 21, 2012, accessed March 12, 2017 from http://www.cnn.com/2012/08/20/world/meast/syria-unrest/.

184 The Telegraph, "US President Barack Obama in 'Red Line' Warning to Syria Over Chemical Weapons," Filmed [August 21, 2012], YouTube video, 01:36, Posted [August 2012], https://www.youtube.com/watch?v=avQKLRGRhPU.

185 Panetta, *Worthy Fights, 450.*

186 Jack Anderson, "The Growing Chemical Club," Washington Post, August 26, 1984, accessed September 9, 2018 from https://www.cia.gov/library/readingroom/docs/CIA-RDP90-00965R000100130055-0.pdf.

187 "Syria's Offensive Chemical Warfare Capability: An Intelligence Assessment," CIA Library, accessed September 9, 2018 from https://www.cia.gov/library/readingroom/docs/CIA-RDP86T00587R000400550004-2.pdf.

188 "Syria's Offensive Chemical Warfare Capability," CIA Library, November 1985, accessed December 7, 2017 from https://www.cia.gov/library/readingroom/docs/CIA-RDP86T00587R000400550004-2.pdf.

189 "Military Expenditure (% of GDP), The World Bank, accessed December 7, 2017 from https://data.worldbank.org/indicator/MS.MIL.XPND.GD.ZS?contextual=region&end=2007&locations=SY&name_desc=true&start=1960&view=chart.

190 "Syria's Offensive Chemical Warfare Capability," CIA Library, November 1985, accessed December 7, 2017 from https://www.cia.gov/library/readingroom/docs/CIA-RDP86T00587R000400550004-2.pdf.

191 "Politics in Syria," CIA Library, May 1, 1979, accessed December 10, 2017 from https://www.cia.gov/library/readingroom/docs/CIA-RDP80T00942A001000030001-0.pdf.

192   Laura Smith-Spark and Tom Cohen, "U.S., Russia Agree to Framework on Syria Chemical Weapons," CNN, September 15, 2013, accessed May 14, 2017 from http://www.cnn.com/2013/09/14/politics/us-syria/.

193   "Security Council Requires Scheduled Destruction of Syria's Chemical Weapons, Unanimously Adopting Resolution 2118 (2013)," United Nations, September 27, 2013, accessed March 19, 2017 from http://www.un.org/press/en/2013/sc11135.doc.htm.

194   "Resolution 2118," accessed March 19, 2017 from http://www.un.org/press/en/2013/sc11135.doc.htm.

195   "Chapter VII," United Nations, accessed March 20, 2017 from http://www.un.org/en/sections/un-charter/chapter-vii/.

196   "Nobel Peace Prize," OPCW, About Us, accessed November 26, 2018 from https://www.opcw.org/about-us/nobel-peace-prize.

197   Stephanie Nebehay, "Assad Tops List of Syria War Crimes Suspects Handed to ICC: Former Prosecutor," Reuters, June 10, 2014, accessed June 5, 2017 from http://www.reuters.com/article/us-syria-crisis-warcrimes-idUSKBN0EL25020140610.

198   "Government Assessment of the Syrian Government's Use of Chemical Weapons on August 21, 2013, The White House: President Barack Obama, accessed June 5, 2017 from https://obamawhitehouse.archives.gov/the-press-office/2013/08/30/government-assessment-syrian-government-s-use-chemical-weapons-august-21.

199   "Destruction of Declared Syrian Chemical Weapons Completed," OPCW, News, January 4, 2016, accessed June 5, 2017 from https://www.opcw.org/news/article/destruction-of-syrian-chemical-weapons-completed/.

200   "Syria Peace Talks Break Up as UN Envoy Fails to End Deadlock," The Guardian, February 15, 2014, accessed June 10, 2017 from https://www.theguardian.com/world/2014/feb/15/syria-peace-talks-break-up-geneva.

201   "Syria Peace Talks Break Up as UN Envoy Fails to End Deadlock," The Guardian, February 15, 2014, accessed June 10, 2017 from https://www.theguardian.com/world/2014/feb/15/syria-peace-talks-break-up-geneva.

202   "Bashar Assad Wins Re-election in Syria as Uprising Against Him Rages On," Associated Press, June 4, 2014, accessed June

10, 2017 from https://www.theguardian.com/world/2014/jun/04/
bashar-Assad-winds-reelection-in-landslide-victory.

203 "Russia Joins War in Syria: Five Key Points," BBC News, October
1, 2015, accessed June 14, 2017 from http://www.bbc.com/news/
world-middle-east-34416519.

204 "Russia Shirks Reconstruction Costs in Syria, Asks Central Asian
Countries to Pay Up," Caravanserai, June 12, 2018, accessed January
24, 2019 from http://central.asia-news.com/en_GB/articles/cnmi_ca/
features/2018/06/12/feature-01.

205 Khalil Ashawi, "Kremlin Says All of Syria Must Be 'Liberated,'" CBS
News, October 23, 2016, accessed April 23, 2017 from http://www.
cbsnews.com/news/kremlin-says-all-of-syria-must-be-liberated/.

206 Lewis, *Crisis, 96-7.*

207 Lewis, *Crisis, 97.*

208 Gates, *From the Shadows, 351.*

209 "Recent Soviet Activity in Syria," CIA Library, October 5, 1972, accessed
December 23, 2018 from https://www.cia.gov/library/readingroom/docs/
CIA-RDP79B01737A002000010065-8.pdf.

210 Robert Gates, *From the Shadows: The Ultimate Insider's Story of Five
Presidents and How They Won the Cold War (New York: Simon & Schuster,
1996), 274.*

211 Andrew Osborne, "Vladimir Putin Saved KGB Offices from East
German Looters," The Telegraph, October 29, 2009, accessed April
17, 2017 from http://www.telegraph.co.uk/news/worldnews/europe/
russia/6455858/Vladimir-Putin-saved-KGB-offices-from-East-German-
looters.html.

212 Gates, *Duty, 530.*

213 Gates, *Duty, 530.*

214 Damien Sharkov, "Russia Announces Plans for Permanent
Naval Base in Syria," Newsweek, October 10, 2016,
accessed June 14, 2017 from http://www.newsweek.com/
russia-plans-permanent-naval-base-syria-tartus-tension-airstrikes-508436.

215   Brendan Cole, "Russia Will Keep Nuclear-Armed Missiles on NATO Border to Counter 'Alliance's Expansion,'" International Business Times, November 22, 2016, accessed June 11, 2017 from http://www.msn.com/en-us/news/world/russia-will-keep-nuclear-armed-missiles-on-nato-border-to-counter-alliances-expansion/ar-AAkBdpd?li=BBnb7Kz&ocid=iehp.

216   "Note to Correspondents: Statement of the International Syria Support Group," United Nations, Statements/Reports, May 17, 2016, accessed June 18, 2017 from https://www.un.org/sg/en/content/sg/note-correspondents/2016-05-17/note-correspondents-statement-international-syria-support.

217   "Joint Statement: Final Declaration on the Results of the Syria Talks in Vienna as Agreed by Participants," The Saker, November 2, 2015, accessed October 2, 2017 from http://thesaker.is/joint-statement-final-declaration-on-the-results-of-the-syria-talks-in-vienna-as-agreed-by-participants/.

218   Security Council Unanimously Adopts Resolution 2254 (2015), Endorsing Road Map for Peace Process in Syria, Setting Timetable for Talks, United Nations, December 18, 2015, accessed on December 3, 2017 from https://www.un.org/press/en/2015/sc12171.doc.htm.

219   Aron Lund, "Riyadh, Rumeilan, and Damascus: All You Need to Know About Syria's Opposition Conference," Carnegie Middle East Center, December 9, 2015, accessed June 17, 2017 from http://carnegie-mec.org/diwan/62239?lang=en.

220   "Syria's War: HNC Unveils Road Map For Transition," Al-Jazeera, September 7, 2016, accessed June 17, 2017 from http://www.aljazeera.com/news/2016/09/syria-war-hnc-unveils-road-map-transition-160907140127669.html.

221   Thucydides, *History of the Peloponnesian War, translated by Rex Warner (New York: Penguin Books, 1972), 402.*

222   "Hagel: Military Remains Ready to Assist Iraq, Protect Americans," Department of Defense, August 7, 2014, accessed February 24, 2018 from http://archive.defense.gov/news/newsarticle.aspx?id=122874.

223 Steven W Hook and John Spanier, "American Foreign Policy Since World War II, Eighteenth Edition (CQ Press: Washington, DC, 2010) 103.

224 50 U.S.C § 1541 (1973).

225 "War Powers," Library of Congress, Legal Reports, accessed February 24, 2018 from https://www.loc.gov/law/help/war-powers.php.

226 Public Law 107-40, 2001, Library of Congress, September 18, 2001, accessed February 24, 2018 from https://www.gpo.gov/fdsys/pkg/PLAW-107publ40/pdf/PLAW-107publ40.pdf.

227 Paul Sperry, "Saudi Government Allegedly Funded a 'Dry Run' for 9/11," New York Post, September 9, 2017, accessed February 24, 2018 from https://nypost.com/2017/09/09/saudi-government-allegedly-funded-a-dry-run-for-911/.

228 Jeremy Diamond, "First on CNN: Trump Slams Obama Over Ground Troops in Syria," CNN, October 31, 2015, accessed October 7, 2018 from https://edition.cnn.com/2015/10/31/politics/donald-trump-syria-super-pacs/index.html.

229 "A Provocation Contingency in Lebanon: Intensified Attacks on Marine Positions to Force U.S. Air and Naval Strikes," CIA Library, September 19, 1983, accessed December 24, 2018 from https://www.cia.gov/library/readingroom/docs/CIA-RDP88B00443R001404090136-7.pdf.

230 Bill Clinton, My Life (New York: Alfred A. Knopf, 2004), 552.

231 Ellen Mitchell, "U.S. May Distribute Arms to Syrian Kurds 'Very Quickly,'" The Hill, May 10, 2017 accessed May 10, 2017 from http://www.msn.com/en-us/news/world/us-may-distribute-arms-to-syrian-kurds-very-quickly/ar-BBAZ7Gy.

232 John Bacon, "Erdogan Rips U.S. Plan to Arm Kurds; Mattis Downplays Turkey Rift," USA Today, May 10, 2017, accessed May 10, 2017 from https://www.usatoday.com/story/news/world/2017/05/10/turkey-miffed-us-decision-arm-kurds-mattis-downplays-rift/101503304/.

233 Greg Bruno, "Inside the Kurdistan Workers Party (PKK)," Council on Foreign Relations, October 19, 2007, accessed May10, 2017 from http://www.cfr.org/turkey/inside-kurdistan-workers-party-pkk/p14576.

234 Ivan Angelovski and Lawrence Marzouk, "Revealed: The Pentagon is Spending $2.2 Billion on Soviet-Style Arms for Syrian Rebels," OCCRP, September 12, 2017, accessed July 22, 2018 from https://www.occrp.org/en/makingakilling/the-pentagon-is-spending-2-billion-on-soviet-style-arms-for-syrian-rebels.

235 Cale Salih, "Is Tal Abyad a Turning Point for Syria's Kurds?," BBC News, June 16, 2015, accessed September 10, 2018 from https://www.bbc.com/news/world-middle-east-33146515.

236 Yusuf Selman Inanc, "FSA Disappointed with US Airdropping Weapons to Kurds, Daily Sabah, Middle East, October 23, 2014, accessed March 20, 2018 from https://www.dailysabah.com/mideast/2014/10/23/fsa-disappointed-with-us-airdropping-weapons-to-kurds.

237 John Irish, "Too Much Focus on Kobane in Anti-ISIS Campaign: Erdogan," Al Arabiya English, October 31, 2014, accessed July 18, 2018 from http://english.alarabiya.net/en/News/middle-east/2014/10/31/Too-much-focus-on-Kobani-in-anti-ISIS-campaign-Erdogan.html.

238 Humeyra Pamak, "Erdogan Says Turkey Won't Let Kurds 'Seize' Northern Syria," Reuters, October 24, 2015, accessed July 17, 2018 from https://www.reuters.com/article/us-mideast-crisis-turkey-erdogan/erdogan-says-turkey-wont-let-kurds-seize-northern-syria-idUSKCN-0SI0IZ20151024.

239 Cale Salih, "Is Tal Abyad a Turning Point for Syria's Kurds?," BBC News, June 16, 2015, accessed September 10, 2018 from https://www.bbc.com/news/world-middle-east-33146515.

240 "Everything We Know About the San Bernardino Terror Attack Investigation So Far," LA Times, December 14, 2015, accessed December 8, 2015 from https://www.latimes.com/local/california/la-me-san-bernardino-shooting-terror-investigation-htmlstory.html.

241 Roy Gutman, "Syria Cease-Fire Brings Turkey Closer to War," Foreign Policy, February 16, 2016, accessed September 15, 2018 from https://foreignpolicy.com/2016/02/16/syria-ceasefire-brings-turkey-closer-to-war/.

242 Roy Gutman, "Syria Cease-Fire Brings Turkey Closer to War," Foreign Policy, February 16, 2016, accessed September 15, 2018 from https://foreignpolicy.com/2016/02/16/syria-ceasefire-brings-turkey-closer-to-war/.

243 "UN Special Envoy's Paper on Points of Commonalities," Voltaire
     Network, March 24, 2016, accessed September 22, 2018 from http://www.
     voltairenet.org/article190914.html.

244 Mark Mazzetti, Adam Goldman, and Michael S. Schmidt, "Behind the
     Sudden Death of a $1 Billion Secret C.I.A. War in Syria," The New York
     Times, August 2, 2017, accessed December 29, 2018 from https://www.
     nytimes.com/2017/08/02/world/middleeast/cia-syria-rebel-arm-train-
     trump.html.

245 Nick Tattersall and Humeyra Pamuk, "After Aleppo, a Chapter
     Closes on Turkey's Ambitions in Syria," Reuters, December 15,
     2016, accessed April 17, 2017 from http://www.reuters.com/article/
     us-mideast-crisis-syria-turkey-idUSKBN14422U.

246 "Turkey Wants to See FSA Replace SDF in Raqqa Battle," Rudaw,
     February 21, 2017, accessed December 24, 2018 from http://www.rudaw.
     net/english/middleeast/syria/21022017.

247 Jane Coaston, "New Evidence Shows the Pulse Nightclub
     Shooting Wasn't About Anti-LGBTQ Hate," Vox, April
     5, 2018, accessed December 9, 2018 from https://
     www.vox.com/policy-and-politics/2018/4/5/17202026/
     pulse-shooting-lgbtq-trump-terror-hate.

248 Ralph Ellis, Ashley Fantz, Faith Karimi, and Elliott C. McLaughlin,
     "Orlando Shooting: 49 Killed, Shooter Pledged ISIS Allegiance," CNN,
     June 13, 2016, accessed December 9, 2018 from https://www.cnn.
     com/2016/06/12/us/orlando-nightclub-shooting/index.html.

249 Louis Nelson and Daniel Strauss, "Libertarian Candidate Gary
     Johnson: 'What is Aleppo?'," Politico, September 8, 2016, accessed
     December 23, 2017 from https://www.politico.com/story/2016/09/
     gary-johnson-aleppo-227873.

250 "Opinions on U.S. International Involvement, Free Trade, ISIS and
     Syria, Russia and China," Pew Research Center, U.S. Politics, October
     27, 2016, accessed October 7, 2018 from http://www.people-press.
     org/2016/10/27/7-opinions-on-u-s-international-involvement-free-
     trade-isis-and-syria-russia-and-china/.

251   "Israeli Strike on Rocket Launcher in Syria Kills Islamic State Terrorists," Jewish Telegraphic Agency, July 26, 2018, accessed February 3, 2019 from https://www.jta.org/2018/07/26/israel/israel-strikes-rocket-launcher-syria-belonging-islamic-state.

252   Karen DeYoung and Missy Ryan, "Pentagon Grudgingly Accepts Syria Deal Amid Deep Mistrust of Russia," The Washington Post, September 15, 2016, accessed January 2, 2019 from https://www.washingtonpost.com/world/national-security/pentagon-grudgingly-accepts-syria-deal-amid-deep-mistrust-of-russia/2016/09/15/e2ac735c-7a98-11e6-beac-57a4a412e93a_story.html?utm_term=.c9930740e5bb.

253   "UN Council Welcomes Syria Ceasefire Move by Russia and Turkey," The Guardian, December 31, 2016, accessed March 7, 2018 from https://www.theguardian.com/world/2016/dec/31/russia-syria-ceasefire-un-security-council-damascus-kazakhstan.

254   "Russia in Power-Broking Role as Syria Peace Talks Begin in Astana," The Guradian, January 23, 2017, accessed March 7, 2018 from https://www.theguardian.com/world/2017/jan/22/russia-syria-talks-astana-kazakhstan-.

255   "Syria War: Twin Suicide Attacks Kill Dozens in Damascus," Al-Jazeera, March 15, 2017, accessed March 10, 2018 from https://www.aljazeera.com/news/2017/03/suicide-attack-hits-justice-palace-syria-damascus-170315114623986.html.

256   "Dozens Killed in Double Suicide Attack in Syrian Capital," Reuters, March 15, 2017, accessed March 10, 2018 from https://www.reuters.com/article/us-mideast-crisis-syria-blast/dozens-killed-in-double-suicide-attack-in-syrian-capital-idUSKBN16M1J0.

257   Thomas Joscelyn, "Al Qaeda and Allies Announce 'New Entity' in Syria," Long War Journal, January 28, 2017, accessed March 8, 2018 from https://www.longwarjournal.org/archives/2017/01/al-qaeda-and-allies-announce-new-entity-in-syria.php.

258   Angus McDowall and Tom Perry, "Syrian Rebels Press Major Assault Near Hama," Reuters, March 22, 2017, accessed March 10,

2018 from https://www.reuters.com/article/us-mideast-crisis-syria/ syrian-rebels-press-major-assault-near-hama-idUSKBN16T13P.

259 Suleiman al-Khalidi and Tom Perry, "Syrian Rebels Launch Second Damascus Attack in Three Days," Reuters, March 21, 2017, accessed March 10, 2018 from https://www.reuters.com/article/ us-mideast-crisis-syria-damascus/syrian-rebels-launch-second-damas-cus-attack-in-three-days-idUSKBN16S0JW.

260 Dylan Collins, "Geneva 4 and the Shifting Shape of Syria Diplomacy," Al-Jazeera, March 11, 2017, accessed March 8, 2018 from https://www. aljazeera.com/indepth/features/2017/03/geneva-4-shifting-shape-syr-ia-diplomacy-170311081959353.html.

261 "Syria: Twin Attacks on Homs Security Bases Kill Dozens," BBC News, February 25, 2017, accessed March 7, 2018 from http://www.bbc.com/ news/world-middle-east-39089013.

262 "At Least 72 Dead in Suspected Chemical Attack in Syria," Fox News, April 5, 2017, accessed April 7, 2017 from http://www.foxnews.com/ world/2017/04/05/at-least-72-dead-in-suspected-chemical-attack-in-syria.html.

263 AFP, "Arab League Calls for 'De-escalation' in Syria," The Times of Israel, April 8, 2017, accessed April 9, 2017 from http://www.timesofisrael.com/ arab-league-calls-for-de-escalation-in-syria/.

264 "Program Acquisition Cost by Weapon System, United States Department of Defense Fiscal Year 2016 Budget Request," Undersecretary of Defense (Comptroller), page 5-14, accessed April 7, 2017 from http://comptroller.defense.gov/Budget-Materials/Budget2016/.

265 Robert Burns, "Official: Russia Knew Syrian Chemical Attack Was Coming," Associated Press, April 10, 2017, accessed April 10, 2017 from http://www.msn.com/en-us/news/world/offi-cial-russia-knew-syrian-chemical-attack-was-coming/ ar-BBzFdx8?li=BBnb7Kz.

266 Alec Luhn and Patrick Wintour, "Syrian Rebels Walk Out of Press Conference as 'Safe Zone Deal is Signed," The Guardian, May 4, 2017, accessed March 11, 2018 from https://www.theguardian.com/world/2017/ may/04/syrian-opposition-rejects-deal-to-create-safe-zones.

267 "Assad Retains Hundreds of Tons of Chemical Weapons, Says Defected General," The Times of Israel, April 15, 2017, accessed April 17, 2017 from http://www.timesofisrael.com/defected-syrian-generAssad-retains-hundreds-of-tons-of-chemical-weapons/.

268 Sam La Grone, "Russia Sends Frigate to Mediterranean Following U.S. Retaliation Strike; U.S. Destroyers Remain on Station," USNI News, April 7, 2017, accessed April 9, 2017 from https://news.usni. org/2017/04/07/russia-sends-frigate-mediterranean-following-u-s-retaliation-strike-u-s-destroyers-remain-station.

269 AFP, "Arab League Calls for 'De-escalation' in Syria," The Times of Israel, April 8, 2017, accessed April 9, 2017 from http://www.timesofisrael.com/arab-league-calls-for-de-escalation-in-syria/.

270 "Syrian Opposition Walks Out of Astana Meeting," Al-Jazeera, May 3, 2017, accessed July 2, 2017 from http://www.aljazeera.com/news/2017/05/syrian-opposition-walks-astana-talks-170503104347398. html.

271 Aria Bendix, "Safe Zones in Syria," The Atlantic, May 4, 2017, accessed July 2, 2017 from https://www.theatlantic.com/news/archive/2017/05/russia-iran-and-turkey-agree-on-safe-zones-in-syria/525486/.

272 Alec Luhn and Patrick Wintour, "Syrian Rebels Walk Out of Press Conference as 'Safe Zone' Deal is Signed," The Guardian, May 4, 2017, accessed March 11, 2018 from https://www.theguardian.com/world/2017/may/04/syrian-opposition-rejects-deal-to-create-safe-zones.

273 Patrick Wintour, "Syria Safe Zones on Hold Amid Concern Over How Deal Will Be Enforced," The Guardian, May 9, 2017, accessed July 2, 2017 from https://www.theguardian.com/world/2017/may/09/syria-safe-zones-on-hold-amid-concern-over-how-deal-enforced-russia-sergei-lavrov.

274 "US Airstrikes Pound Pro-Assad Forces in Syria," Fox News, World, May 18, 2017, accessed March 11, 2018 from http://www.foxnews.com/world/2017/05/18/us-air-strikes-pound-pro-assad-forces-in-syria.html.

275 Nabih Bulos and W.J. Hennigan, "US Warplanes Shoot Down Syrian Jet Near Raqqah," MSN News, June 18, 2017, accessed June 18, 2017 from http://www.msn.com/en-us/

news/world/us-warplane-shoots-down-syrian-jet-near-raqqah/
ar-BBCRhpv?li=BBnbfcL.

276   Dana Khraiche, Ilya Arkhipov, and Jennifer Epstein, "U.S. Moves
       Jets to Ease Syria Tensions Amid Russian Threat," Bloomberg, June
       19, 2017, accessed June 19, 2017 from http://www.msn.com/en-us/
       news/world/us-moves-jets-to-ease-syria-tensions-amid-russian-threat/
       ar-BBCT7zf?li=BBnb7Kz.

277   Patrick Wintour, "Syrian Peace Talks Break Up After Making Only
       'Incremental Progress,'" The Guardian, May 19, 2017, accessed March
       11, 2018 from https://www.theguardian.com/world/2017/may/19/
       syrian-peace-talks-break-up-after-making-only-incremental-progress.

278   "US Reassures Turkey: We Will Keep Account of Weapons Provided to
       Syrian Kurds," ARA News, June 4, 2017, accessed June 17, 2017 from
       http://aranews.net/2017/06/us-reassures-turkey-we-will-keep-account-
       of-weapons-provided-to-syrian-kurds/.

279   "IS Retakes Raqa District from US-backed Forces: Monitor," AFP, June
       30, 2017, accessed June 30, 2017 from http://www.msn.com/en-us/
       news/world/is-retakes-raqa-district-from-us-backed-forces-monitor/
       ar-BBDu2us.

280   Catherine Putz, "5th Round of Astana Syria Peace Talks End Without
       Agreement," The Diplomat, July 7, 2017, accessed March 11, 2018 from
       https://thediplomat.com/2017/07/5th-round-of-astana-syria-peace-talks-
       end-without-agreement/.

281   "Russia Shirks Reconstruction Costs in Syria, Asks Central Asian
       Countries to Pay Up," Caravanserai, June 12, 2018, accessed January
       24, 2019 from http://central.asia-news.com/en_GB/articles/cnmi_ca/
       features/2018/06/12/feature-01.

282   Jeff Mason and Denis Dyomkin, "Partial Ceasefire Deal Reached
       in Syria, in Trump's First Peace Effort," Reuters, July 7, 2017,
       accessed September 25, 2018 from https://www.reuters.com/article/
       us-mideast-crisis-syria-ceasefire-idUSKBN19S2DG.

283   Jeff Mason and Denis Dyomkin, "Partial Ceasefire Deal Reached
       in Syria, in Trump's First Peace Effort," Reuters, July 7, 2017,

accessed September 25, 2018 from https://www.reuters.com/article/
us-mideast-crisis-syria-ceasefire-idUSKBN19S2DG.

284   "Syria Talks Conclude in Geneva With No Breakthrough," Al-Jazeera,
       July 15, 2017, accessed March 11, 2018 from https://www.aljazeera.com/
       news/2017/07/ends-syria-breakthrough-170715133937590.html.

285   Geoffrey Aronson, "The Syrian Opposition Meeting in Cairo: One
       Small Step," Middle East Institute, January 31, 2015, accessed
       December 24, 2018 from https://www.mei.edu/publications/
       syrian-opposition-meeting-cairo-one-small-step.

286   Zvi Bar'el, "In Blow to Iran, Egypt Becomes Surprise New
       Player in Syria," Haaretz, August 21, 2017, accessed December
       24, 2018 from https://www.haaretz.com/middle-east-news/syria/
       in-blow-to-iran-egypt-becomes-surprise-new-player-in-syria-1.5444424.

287   "Final De-escalation Zones Agreed on in Astana," Al-Jazeera,
       September 15, 2017, accessed March 13, 2018 from https://www.
       aljazeera.com/news/2017/09/final-de-escalation-zones-agreed-as-
       tana-170915102811730.html.

288   Anne Barnard, "Syrian Peace Talks in Russia: 1,500 Delegates, Mostly
       Pro-Assad," New York Times, January 30, 2018, accessed March 13, 2018
       from https://www.nytimes.com/2018/01/30/world/middleeast/syria-rus-
       sia-sochi-talks.html.

289   Assel Satubaldina, "Ninth Round of Astana Process Syrian Peace
       Talks Reaffirm Previous Agreements," The Astana Times, May 17,
       2018, accessed June 4, 2019 from https://astanatimes.com/2018/05/
       ninth-round-of-astana-process-syrian-peace-talks-reaffirm-previ-
       ous-agreements/.

290   Ryan Browne and Barbara Starr, "ISIS Creating Chemical Weapons
       Cell in New De Facto Capital, US Official Says," CNN, May 17, 2017,
       accessed May 17, 2017 from http://www.cnn.com/2017/05/17/politics/
       isis-chemical-weapons/index.html.

291   "Raqqa: IS 'Capital' Falls to US-Backed Syrian Forces," BBC News,
       October 17, 2017, accessed July 21, 2018 from https://www.bbc.co.uk/
       news/world-middle-east-41646802.

292 "Joint Statement by the President of the United States and the President of the Russian Federation," Department of State, November 11, 2017, accessed July 23, 2018 from https://www.state.gov/r/pa/prs/ps/2017/11/275459.htm.

293 "'Heavy Clashes' as US-backed Forces Battle IS in Syria: Monitor," AFP, February 11, 2019, accessed February 19, 2019 from https://www.msn.com/en-us/news/world/heavy-clashes-as-us-backed-forces-battle-is-in-syria-monitor/ar-BBTonsb?ocid=spartanntp.

294 Rukmini Callimachi, "Why a 'Dramatic Dip' in ISIS Attacks in the West is Scant Comfort," The New York Times, September 12, 2018, accessed December 24, 2018 from https://www.nytimes.com/2018/09/12/world/middleeast/isis-attacks.html.

295 "Syria: US Ally's Razing of Villages Amounts to War Crimes," Amnesty International, October 13, 2015, accessed July 19, 2018 from https://www.amnesty.org/en/latest/news/2015/10/syria-us-allys-razing-of-villages-amounts-to-war-crimes/.

296 "Operation Olive Branch," Global Security.org, accessed October 8, 2018 from https://www.globalsecurity.org/military/world/war/syria-olive-branch.htm.

297 Idrees Ali, "Turkish Offensive in Syria Leads to Pause in Some Operations Against IS: Pentagon," Reuters, March 5, 2018, accessed March 13, 2018 from https://www.reuters.com/article/us-mideast-crisis-syria-turkey-pentagon/turkish-offensive-in-syria-leads-to-pause-in-some-operations-against-is-pentagon-idUSKBN1GH2YW.

298 Tuvan Gumrukcu and Ece Toksabay, "Turkey, U.S. Agree Roadmap to Avert Crisis in Syria's Manbij, Few Details," Reuters, June 4, 2018, accessed October 8, 2018 from https://www.reuters.com/article/us-usa-turkey/turkey-u-s-agree-roadmap-to-avert-crisis-in-syrias-manbij-few-details-idUSKCN1J01ZC.

299 "All Eyes on Manbij as More Forces Deployed Near Syrian Flashpoint," Hurriyet Daily News, December 26, 2018, accessed December 27, 2018 from http://www.hurriyetdailynews.com/all-eyes-on-manbij-as-more-forces-deployed-near-syrian-flashpoint-140042.

300 "Tens of Displaced Syrians Return to Liberated Villages Near Manbij," Syrian Observatory for Human Rights, January 4, 2019, accessed January 15, 2019 from http://www.syriahr.com/en/?p=111429.

301 Richard Engel, Caroline Radnofsky, Courtney Kube, Mosheh Gains, and Saphora Smith, "4 Americans Among Those Killed by Explosion in Manbij, Syria," NBC News, January 18, 2018, accessed January 27, 2019 from https://www.nbcnews.com/news/world/u-s-service-members-wounded-explosion-manbij-syria-n959231.

302 Richard Engel and Kennett Werner, "US Troops Who Repelled Russian Mercenaries Prepare for More Attacks," NCB News, March 15, 2018, accessed March 16, 2018 from https://www.msn.com/en-us/news/world/us-troops-who-repelled-russian-mercenaries-prepare-for-more-attacks/ar-BBKgLTt.

303 "Putin Ally's Private Army Behind Attack on U.S.-Backed Forces?," CBS News, February 23, 2018, accessed March 15, 2018 from https://www.cbsnews.com/news/russia-vladimir-putin-yevgeny-prigozhin-wagner-group-attack-us-allies-syria/.

304 Bill Gertz, "Casey Sees Syria, Libya as Proxies in Soviets' Plan," The Washington Times, April 7, 1986, accessed December 10, 2017 from https://www.cia.gov/library/readingroom/docs/CIA-RDP90-00965R000302320046-5.pdf.

305 "Fact Sheet: U.S. Assistance for the People of Syria," USAID, News and Information, January 26, 2018, accessed March 18, 2018 from https://www.usaid.gov/news-information/press-releases/jan-26-2018-fact-sheet-us-assistance-people-syria.

306 Kim Hjelmgaard, "Syria's Civil War Has Been Raging for 7 Years and No End in Sight," USA Today, March 14, 2018, accessed November 29, 2018 from https://www.usatoday.com/story/news/world/2018/03/14/syrias-war-enters-eighth-year/423821002/.

307 Carol Morello, "US Prepared for Military Action in Syria if United Nations Doesn't Stop the Bloodshed, Haley Warns," The Washington Post, March 12, 2018, accessed March 13, 2018 from https://www.msn.com/en-us/news/world/us-prepared-for-military-action-in-

syria-if-united-nations-doesn't-stop-the-bloodshed-haley-warns/
ar-BBK8RfF.

308   Ali Alfoneh, "What is Iran Doing in Syria?," Foreign Policy,
September 25, 2012, accessed May 14, 2017 from https://web.
archive.org/web/20120925053921/http://www.foreignpolicy.com:80/
articles/2012/09/21/what_is_iran_doing_in_syria.

309   Jonathan Schanzer, "Russia Risks a Showdown with Israel
over Hezbollah in Syria," Newsweek, April 29, 2017,
accessed May 17, 2017 from http://www.newsweek.com/
russia-risks-israel-showdown-over-hezbollah-syria-590991.

310   Max Boot, *Invisible Armies: An Epic History of Guerrilla Warfare from
Ancient Times to the Present (New York: Liverlight Publishing Corporation,
2013), 512.*

311   "Jordanians 'Won't Support Ground Intervention in Syria,'" Al Jazeera,
May 10, 2017, accessed May 10, 2017 from http://www.msn.com/en-us/
news/world/jordanians-wont-support-ground-intervention-in-syria/
ar-BBAZ6k7.

312   Hugh Naylor, "In Syria's Aleppo, Shiite Militias Point to Iran's
Unparalleled Influence," The Washington Post, November
21, 2016, accessed June 15, 2017 from http://www.msn.com/
en-us/news/world/in-syria%e2%80%99s-aleppo-shiite-mi-
litias-point-to-iran%e2%80%99s-unparalleled-influence/
ar-AAkxHSp?ocid=iehp.

313   Ben Hubbard and David M Halbfinger, "Iran-Israel Conflict Escalates
in Shadow of Syrian Civil War," The New York Times, April 9, 2018,
accessed February 3, 2019 from https://www.nytimes.com/2018/04/09/
world/middleeast/syria-russia-israel-air-base.html.

314   Steve Almasy, Jennifer Hauser, and Natalie Gallon, "Airstrikes Hit Syrian
Enclave Where Many are Fleeing, Activists Say," CNN, March 17, 2018,
accessed March 18, 2018 from https://www.cnn.com/2018/03/17/mid-
dleeast/syria-ghouta-evacuations-afrin-hospital/index.html.

315   "Ahrar al-Sham," Stanford University, Mapping Militant Organizations,
accessed February 4, 2019 from http://web.stanford.edu/group/
mappingmilitants/cgi-bin/groups/view/523#cite10.

316 Alia Chughtai, "Syria's War: Who Controls What," Al-Jazeera, December 19, 2018, accessed December 26, 2018 from https://www.aljazeera.com/indepth/interactive/2015/05/syria-country-divided-150529144229467.html.

317 "Syria War: What We Know About Douma 'Chemical Attack,'" BBC, July 10, 2018, accessed October 6, 2018 from https://www.bbc.com/news/world-middle-east-43697084.

318 Michel Moutot, "Al-Qaeda's Shadow Still Hangs Over Syria's Idlib: Analysts," AFP, January 15, 2019, accessed January 15, 2019 from https://www.msn.com/en-us/news/world/al-qaedas-shadow-still-hangs-over-syrias-idlib-analysts/ar-BBSfbTI.

319 "Syria's Assad Rejects Key Opposition Demand," CBS News, March 30, 2016, accessed June 18, 2017 from http://www.cbsnews.com/news/syria-bashar-assad-rejects-transitional-body-opposition-geneva-peace-talks/.

320 CIA World Factbook, The Middle East, Syria, accessed April 23, 2017 from https://www.cia.gov/library/publications/resources/the-world-factbook/geos/sy.html.

321 "Syria," The Economist, Intelligence Unit, September 7, 2016, accessed April 22, 2017 from http://country.eiu.com/article.aspx?articleid=1594612543&Country=Syria&topic=Risk&subtopic=Credit+risk&subsubtopic=Overview.

322 Holly Ellyatt, "This is How Much Russia's 'War' in Syria Costs," CNBC, October 21, 2015, accessed April 22, 2017 from http://www.cnbc.com/2015/10/21/this-is-how-much-russias-war-in-syria-costs.html.

323 CIA World Factbook, The Middle East, Syria, accessed April 23, 2017 from https://www.cia.gov/library/publications/resources/the-world-factbook/geos/sy.html.

324 Syrian Refugees, Home, accessed June 18, 2017 from http://syrianrefugees.eu/.

325 "UN Says 250,000 Refugees Could Return to Syria in 2019," Al Jazeera, December 11, 2018, accessed February 4, 2019 from https://www.aljazeera.com/news/2018/12/250000-refugees-return-syria-2019-181211134022694.html.

326 "UN Says 250,000 Refugees Could Return to Syria in 2019," Al Jazeera, December 11, 2018, accessed February 4, 2019 from https://www.aljazeera.com/news/2018/12/250000-refugees-return-syria-2019-181211134022694.html.

327 Andrew Osborn, "Assad Advisor Rejects Idea of Granting Syrian Kurds Autonomy," Reuters, February 19, 2019, accessed June 15, 2019 from https://www.reuters.com/article/us-mideast-crisis-syria-adviser/assad-adviser-rejects-idea-of-granting-syrian-kurds-autonomy-idUSKCN-1Q81QA.

328 Henry Meyer and Stepan Kravchenko, "Syrian Kurds Demand Autonomy Before Merger With Assad's Army, Bloomberg, March 26, 2019, accessed June 16, 2019 from https://www.bloomberg.com/news/articles/2019-03-26/syrian-kurds-demand-autonomy-before-merger-with-assad-s-army.

329 "Jerusalem Embassy Act of 1995," US Congress, Public Law 104-45, November 8, 1995, accessed January 22, 2017 from https://www.congress.gov/104/plaws/publ45/PLAW-104publ45.pdf.

330 "Full Video and Transcript: Trump's Speech Recognizing Jerusalem as the Capital of Israel," The New York Times, December 6, 2017, accessed December 6, 2017 from https://www.nytimes.com/2017/12/06/world/middleeast/trump-israel-speech-transcript.html.

331 "Israel Passes Law to Strip Residency of Jerusalem's Palestinians," Al-Jazeera, March 7, 2018, accessed March 10, 2018 from https://www.aljazeera.com/news/2018/03/israel-passes-law-strip-residency-jerusalem-palestinians-180307153033538.html.

332 "US Plans to Close PLO Office in D.C., Bolton Blasts Int'l Criminal Court," Associated Press, September 10, 2018, accessed September 30, 2018 from https://www.nbcnews.com/politics/white-house/u-s-plans-close-plo-office-washington-n908181.

333 Bethan McKernan, "Outrage Over New Israeli Law Allowing Palestinians in Jerusalem to be Stripped of Residency," Independent, March 8, 2018, accessed March 10, 2018 from http://www.independent.co.uk/news/world/middle-east/israel-jerusalem-palestinians-residency-stripping-law-latest-a8246336.html.

334   "Palestine Liberation Organization (PLO): History & Overview," Jewish Virtual Library, accessed December 4, 2018 from https://www.jewishvirtuallibrary.org/history-and-overview-plo.

335   Jonathan Ferziger, "Israeli Settlements," Bloomberg, March 22, 2018, accessed October 2, 2018 from https://www.bloomberg.com/quicktake/israeli-settlements.

336   Tovah Lazaroff, "Israel to Advance Plans for 3,900 West Bank Settler Homes," The Jerusalem Post, May 24, 2018, accessed March 16, 2019 from https://www.jpost.com/Arab-Israeli-Conflict/Israel-to-advance-plans-for-3900-settler-homes-558243.

337   Loveday Morris, "US Ambassador Breaks with Policy: 'I Think the Settlements are Part of Israel,'" Washington Post, September 29, 2017, accessed September 30, 2018 from https://www.washingtonpost.com/news/worldviews/wp/2017/09/29/u-s-ambassador-breaks-with-policy-i-think-the-settlements-are-part-of-israel/?utm_term=.1e5d725e8526.

338   Ben Lynfield, "Israel to Build Almost 4,000 New West Bank Settlement Units," The National, May 24, 2018, accessed July 22, 2018 from https://www.thenational.ae/world/mena/israel-to-build-almost-4-000-new-west-bank-settlement-units-1.733731.

339   Amir Tibon, "In First, U.S. Votes Against UN Resolution Condemning Israeli Control of Golan Heights," Haaretz, November 16, 2018, accessed December 4, 2018 from https://www.haaretz.com/us-news/in-first-u-s-votes-against-un-resolution-condemning-israeli-control-of-golan-heights-1.6657881.

340   "Russia Establishing Permanent Presence at Its Syrian Bases: RIA," Reuters, December 26, 2017, accessed February 4, 2019 from https://www.reuters.com/article/us-mideast-crisis-syria-russia-bases/russia-establishing-permanent-presence-at-its-syrian-bases-ria-idUSKBN1EK0HD.

341   Damien Sharkov, "Russia Announces Plans for Permanent Naval Base in Syria," Newsweek, World, October 10, 2016, accessed February 4, 2019 from https://www.newsweek.com/russia-plans-permanent-naval-base-syria-tartus-tension-airstrikes-508436.

342   Emily Birnbaum, "Trump Defends Decision to Leave Syria During Visit to Iraq," The Hill, December 26, 2018, accessed December 26, 2018 from

https://thehill.com/policy/defense/422936-trump-defends-decision-to-leave-syria-during-visit-to-iraq.

343 Joost Hiltermann, "The Kurds Once Again Face American Abandonment," The Atlantic, August 30, 2018, accessed December 29, 2018 from https://www.theatlantic.com/international/archive/2018/08/syria-kurds-assad-ypg-isis-iraq/569029/.

344 Robin Wright, "A Victory in Kobani?" The New Yorker, January 27, 2015, accessed October 2, 2015 from https://www.newyorker.com/news/news-desk/victory-kobani.

345 Samantha Raphelson, "Fall of Raqqa Delivers Sharp Blow to Islamic State's Media Operation," NPR, November 6, 2017, accessed July 21, 2018 from https://www.npr.org/2017/11/06/562326147/fall-of-raqqa-delivers-sharp-blow-to-islamic-states-media-operation.

346 "The Islamic State Releases New Recording Purportedly Carrying Message From Leader al-Baghdadi," Haaretz, August 23, 2018, accessed September 27, 2018 from https://www.haaretz.com/middle-east-news/isis/isis-releases-new-audio-purportedly-carrying-message-from-al-baghdadi-1.6410102.

347 "Evaluation of Embassy Baghdad's Implementation of Line of Effort 6 in the President's Strategy to Counter ISIL: Exposing ISIL's True Nature," State Department Office of Inspector General, March 2016, accessed September 30, 2018 from https://www.stateoig.gov/system/files/isp-i-16-10.pdf

348 Tamer el-Gobashy, "Trump's Decision on Syria is Worrying Allies in Iraq and Emboldening Opponents, The Washington Post, December 20, 2018, accessed December 26, 2018 from https://www.washingtonpost.com/world/middle_east/trumps-decision-on-syria-is-worrying-allies-in-iraq-and-emboldening-opponents/2018/12/20/61bbeb62-045f-11e9-958c-0a601226ff6b_story.html?utm_term=.164dd051ed3f.

349 Gates, *Duty, 591.*

350 "At Least 72 Dead in Suspected Chemical Attack in Syria," Fox News, April 5, 2017, accessed April 7, 2017 from http://www.foxnews.com/world/2017/04/05/at-least-72-dead-in-suspected-chemical-attack-in-syria.html.

351   Brian Rohan, "Egypt Launches Regional Gas Forum, Including Israel in Fold," AP News, January 14, 2019, accessed June 17, 2019 from https://www.apnews.com/419b7ed277354b3fa3d2239e33dd2e09.

ABOUT THE AUTHOR

Christopher J Hill is a veteran of the US Army and holds a Master's degree in National Security Studies and a Bachelor's degree in History. Syria on the Brink is his first book; he currently resides in Houston, Texas.

www.ingramcontent.com/pod-product-compliance
Lightning Source LLC
Chambersburg PA
CBHW060838280326
41934CB00007B/831